# Fishing for Heritage

For Judy –
from my
previous incarnation.

Jane

# Fishing for Heritage

## Modernity and Loss Along the Scottish Coast

### Jane Nadel-Klein

*Oxford • New York*

First published in 2003 by
**Berg**
Editorial offices:
150 Cowley Road, Oxford, OX4 1JJ, UK
838 Broadway, Third Floor, New York NY 10003-4812, USA

Berg is an imprint of Oxford International Publishers Ltd.


**Library of Congress Cataloging-in-Publication Data**
Nadel-Klein, Jane, 1947–
    Fishing for heritage : modernity and loss along the Scottish coast /
Jane Nadel-Klein.
        p. cm.
Includes bibliographical references (p.  ) and index.
        ISBN 1-85973-562-2 – ISBN 1-85973-567-3 (pbk.)
    1. Tourism–Scotland–History–20th century. 2. National characteristics,
Scottish–History–20th century. 3. Historic sites–Interpretive programs–
Scotland–Public opinion. 4. Cultural property–Protection–Scotland–Public
opinion. 5. Heritage tourism–Scotland–Public opinion. 6. Scotland–
Economic conditions–1973– 7. Fishing villages–Scotland. 8. Public
opinion–Scotland. 9. Coasts–Scotland. I. Title.

DA867.5 .N33 2003
941.1085–dc21

                                                                        2002013469



**British Library Cataloguing-in-Publication Data**
A catalogue record for this book is available from the British Library.


ISBN  1 85973 562 2 (Cloth)
          1 85973 567 3 (Paper)


Typeset by JS Typesetting Ltd, Wellingborough, Northants.
Printed in the United Kingdom by Biddles Ltd, Guildford and King's Lynn.

# Contents

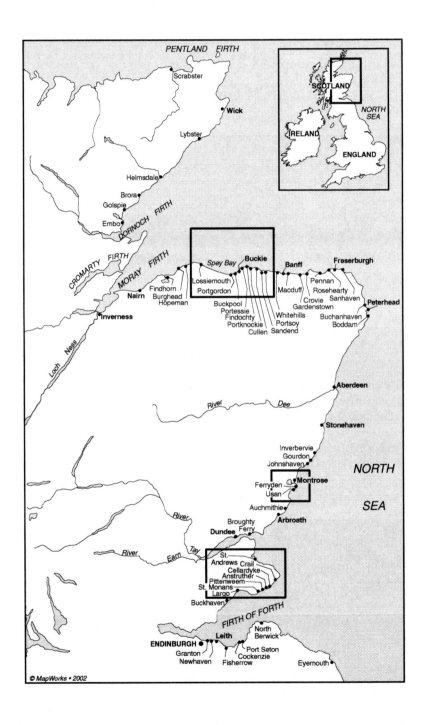

# Acknowledgements

This book has had a long gestation period. Many people have helped to give it birth. My first thanks go to my husband, Bradley S. Klein, who, by dint of loving, nagging, browbeating and encouraging me (as well as by brewing endless cups of coffee) gave me the strength and persistence to complete the task. He is also a ruthless editor. My next thanks go to my dear friends and colleagues, Deborah Gewertz and Frederick Errington, whose brilliant, patient and painstaking editing skills rescued me from many blind alleys. Their courage has also taught me much about the meaning of loss and resilience.

Others have also given very helpful critiques along the way, in particular: Joan Hedrick, Margo Perkins and Barbara Sicherman, from Trinity College, with whom I spent many productive afternoons as part of a writers' circle. With Dona Davis of the University of South Dakota, I have had countless stimulating discussions comparing Scottish fishing communities to those in Newfoundland and Norway.

I owe an incalculable debt to the fisherfolk of Scotland. Many people in Ferryden, Anstruther, Pittenweem, Eyemouth, Buckie and Nairn endured my questions with great patience and good humor. They have given generously of their hospitality, time and information. I must particularly thank members of the Buckie Heritage Society, the Nairn fishertown museum, and the Scottish Fisheries Museum. In Anstruther, David Smith and James Tarvit have been especially helpful in explaining the very complex workings of a fisherman's life. I thank them and also apologize for never being able to keep straight the differences between a Zulu and a Fifie. The errors and omissions here are mine alone.

I cannot find words to express my affection for and gratitude to James and Olive Halliday of Broughty Ferry. They have been my true friends, surrogate family and key interpreters of Scottish life and politics for a quarter of a century. We have logged many miles on Scottish roads together. Also, Sheila and Richard Suddaby of Buckie have been good friends and hosts.

The research has been generously supported by grants from the National Endowment for the Humanities; first through their Summer Stipend program and later through the College Teachers Fellowship program. I must also thank the Faculty Research Program of Trinity College, which has supported this effort with funding and leave time. In Scotland, I wish to thank the following at the University of Edinburgh: the International Social Science Institute for giving me office space and institutional affiliation; the Department of Social Anthropology (particularly Alan Barnard, Charles Jedrej, Iris Jean-Klein and Jean Cannizzo) for their warm reception of a foreign colleague; and the School of Scottish Studies and its Director, Margaret McKay, who gave me full access to the School's wonderful library.

In writing this book I felt the difficulty of my position as ethnographer, knowing full well that, no matter how sincere and strenuous my attempts to present my informants' points of view as I think they would want them presented, I have made mistakes and committed serious transgressions in reflecting their views of truth. For this, I can only apologize.

Our daughter, Cory-Ellen, who almost became an anthropologist but wisely chose instead to be a poet, endured many fieldwork absences during her childhood, but also learned many obscure Scottish folk songs. I dedicate this book to Brad and to Cory-Ellen, with all my love.

# –1–

# Archetypes, Fantasies and Ethnographic Destinations

"In Viking days they put all the social anthropologists to the sword"

Cooper, *The Road to Mingulay*

## Introduction

Some might think a book on Scottish fishing villages to be a mite esoteric, even obscure. How many could there be, after all, and why should we care about them, other than as pretty places to visit on a holiday? I have spent a quarter of a century studying these villages and the people who live there, thinking about them almost daily. I have come to know many as informants and some as friends, so I feel entitled to give an answer. Actually, three answers.

The first is simply the one that any right-minded anthropologist or humanist might give, that all people, "great and small," deserve our attention, not least because "human populations construct their cultures in interaction with one another, and not in isolation," as Eric Wolf said in his preface to *Europe and the People Without History* (1982: ix). Fishers have been part of the larger story of Scotland, Europe and the world beyond.

The second is that by studying Scottish fishing villagers we learn something about the conundrums of modernity and perhaps of post-modernity (should it exist); for in their histories and in their present circumstances, they have experienced how capitalism can create and then dismiss a way of life. Living in small places initially adapted to a small-scale, decentralized industry, they now find themselves struggling to stay afloat in a world run by much larger players. Adapting to these changes over the years has given the fishers a toughness and resilience as well as a sharply critical eye and tongue. As I have said elsewhere, they are not about to watch their eclipse happen silently (Nadel-Klein 1991a). They see themselves as survivors. They are not sure, however, what legacy they can leave to their children.

Thirdly, I also know, as an anthropologist, that ethnographic investigation can teach us much about the experience of what it is now fashionably called globalism. To understand the consequences of public attitudes, policies, national agendas and transnational economic forces upon localities, we cannot afford to look only at statistics on employment and migration. We must remember Geertz's exhortation that ethnography is a "craft of place" (1983: 167) and look at – and listen to – people. The fisherfolk are fabulous – and generous – storytellers who can teach us much about survival, integrity and strength in the face of hardship. By listening to them and by setting their tales in present-day, as well as in historical context, we engage with memory as a tactic that builds and rebuilds identity. For it is not just the body that must perpetually renew itself; it is our sense of self, as well.

The best way to find local experience is to live with people in the places they call "home." My strategy here is to let my informants speak about identity, time, place and community and to set their views against those of "outsiders" as much as possible. In this way, I examine how Scottish fishing people define themselves, how others define them, and how these contrasting perceptions shape an ongoing, but rarely equal dialogue, similar in many ways to that encompassing Highlanders, Celts, Gypsies and others who occupy stereotyped and often stigmatized categories.

Identity-in-dialogue is a never-completed process, rather than an object, so my book is historical as well as ethnographic. Stereotype, stigma and, indeed, marginalization, have molded fishers' lives. Scholarly, popular and touristic descriptions have, each in their own way, contributed to that marginalizaton. Nonetheless, the people of fisher communities have managed to construct a positive sense of their own value. They do not regard the past as something to be transcended or forgotten but as an educational resource, a school of hard knocks that helps them to endure modern burdens. For them, the past is not so much a foreign country (cf. Lowenthal 1985) as a familiar attic in which they rummage at will, pulling out bits and pieces that can be recycled for present use. These bits and pieces are not randomly chosen, but provide evidence of a strategy of negotiation in the face of long-term social stigma and economic struggle.

The rise, decline and transformation of Scottish fishing villages provides the book's framework. Each chapter looks both at material circumstances as well as at different ways that fishers have responded to power. In this first chapter, I introduce the intersecting layers of discourse, the community imaginings in which fishers are embedded (Anderson 1983). To reach the local level, so as to achieve an anthropological understanding, we must move through the national; we are helped along the way by fictional and poetic, as well as ethnographic accounts. Chapter 2 addresses cases, examining historically how the east coast fishing communities were established as objects of social stigma. Gender forms the core of Chapter 3, where I look at how fisherwomen's complex, public roles helped to reinforce the idea that fishers were "different."

In Chapter 4, I hone in on Ferryden, site of my first Scottish fieldwork. It is a village whose claim to be a fishing community now hangs by a thread, so eclipsed by others' agendas that it has even disappeared from many maps. In Chapter 5, I broaden the focus again to confront crisis, an idea with which fishers everywhere are only too familiar. I set the current moment of crisis in a more general North Atlantic context to show that the Scottish fishers' experience is not unique, but also to demonstrate the enormous complexity of their current predicament.

Finally, in Chapter 6, I tie these threads together, reprising themes of representation by looking at how tourism and the "heritage industry" (Hewison 1987) are producing new imaginings about fisher people. While these allow local voices to be heard in new venues, the fishers seldom get to control who hears them, where the message goes, or how it is interpreted. As Sharon MacDonald (1997: 246), in her book on cultural "reimagining" on the Isle of Skye, points out, "People are being called upon to revive, maintain and express the cultural particularity that it is assumed that they have somehow lost touch with: they are being called upon to expressively individuate themselves as 'cultures'." In the tensions that arise during this process along the east coast, we can see the latest in the series of struggles that have, in some measure, pitted fisherfolk against those who would appropriate cultural resources for their own ends.

## Situating the Ethnographer: a Brief Cultural Autobiography

I wish to ground the following discussion in a little cultural autobiography, to say something about some of the factors that have influenced my choice of topic as well as the approach I take to it. This is not a confessional, but an exercise in context building, a bow to the importance of reflexivity, particularly when examining others' ideological constructions. As I began this work as a graduate student, and am writing this book over a quarter of a century later, it seems appropriate to say something about how the field has changed in that time, particularly the field of British ethnography.

But more is needed: ethnographers, like other people, do not live in protective bubbles. We travel, read novels and newspapers, see films, listen to (and sing) songs, and watch television. So here, as well as elsewhere in the book, I will also refer to some of the popular, as well as scholarly, sources of ideas about British and Scottish society that have provoked me, one way or another, into thinking about identity and representation. From this beginning, I will reflect upon the dialogue that has emerged between fishing villagers and those who describe and objectify them, to deconstruct the assumptions underlying that dialogue, and then to consider how the whole conceptual apparatus of difference actually impinges upon fishers' lives.

Scotland is a hallowed place for many North Americans. The country attracts tourists like a magnet, many of them apparently expecting to find the ghosts of ancestral Celtic clansmen striding the hills and bagpipes skirling on every corner. A place so laden with fodder for the foreigner's imagination can prove a special challenge for the ethnographer. I have learned in recent years to take seriously the question I am so often asked: "how did you choose Scotland, and Scottish fishing villages, for your field research?" A part of the honest answer (which I sidestepped for years) is that twenty odd years ago, as a graduate student, I simply loved the country for my sense of its romance: for the folk songs and the heather, the bleak hills and the ever-present sea. The picture of Scotland I held then was built upon many of the images that travel agents and tourist boards so lyrically promote, upon those myths and dreams of venturing to a land of spiritual allure and exhilarating scenery that make tourism today one of Scotland's most important industries. As Michael Russell, Chief Executive of the Scottish National Party, says, "It has never been difficult to travel in an imaginary Scotland" (1998: xiii).

Unlike many sojourners in this realm, I have no Scottish ancestry. Acquaintances – particularly Scottish ones – often assume this in queries about my ethnographic choice: must I not be engaged in a quest for Scottish "roots?" But I have never been tempted to see myself as the scion of some lost Russian-Jewish branch of a clan, complete with "documented" genealogy – the MacHurwitzes, perhaps. From childhood, however, I had clung to another kind of legacy: an imagined world constructed chiefly through literary and musical sources as miscellaneous as stories of bravehearted (and extraordinarily intelligent) collies, some of Robert Burns' politer songs (for years, I wondered what a gloaming was), and tales of twentieth century children encountering ancient sources of Celtic wizardry.[1]

A visit to the Scottish Highlands in 1967 brought to life all my adolescent imaginings and readings about a wild and older world still somehow accessible to the adventurous traveler. Succumbing to the all-too-common conflation of Scotland as a whole with its northern and western parts, I saw the country, then, not only in purely Highland terms, but also as a place outside of modernity, a place where humans had stepped lightly. It seemed no less than magical.

Such fantasies concern me now. Ethnographers today are expected to be reflexive, to reveal something of their own intellectual and emotional subjectivity in the course of writing about some "other." Acknowledging oneself and one's position as a writer in the course of writing is key to approaching the partiality (in the senses both of bias and of incompleteness or provisionality) of the "truths" (Clifford 1986; Rosaldo 1993) that we portray. However, my early images of a romantic, somehow timeless Scotland – of a maritime Brigadoon (see Bruce 1996; Carrier and Carrier 1987; Gold and Gold 1995; Hardy 1990) – were not merely idiosyncratic. They were part of a much larger, historically and culturally constructed scenario that has itself been the occasion for significant social transformation in many Scottish communities. We have only to consider, for example, the vast unpopulated estates of the north, kept "cleared" for lucrative, open-air leisure pursuits (Callander 1998, McEwen 1981; Wightman 1997).

Indeed, with respect to the distribution of land, Scotland appears downright archaic (Callander 1998; McEwen 1981; Wightman 1997: 189). In fact, Callander tells us, "Scotland is both the only country *in the world* with a feudal system of land tenure and the country with the most concentrated pattern of large-scale private estates" (italics mine; Callander 1998: 7; see also Short 1997: 310–32). Characterizing a late twentieth century European nation as feudal may seem like invective. Such usage stems, however, from the complex history of relationships between landholders and the general population. A small number of landowners has wielded great power, buying and selling enormous estates that may include a number of villages and that affect thousands of people.

In the western Highlands, for example, a community organization representing the seventy residents of Knoydart finally managed to buy the estate, which had deteriorated sadly over the past fifty years. They only managed to do so with outside help donated by lovers of nature and wilderness. However, a local man put it in historical terms. "The people of Knoydart are now free from the threat of suffering and injustice which was once so brutally inflicted by its owners during the Clearances of 1853 and the time of the land raiders" (Ross 1999: 7). Needless to say, the event got considerable press. It also aroused the fears of many landlords (McBeth 1998). However, locally driven possibilities for economic development usually remain extremely tenuous.

As the quote above reveals, sales of large estates, or announcements of new plans to extract capital from the land continue to call up the spectre of the Highland clearances and the prospect of displacement and landlessness. One often hears that the nineteenth-century era of mass evictions has not, in fact, ended.

Ideas of what Scotland, and Scotland's inhabitants, particularly in their more rural manifestations, are supposed to be, have played a significant role in how the political economy of many Scottish places has been shaped. We can see these ideas at work in the goals of those eighteenth- and nineteenth-century rural social engineers called the Improvers (whom I discuss in the next chapter); in Sir Walter Scott's powerful effect upon public perceptions of the Highlands[2] and the successful efforts of Thomas Cook to lure tourists there; in the pastoral revels of Queen Victoria. This last has been excoriated mercilessly by playwright John McGrath in *The Cheviot, the Stag, and the Black, Black Oil* (1974) in which North Sea oil development is depicted as a modern version of internal colonialism (so quaintly represented in the gentle humor of the film *Local Hero*).

I cannot pretend that romanticism and/or the projection of my own escapist fantasies had nothing to do with my later selection of a Scottish fishing village – albeit one outside the Highlands – for field research. For one thing, I have always been intrigued by the sea as a symbol of both freedom and danger, of raw, untamed "nature" at the doorstep, proclaiming the illusion of a frontier. For another, there is no denying that fishing villages are probably as close as one can get in the eastern Lowlands to a visual illusion that modernity has been kept at bay. These coastal communities appear to be discrete, even autonomous, with their distinctive architecture: narrow, winding streets, small, crowded houses and little commercial life beyond a post office and village shop. They have no chain stores – no Boots, no Marks and Spencer – and none of the ubiquitous shoe stores that seem to line virtually every British High Street. While many of them now house substantial populations of "incomers" who know nothing about fishing as a way of life, the public image of these places as fishing villages somehow survives. Indeed, in many places it is being highlighted for tourist consumption, as we shall see in Chapter 6.

Contemplating my own early ideas about Scotland has led me to consider more generally how romantic fantasies have informed the ways popular and ethnographic ideas about the rural/peasant/marginal/peripheral have affected the people designated as such. Each part of the world has had its share of representations that have been variously described as colonialist, romantic, orientalist, or occidentalist (Asad 1973; Carrier 1992, 1995; Clifford 1986; Pratt 1986; Said 1978), characterizations that reveal these as stereotyped essentialisms. This prompts us to ask how such images have conditioned ethnographers' interpretations of what we see in

Britain, to search for points of articulation between the belief in "folk" with more general ideas about British rural life. Specifically, we must wonder whether we are yet free from Redfield's unidirectional and polarizing paradigm of the folk/urban continuum (Redfield 1955). Do we still subscribe in some subtle way to Frankenberg's (1966) recasting of this paradigm as a "morphological continuum" of the truly rural to the urban? And what is at work here besides what Cohen refers to as a "powerful compulsion of anthropologists, inherited from their Victorian forebears, to taxonomy" (Cohen 1990: 204)?

## Imagining Fishers: "Folk" Tales

Long before the current popularity of "heritage" as an economic resource and nation-building device for Scotland, the fisherfolk have been constituting themselves as a people of strength and adaptability. If they have a totem, it is hard work. In daily conversation they argue, reminisce and dwell upon the dangers and importance of their bygone occupation. They cast themselves as the central characters in their own universe of meaning, even as they remain keenly aware that others have not always appreciated their skills and sacrifices. A difference now is that some of the fisherfolk's self-constructions are finding their way into the popular view. Emblems of their identity such as dress, boat models, and songs (Macdonald's nice phrase for this is a "cultural 'identikit'"; 1997: 246), in short, anything that can be captured and used for display, are now being used to sell the idea of fishing villages as desirable visitor attractions. This is not altogether an unwelcome development from many fisherpeople's point of view, as we shall see, but it is one that, rather ironically, depends upon maintaining the image of fishers as "folk."

What is this rather archaic category of "folk" life, from which others, particularly middle-class and urban others, are normally excluded? How has it become an archetype and what use is being made of it in the present day? And why are some folk "folk," and other folk not? The prism of modernity refracts "folk" into multiple meanings. David Buchan (1984: 1) glosses folk as referring to "anything old, or earthy or couthy or even, in the Scottish context, vernacular". McKinney (1999) adopts a similar view, saying that the boundaries between what counts as folk music are nearly impossible to pin down. Pre- or non-literacy has been invoked as a criterion. Only oral tradition counts. Colls (1977: 19) tells us, for example, that the great nineteenth-century folksong collector Cecil Sharp insisted that folk culture must be uncontaminated by print, and averred, moreover, that "folk music is the product of a race and reflects feelings and tastes that are communal rather than personal". Boyes (1993: 3) suggests that the counter-cultural folksong revival of the mid-twentieth century relied upon idealized notions of folk culture. "Old, lost, rural 'organic communities', rather than newly developed urban existence could, therefore, be held up as the only valid source of an alternative, uncultivated art". Folk have also stood as emblems of the nation. Herzfeld (1987) notes nineteenth century nationalists' belief that in folklife they could find the essence of national character, reducing local and ethnic differences to a single "a moralistic canon of texts that reduced diversity to uniformity". I will return to this question when I discuss the rise of folk museums in Chapter 6.

"Fisherfolk" is an occupationally centered cultural identity marked today by both dilemma and irony: dilemma because, as Chapter 5 will show, North Atlantic fishing communities are economically threatened as never before; and irony because, as we shall see in Chapter 6, their salvation may well lie in transforming themselves into cultural showcases or icons of one particular variety of Scottish "heritage," where aspects of the fishery are displayed and performed, yet where fish are no longer locally caught and sold. As the source of fisherfolk identity moves from fishers' material status as primary producers of food to their symbolic status as objects of "the tourist gaze" (Urry 1990), they come to stand "in opposition to the aesthetic ideal of a creative producer" (D. Miller 1995: 1). Putting it another way, once they were *fisher*folk; now they are becoming fisher*folk*, with all that the "folk" metaphor implies about essentialized tradition, about authenticity and putative antiquity at the end of the twentieth century (cf. Herzfeld 1987; Hobsbawm and Ranger 1983). What it means to be a member of a stereotyped and marginalized category like "the fisherfolk" in modern-day Britain, and how this stereotype becomes grounded in locale, I take to be one of my central theoretical, as well as empirical tasks. How long the fisherfolk can hold on to the idea of – and belief in – themselves *as fisherfolk*, even with its newly transposed emphasis, is a matter of considerable doubt and great local concern. In this sense, Scottish fisherfolk can be added to the list of peoples for whom cultural survival is an issue.

The "folk" label – highly loaded, indeed, antiquarian – says much about the survival of our own folk models of the West, of which fishers form a particularly instructive example (cf. Holy and Stuchlik 1981). Whatever else they might be, "folk" are almost always rural. As I have argued previously (Nadel-Klein 1995), images of British rural life as set in pristine circumstances occupy a special and privileged niche in the

Western imagination of place. They provide an internalized, exotic other that stands for a past of virtue and predictability. A comforting counter-weight to the confusions and burdens of modern life, one can point to them and say "Look! How wonderful that such simple places still exist; how lucky we are to be able to visit them."

"Folk" is a term that separates, one that implies a sense of difference, not just of residence or occupation, but of kind, a difference resembling the equally vague, but more academically respectable, notion of ethnicity. But "folk" is clearly not a neutral term and carries with it some heavy cultural baggage about backwardness. Folk are most widely known through two organizing ideas. The first is the notion of the country bumpkin: folk are simple. The second is the notion of special material culture: folk look and act different from the rest of us. As an American schoolchild in the 1950s, I can remember learning about European "folk" through textbook images of quaint, ceremonial peasant dress. Starched Swiss aprons, lederhosen, and kilted bagpipers come immediately to mind. Such images conjured up not only foreignness, but festivity. The people in the pictures always looked "historical," though no one ever said that they were dead or even obsolete.

Anthropologists of Europe need to address the folk category head on and consider how it resonates within our own discourses of Europe, as Herzfeld (1987) has said. While it may appear to be an archaism on one level, on another, it is very much a part of present usage within Europe itself and cannot be dismissed as a Tylorian "survival" within academia, a point that Herzfeld makes powerfully with respect to the ethnography of Greece and the idea of how we construct the very boundaries of the West (Herzfeld 1987).

More often, attention to problems of social marginalization and cultural survival has been directed to those places and peoples of the "Third" or "Fourth" Worlds, where Europeans have ventured and whose land and resources they have, in various ways, appropriated. Herzfeld's ground-breaking contribution was to redirect some of those concerns towards Europe itself. In *Anthropology Through the Looking Glass*, Herzfeld brought us "part-way home" (*pace* Cole 1977), as it were, to look at Greece as not-quite-Europe, not-quite-"Other." Standing on the margins of the continent, at the crossroads of many cultural encounters, Greece has had the ambiguous distinction of embodying both ancient (Western) glory and premodern (Eastern) backwardness in the eyes of its European neighbors. In a world where to be European has been to be presumed powerful, such conceptual marginalization has social and public policy consequences (Herzfeld 1987).

Malcolm Chapman (1992: 128) takes this line of reasoning both north and west, noting that "romanticisation of internal ethnic variety is a British invention" of the nineteenth century, particularly as applied to those rather amorphous creatures known as Celts. He examines their construction as an other worldly and primitively-derived folk survival within modern Britain, Ireland, and France. He takes it as "no surprise, then, that 'Celts' and the 'folk' should often seem virtually co-terminous categories" (1992: 116).

One does not have to go to the geographical periphery to find the cultural margin, however. The "other" may be found whenever class and power differences become conflated with localized identities. At such junctures, "locals" easily become either vilified or exoticized (or both). Thus in their stigmatized and dependent positions, they resemble other, less localized, but even more marginalized or pariah groups, such as the Gypsies of Europe (Barth 1969; Gmelch 1985; Okeley 1983). They remain the objects of fantasy, scorn or charity rather than empathy. The symbolic boundaries that define their communities are constructed in a chronic dialogue between "inside" and "outside" (cf. Cohen 1985), where being "inside" confers both rights and deprivation. In Britain, localized identities are often presumed to reside in villages, sites that have become virtually coterminous with the concept of the folk but that also provide microcosmic examples of the wider class system.

## Encountering Villages

Margaret Mead once worried that villages, like tribal societies, might be endangered in the modern world. She saw in them a special kind of social value perhaps unavailable elsewhere (Mead 1980). She has not been alone in her concern. It has been widely observed that the British – particularly the English – seem to worship the pastoral. Contemporary scholars of rural life have approached the subject from different critical perspectives and with various degrees of skepticism. Newby (1987: 3) sees in the romantic-ization of villages something pernicious, a refusal to acknowledge the brute impact of the social inequalities underlying rural life that he calls "one of the major protecting illusions of our time". On the other hand, Raymond Williams (1973), regarding the polarities and contrasts of city and country in constructing the pastoral perspective, sees an ambivalence about rural life unfolding through many centuries of Western literature, vacillating from the idea of the idyllic pastoral to the notion of rural parochialism, or even idiocy.

In my mind's eye, the popular image of the British village is a pallid, two-dimensional watercolor sketch rather than a robust oil painting full of color, depth, perspective and variety: white-washed cottages and gardens signal a community that is small, self-contained, and family-like in its dense web of harmonious relationships. It sits securely within its tidy lanes. The sketch itself, however, is a metaphor for all kinds of messages that are both widely disseminated and very seductive. They come to us strongly through many sources. Investigating these sources is an anthropological challenge of no mean significance; indeed it is at the core of the reflexive dilemma and of debates about the ontological status of cultural authenticity. Ethnographers are as susceptible as anyone else to the pictures that are drawn for them. The advantage of fieldwork is that it provides the chance to explore how these pictures have been drawn – and who is drawing them.

Literature, whether high, low or academic, has contributed substantially to this vision. Murder mysteries are one of my favorite examples because I am personally quite addicted to them. For years, I was particularly fond of the classic "English village" genre that depends upon a small community setting for the unfolding of its plot and characters (see Nadel-Klein 1995). Indeed, it is the stereotypical English village, with its nucleated settlement, resident squirearchy, and Norman church that informs the image embedded in what Raymond Williams (1973: 249) calls the "middle-class detective story". Here a timeless and traditional, comfortingly hierarchical social order is taken for granted. Such stories are, as he says, sometimes "combined with middle-class fantasies about the human nature of the traditional inhabitants" (1973: 249). In such stories, villages embody social stability and intimacy. Newby (1987: 1) describes this view as "the pastoralism of merrie rustics, safely-grazing sheep and stolid yeomanry". Villages thus appear to stand, not only for mystery readers but for a wider public as well, for the survival of our essential, "good" past, the place and time when social relations were safe, or at least predictable. In this view, inequalities are traditional and thus, somehow, inconsequential.

My naive, Edenic vision of Britain was also reinforced through my anachronistically constructed experiences as a tourist. Visitors anywhere in rural Britain, after all, are encouraged to sidestep anything that mars their preconceived, pastoral visions of unchanging village simplicity. Those who trumpet British destinations play this note very loudly. Consider, for example, the following advertisement that appeared in *The New Yorker*:

English Adventures. *Travel back in time* on our luxury tours to the enchanted villages and spectacular mountains of Wordsworth's Lake District, including visits to the Roman Wall and Yorkshire Dales. (28 September 1992; italics mine)

The British National Trust, which preserves over half a million acres of historic properties in England, Wales, and Northern Ireland, also embraces this approach, assuring readers of their magazine that "the British remain one of the most past-loving societies on earth" (Lohr 1989: 45). And where else but in a "village" could one find the living past, shored up by old walls and old ways?

However, it is not only tourism developers, mystery writers and wistful singers who have been obsessed by the village. By the 1960s, villages had begun to surpass tribes as archetypal anthropological units of study, our disciplinary preserve in the then largely sociological wilderness of "complex societies." Searching for manageable units in which to practice participant observation, ethnographers not surprisingly have gravitated to small communities with visibly accessible boundaries. Pioneered by Arensberg and Kimball in County Clare, early British and Irish studies focused on distinguishing rural from urban communities, identifying their salient structural and functional features (Arensberg 1959; Arensberg and Kimball 1968).

For them, as for Littlejohn in his study of the Border parish of Westrigg, village-ness and rurality apparently inhered in kinship ties, an egalitarian ethos, and a relatively "undifferentiated" economy, as well as in the shared built environment. Littlejohn appears to have found Westrigg somewhat disappointing in this respect (Littlejohn 1963). It was undeniably located in the countryside, but was distinctly lacking in *gemeinschaft* or community (Tonnies 1955 [1887]). Similarly, Frankenberg's revealingly titled chapter, "The Town That is a Village," expresses the notion that village-ness has an essential, moral quality. As he says of the Welsh mining town of Ashton, "It remains a village, but combines *multiplicity of ties and sense of community* with urban values and environment" (1966: 139; emphasis mine).

As Arensberg (1961) noted, such communities were recognized not merely as encapsulated "objects" in and of themselves but as "samples" of a wider social context. However, discussions about how to define that context, about the ways in which a part could stand for the whole, and about the relationship of locality to nation have never ceased to tax us. The very word, "village," suffered for years from very nearly the same epistemological ambiguity that has bedeviled the notion of "tribe" (Fried

1975). That is, everyone used it, and few bothered to define it. What assumptions were tacitly made about the nature of villages? Was the concept being reified according to some essentialist archetype?

A paradigm of village-ness is difficult to pin down. Nineteenth-century attempts to classify villages tended to take an evolutionist stance. Gomme (1890: 2), for example, insisted that "the village community is of primitive origin . . . its later existence a survival." Matless (1994) suggests that these ideas may not have disappeared as thoroughly as one might expect. He subtitles his Foucauldian genealogy of postwar geographical writing on the English village, "An Essay in Imaginative Geography". Such writing, he argues, colludes in an effort to present the village as a place of peace and stability, where form is valued over function and where tradition persists for its own sake. Behind this is the ideal of the rural as "a site of potential and actual [aesthetic and ecological] redemption" (1994: 49). Astutely questioning the meanings behind this representation, Matless also points to the idea that a village is situated within a rural landscape, highlighting its perception as a bounded, separate place, the non-urban and the non-suburban (1994: 77).

Size might be another vague criterion: Westerners think of villages as small places. However, village populations and areas vary considerably; there is seldom any problem in distinguishing them from cities, but they sometimes approach the dimensions of what might ordinarily be thought of as a town. But this is to objectify and essentialize the concept of size, which of course is itself relative to context and the experience of the observer. A village may be the largest or the smallest residential segment a person or society recognizes or experiences, depending on whether we're talking about Anglo-Saxon or nineteenth-century England, for example.

Most problematic is the notion of a village boundary. The word "village" conjures up an immediate impression of geographic coherence and limit-ation. A settlement called a village may be seemingly isolated – accessible only by sea, perhaps – or it may be obviously engulfed within an urban matrix. But the significance of geography is quickly changing, with electronic communications making it possible for computer operators in Ireland or the Philippines to deliver text to publishers in New York or Edinburgh and thus to help sustain their local economies. Where do cyber-commuters really work? Social boundaries are no clearer. Villages today house farmworkers, coal miners, and/or commuting stockbrokers, multi-parish vicars and retired physicians.

But the characteristic most often presumed intrinsic to village life remains the idea of community, of shared, overlapping ties and roles, of an ethos of "belonging" (Cohen 1982). Redfield spoke of it in terms of a way of "living, thinking and feeling" (Redfield 1955: 147). Certainly this was my unconscious mind set when I embarked upon my first fieldwork experience, which was not in Scotland but in England. As I was only an undergraduate at the time, my memories can have neither the richness nor the layering of Barbara Anderson's instructive memoir about *First Fieldwork* (1990). Still, I recall them here as a backdrop to my later encounter with Ferryden, my first Scottish field site and the subject of Chapter 3. It was in Puttenham, a small village in Surrey, that I first became truly aware of class and power. Following my junior year at Barnard College, I set off in 1967 to spend a summer in this prosperous little Green Belt village about 30 miles south of London. Puttenham fulfilled most fantasies: small and intimate, with flowers at every front gate. There was a Manor, a Squire, and even a thatched cottage or two. I kept expecting to meet Miss Marple. (And to this day, whenever I recall Agatha Christie's descriptions of St Mary Mead, I see Puttenham.)

A nucleated village, its single street (called, in fact, The Street) linked an 800-year-old church at one end with a tidy Council housing estate tucked away at the other. The Street wove past *The Good Intent* (a white, half-timbered pub that mystery writer Martha Grimes would appreciate).[3] Set back from The Street along a couple of meandering lanes, some newer and more affluent looking modern houses bespoke the influx of what Watson (1964) called the Spiralists, members of the post-war, upwardly mobile business class now seeking country living and gentility at a comfortable remove from the City. In keeping with Laslett's (1984: 25) observation that the English "still seem to want to live in the structures of the pre-industrial world as the proper place for the proper Englishman to dwell in", residents of Puttenham took great pride in having won the coveted "best-kept village" award for Surrey several years running (see Dugmore 1972 for a resident's account). They earnestly swept up litter and pruned the roses. I had never seen anything like it in my home state of Connecticut. A self-conscious discourse of rural "villageness" animated so much of this benevolent busy-ness. Villagers were determined to keep Puttenham both green and genteel even as it was changing from an agricultural backwater to a middle-class commuters' haven (Newby 1987: 222). Through numerous voluntary associations, they joined together to fulfil their image of how rural society should be.

But there is nothing like fieldwork to sweep away the veils of glamor. I was still enchanted by the lanes and hedgerows, as well as by the kindness with which I was treated. However, I quickly found that Puttenham's image was preserved in large measure through social practices predicated upon a relentless insistence upon social hierarchy. No number of murder mysteries could have adequately prepared me for the English class system: how, for example, the nuances of class were built into every speech event. Not just a matter of vocabulary or pronunciation, the higher ranked person held the reins in every conversation. I have never forgotten, for example, how the word "Quite," spoken softly but authoritatively, can end a discussion.

Now, as I began to ask what underlay this image of pastoral simplicity, the critiques of functionalist community studies I had read in graduate school hit home. Puttenham was not a closed, static or self-regulating social universe. Its 600 people were clearly and sharply divided into social groupings that reflected national hierarchies and history. Class in Puttenham was made manifest through occupation, education, dress, speech, dwelling and membership in voluntary organizations. Living standards ranged from affluent to poor. Some households still lacked indoor toilets whereas others had swimming pools. The landowning gentry; the affluent, London-commuting stockbrokers (See Newby 1987: 221); the shabby-genteel cottage dwellers; and what was once unproblematically described as the "working class" (Thompson 1968); all lived in the same village, but inhabited largely separate social worlds.

So while Puttenham fulfilled my immediate expectations of charm, in the long run, it also raised questions about the kinds of costs such an image entails. The experience of living there, albeit for only a summer, left with me a strong sense of unease, not least because I became aware that my American, undergraduate university-student identity, along with my natural shyness and reserve (the English seem to like these qualities) had saved me from the slights of class; indeed, it had given me access to a much broader range of people than the village inhabitants themselves normally enjoyed. So later, when I went to do fieldwork in Scotland, I was already predisposed to question the idea of community as homogeneous and to ask about the sources and effects of power.

## Finding Ferryden

In 1975 I set out to examine the social impact of North Sea oil development on the community, identity and boundaries of the east coast fishing village of Ferryden and on its relations with the neighboring market town of Montrose. For a graduate student brought up in the early 1970s political economy tradition of anthropology, with its emphasis upon power and the making of the modern world system (Wallerstein 1974), the chance to study local responses to multinational corporations, and to do so in a rich historical context, was enticing. My graduate training at the City University of New York had emphasized the importance – and the difficulty – of studying the ways local and regional elites negotiated processes of change. It also emphasized the importance of working in Europe, a very distinct, even radical, point of view for the discipline at that time. Thus I had not yet quite realized just how marginal the study of Europe still was within conventional ethnographic research.

Actually, my initial goals were somewhat vaguer than I have just presented them. When I first left for the field, I wanted to examine a Scottish coastal community but had no idea which one to choose. I knew only that I was going to the northeast, rather than to the more distant-seeming Highland and Island areas, despite my earlier yearnings for remoteness. For one thing, with a couple of exceptions, that was where the bulk of North Sea oil development was taking place and where its most immediate impacts were likely to be felt. For another, what little Scottish ethnography there was at that time had been done either in the Borders (Littlejohn 1963) or in the Western or Northern Islands (Parman 1972; Goffman 1963).

True to the traditions of our novelty-oriented discipline, I also wished to carve out new ethnographic territory. By that time, of course, I was better versed in Scottish history and wanted to address inequality and local struggles for survival. It seemed apparent that the small communities most directly affected by multinational oil operations would have little to say about the changes swiftly overtaking them. I wished to know what that would mean in people's lives and how they would respond. Would local culture persist in any significant way after the Texan oil drillers had marched through?

My discovery of Ferryden village itself was, in fact, purely serendipitous. After flying from New York to London, I boarded an early morning train to Aberdeen, hoping to consult with scholars at the university there about a possible research site. Previous experience had taught me that it would be unwise to arrive anywhere in Scotland after five or six in the evening (when the tourists' accommodation office had closed) and I hoped to make Aberdeen early enough to secure a bed-and-breakfast through the local tourist board. What I hadn't anticipated was that the train would become stuffed full of people in Edinburgh heading north to Carnoustie, the site that year for the British Open Golf Championship. Despite the collective wish of hundreds of golf enthusiasts and one anthropology graduate student for the train to speed along, it crept ever more slowly along the tortuous coastal route. By the time we reached Carnoustie, I began to worry that I would arrive in Aberdeen far too late to find accommodation. Now the train began to make sudden and inexplicable stops. Finally, word trickled through the compartments that the train ahead of ours had derailed.

Luckily, as it turned out, I had fallen into conversation with a college student on his way home to the town of Montrose, which we were then approaching. Along with a capsule description of the town, he told me that an offshore oil supply base had been recently established there. As we pulled into the station, I made a quick decision. It would be better to get a night's sleep thirty miles from my destination than to be stranded overnight in Aberdeen station. Reaching the Montrose tourist office just minutes before closing time, I was directed to the home of a salmon fisherman and his wife who provided bed-and-breakfast accommodation. Their hospitality proved to the best introduction I could have had to the area. They took pity on the "American lassie" who was traveling all alone and saw to it that I had company, rich, warm food, and tea – a lot of tea. Mr and Mrs Inglis urged me to stay in Montrose for the weekend so that they could take me for a sightseeing drive up into the glens and around the neighboring inland villages.

Our last stop was Ferryden, a place across the river from Montrose that they had described to me as a fishing village. As we crossed the bridge, my hosts pointed out the new Sea Oil Services Base that abutted Ferryden's northern flank. Built in 1973, just two years previously, developers had filled in the tidal "burn" or stream that had flowed past village doorsteps to make a site for the project. The Base gave the village an oddly compressed look. Its cottages seemed huddled together as if for protection, separated as they were only by a narrow road from the warehouses and construction equipment that occupied most of the Base's 40 acres.

The following Monday morning I went on to Aberdeen to spend a few weeks there conferring with regional planners and scholars at Aberdeen University's Center for the Study of Sparsely Populated Areas.[4] They confirmed my suspicions that much of the area north of Aberdeen (where most oil-related development was then located) was already being rather intensively studied by British researchers, primarily sociologists and economists. Little attention was being paid to developments further south, however, and no one had yet looked at the Ferryden and Montrose area; they encouraged me to begin work there. Wishing to avoid a turf war, but also intrigued by what I had seen of Ferryden, I agreed.

In retrospect, I must admit that I was drawn in part by Ferryden's relative obscurity. In my initial visit, it had become apparent that the Sea Oil Services base had wrought major changes in the village that seemingly had gone unremarked by outsiders. For example, I could not help but notice that everyone I met in Montrose, including my hosts, had referred to Ferryden as a fishing village, and yet I had glimpsed no signs of an active commercial fishery. I assumed (wrongly, as it turned out, for the fishery itself had gone a generation earlier) that the oil development was directly responsible for this absence.

The immediate task of figuring out "when is a fishing village not a fishing village" required attending to a problematic set of issues involving the formation and persistence of community identity. A complex historical as well as ethnographic trail lay ahead as the objectives of my research ramified quickly. Instead of looking at Ferryden village as a "thing" to which other "things" happened, I began to seek a more processual exploration that took into account how social and economic power was constructed and organized beyond the village level, and yet articulated within it. The significance of multinational oil companies began to recede somewhat in the context of a dense regional network of landowners and entrepreneurs who had brokered developments in the coastal economy for centuries.

Since the 1970s, Scotland has remained my primary site for fieldwork. I have returned many times over the years for research stays of varying duration, though never in the Highlands. Rather, the eastern and northeastern Lowlands have become my ethnographic bailiwick. I returned to Ferryden in 1984 to find that little had outwardly changed. However, several of my older informants had died and this left me with a curious sense of urgency. It was time to go further afield, to learn more about the wider world of Scottish fishing communities and particularly to investigate ones where the industry was still alive to some degree. So I ventured southward first, to the Fife coast; then I went north to the Moray Firth. A brief stay in the town of Nairn (12 miles east of Inverness) showed me how tourism was beginning to collide with fisher interests. Several longer stays in Buckie (another 20 miles eastward) taught me much more about these collisions.

These later trips (four in all) were, of necessity, shorter. Now I had a young daughter and a teaching position. In 1999, however, a sabbatical afforded me the chance to spend another half year in Scotland. This time I based myself in Edinburgh. I needed to look at things from the institutional and financial center of Scotland. There I learned more clearly than ever how "remote" fishing villages seemed to people outside them.

This book has emerged in part as an attempt to confront my early illusions of romantic Scotland without relinquishing my fascination with the country's extraordinary diversity of place, speech, community, and representation.

In this sense the book is also, in part, an anthropologist's answer to several modern travel writers. I refer here to two writers of very different dispositions: Paul Theroux and Bill Bryson. Each has written a memorable survey of travels around mainland Britain. Each speaks almost entirely in terms of what he saw, rather than of what he heard or learned from the people he met. Theroux, in *Kingdom by the Sea* (1983) writes rather sourly, to say the least:

> I came to hate Aberdeen more than any other place I saw . . . it was an awful city . . . It was only in Aberdeen that I saw kilts and eightsome reels and the sort of tartan tightfistedness that made me think of the average Aberdonian as a person who would gladly pick a halfpenny out of a dunghill with his teeth. (1983: 350)

To be fair, Theroux traveled through Thatcher's Britain, when unemployment had skyrocketed and attention to the quality of life had plummeted. Nonetheless, his account reeks of disappointment, of the failure of places to live up to his expectations.

Bryson penned *Notes from a Small Island* when memories of Tory rule had begun to fade and a lighter spirit prevailed. He wrote hilariously and with great affection. Like Theroux, he found Aberdeen a letdown, but for different reasons.

> If I had come to Aberdeen fresh from another country, it would probably have seemed pleasant and agreeable. It was prosperous and clean. It had bookshops and cinemas and a university and pretty much everything else you could want in a community. It is, I've no doubt, a nice place to live. It's just that it was so much like everywhere else. It was a British city. How could it be otherwise? (1995: 317)

In his own way, each author homogenized his experience because in his travels he did not spend enough time anywhere to get a sense of local knowledge and the particularities that form the substance of people's self-definitions. Places remained inanimate objects, foils for the writer's larger agenda (to critique; to amuse). Each writer is governed by preconceived notions: regarding a site as pleasing or not, according to what it *ought* to look like.

Britain is an entirely modern state, participating in a transnational capitalist economy, so signs of that economy conspicuously affect many towns: chain stores, malls, and some unfathomably ugly architecture. Certainly there is no excuse for the block-like British Home Stores building on Princes Street in Edinburgh, and the appearance of a Blockbuster

Video in Montrose does jar the senses (although everyone has long been used to Woolworths). It is not hard to see how visitors might be disappointed when the timeless images promised them either fail to materialize or are so conspicuously surrounded by reminders of the less picturesque. Where Theroux and Bryson see the obliteration of the local, however, the anthropologist may – no, must – see a more complex reality, one in which people negotiate both the sublime and the ridiculous, the preindustrial and the postmodern. People in the fishing villages are experts in such negotiations.

So now I will turn to the fishing villages themselves: their origins and development as a genre of place, as well as particular localities. Here we will see how fisherpeople became economically and socially marginalized, as well as how they became stigmatized as different and disreputable.

## Notes

1. M. Pardo's *Curtain of Mist*, where English children travel to pre-Roman Scotland, was my earliest encounter with our world's porous border with that of Celtic legend; see also multivolume stories by Cooper (*The Dark is Rising*), Garner (*The Weirdstone of Brisingamen*); O'Shea (*The Hound of the Morrigan*); and Yolen's *The Wild Hunt*. All of these are set in vaguely Celtic territory (mostly Cornwall and Wales) and involve desperate battles between good and evil.
2. In 1999, Jeanne Cannizzo of the University of Edinburgh, curated a wonderful exhibit on Scott and his influences for the National Portrait Gallery in Edinburgh.
3. Many of Grimes' books are named for pubs: *The Horse You Came In On* (1993), *The Old Silent* (1989), for example.
4. I owe thanks to the people associated with the Aberdeen University Institute for Sparsely Populated Rural Areas, particularly Dr Robert Moore and Dr Deirdre Hunt for giving me advice and encouragement at this time. For those interested in following some of the relevant literature on offshore oil, see, for example, Button 1978; Hunt 1976; House 1986; Moore 1982; MacKay 1986; Nadel 1983).

# Stigma and Separation: Fisherfolk as a "Race Apart"

## Introduction

Walk into one of the villages poised along the eastern coast of Scotland and see how the houses cluster close together, each facing the sea. With a slight reach of the imagination, they look like old men and women hunching their shoulders against the rough wind – or is it against the land? The village seems a closed society, with a wary, watching face behind each lace-curtained window. The "clannishness" of fisherfolk is common knowledge. It is also said that fisherfolk are different from other people, perhaps even an inferior breed.

> Even at an early age, one was aware that fishing communities were different. Adults talked about "close brethren" and the singing of fishermen in mission halls; the way the exterior of their houses seemed to sparkle because of their white-washed or painted walls; their lifeboat service; and their habit of only marrying within their own communities; until they almost seemed a race apart (Lockart 1997: xi).

When a middle-class, university-educated man at a Scottish National Party gathering in 1993 said to me that the people of Ferryden village were "odd" and closely inbred, he expressed a widely held stereotype that has a long ancestry. Penelope, an upper-class woman whose house overlooked the village, decried "prejudice" but admitted that "there are some around here who would still disapprove of farmers' sons marrying Ferryden girls. That's one reason they send their boys away to school." Jenny, a young woman from Montrose who had married a salmon-fisher, told me that when she and her husband announced their plans to go house hunting across the bridge in Ferryden, their friends protested that the village was backward, that it didn't even have even indoor plumbing, and joked that she'd have problems because her "ass was too big to fit into a bucket!"

Such comments reveal that Scotland's fishing communities have been assigned to an "invidious" social category (Berreman 1972). Like members of low-ranked castes, classes, races, and ethnic groups in stratified societies around the world, the fishing people of Scotland have been stigmatized. Popular – and formerly, even scholarly – attitudes towards them have been based upon explicitly essentializing understandings of their presumed innate character deficiencies.

This chapter details the early historical context of economic deprivation and dependency within which members of fishing communities became marginalized. In so doing, it reveals how localities may be formed as the unintended consequences of the systemic requirements of capitalism. Along the way, however, such localities take on their own dynamics to become forces in a larger setting. As I said in the first chapter, my task here is to elucidate how this history of marginality has underpinned fishers' identity as a special kind of "folk" who are attached to special kinds of places. With this historical understanding, we will be better placed to see how fishers have been and continue to be caught between competing rhetorics of hierarchy and equality in the modern Scottish nation.

## Fishers, Land and Power

To tease out the particular cultural and institutional factors that have made fisherpeople who they are today, I take a long-range, historical view of fishing as an economic enterprise in Scotland. Fortunately, I have help: several people have intensively examined the details of the fishing industry itself, particularly its technological and economic development over the last three centuries (including Coull 1969, 1972, 1986; Gray 1967, 1978; Miller 1999; Thompson, Wailey and Lummis 1983); others have taken a more ethnographic and contemporary look at specific communities (Baks and Postel-Coster 1977; Cohen 1987; Byron 1986; Dorian 1981; Knipe 1984). My task here is to coordinate these analyses in a systematic way so as to place the commonalities of modern fisher culture and experience within a wider Scottish context.

Some 150 fishing communities once were sprinkled along the Scottish coast from just north of the English border to the northeast corner of the Scottish mainland at Caithness (Anson 1930).[1] Each had its own fleet of boats that brought in the community's livelihood. Today, a small fraction of those living in these communities retains any viable connection to fishing, though many still cling to an image of themselves as fisherfolk. Moreover, many fishermen who still reside in these communities must now commute to work in the larger ports. As we shall see in Chapter 5, only a handful of harbors today provide the kind of market and support facilities that the modern industry requires.

Thus, only a few places appear to have a clearly viable long-term future. Some of the smaller, moderately busy ones may not even be operating a generation from now, depending upon how the industry adjusts to continuing ecological limitations, international competition, and spiraling costs. In short, what was once a widely dispersed, village-based occupation is giving way to the apparently inexorable logic of late twentieth-century capitalism, under the centralizing tyranny of economies of scale.

However, the decline in numbers of fishermen or fishing communities is not yesterday's artifact, or even that of the day before. If we look back before the days of "scientific," state-directed fisheries management, we can see lights along the coast flickering and dimming much earlier in this century, even when there was still, in the lovely words of Orkney writer George Mackay Brown (1995: 78), a "fish-fraught sea".

The early period of east coast, village-based Scottish fishing can be divided into two overlapping phases, marked by different degrees and kinds of community involvement. Roughly speaking, we can identify the first as the time, during the medieval era, when most fishing was carried on within a feudal context, and from a few scattered places along the coast. These fishers often combined fishing with farming, doing both on a small scale. The second phase began in the eighteenth century with the efflorescence of specialized occupational communities. Men from these settlements pursued both "white fish" (an indigenous category referring mainly to cod, ling, haddock, and whiting) and herring. It was during this time that we find observers commenting upon the fishers' "peculiarities."

The modern period that followed these phases began during the nineteenth and twentieth centuries. Here we find these specialized communities increasingly engaged in long-distance, more highly mechanized, commercial fishing that also entailed more proletarianized relations of work. Currently, fishers find themselves in a time of contraction and concentration of the industry, with its associated problems of economic and cultural survival for many villages. But these later developments will be discussed in succeeding chapters. Here I wish to provide the historical background for the fishers' modern predicament.

A proviso: it would be simplistic to regard these phases as marking any straightforward rise and fall or boom and bust of an entire industry. From village to village, they correspond only roughly to a common chronology and must not be considered in any sense as clearly demarcated or absolute. Different communities entered and left different stages of the fishing industry at different times and not all have participated equally in each. Yet, it is the case that the parameters of these phases comprise the ecological, technological, legal and market forces that connect the fisherfolk to their marine resources, to the state, and to the world system of power and organization. Fisherfolk have experienced and interpreted these connections as part of their place in the world, sometimes even as their destiny. This has contributed powerfully to their deeply felt sense of special character and separateness, as well as to their identification by others as a group of people that embodies "difference."

As we shall see, the early history of the fishing communities clearly shows that popular notions of the independent, entrepreneurial and care-free fisherman, cocking a snook at land-based conventions and free of the peasant's burdens of deference, do not work for Scotland. Never in Scotland's recorded history were fishing resources truly common property. Nor were fishermen ever "free," in the sense of having economic autonomy. Whatever the era, the historical record shows a long-standing pattern of landed dominance and fisher subordination. It is only in the latter part of the twentieth century that a few fishers have become truly prosperous when compared to some other segments of the Scottish population. Their most common experience has been that of disempowerment and cultural marginalization.

This low status has come with considerable symbolic baggage. East coast fishers have been seen as society's ragged edge. They have been held up as a contrast to Scotland's emerging modernist preoccupation with respectability, predictability, and social order. The people of the sea have stood for the backward, or even, perhaps, for the wild. Such representations have, of course, said as much about the wider culture in which fisherfolk have been embedded as they have about the fisherfolk, themselves.

## Phase One: The Medieval Era and the Prelude to Modernity

Scotland's ancient coastal riches played a significant part in establishing the hierarchies of wealth and power that began to encapsulate fishing people in medieval times. Records of a trade in salt herring between Scottish or English ports and Europe go back at least a thousand years, as do references to the importance of salmon, shellfish, and near-shore white fish along the east coast. Archaeological evidence reveals that fishing in various forms was practiced at least 9,000 years ago (Coull 1996: 2). Certainly shellfish (limpets, winkles, whelks, mussels, oysters, and scallops) have long been vital to the survival of many coastal populations in times of famine (Martin 1995: 5).

The period from the eleventh through the seventeenth centuries warrants scrutiny as the backdrop to later occupational specialization. The emerging circumstances of fishers during this period provide a view into how growing elites relied upon their ability to manipulate maritime resources. The evidence from so long ago inevitably gives us a rather top-down picture of what was happening, but it forms the only entry point we have towards understanding how and in what ways fishers became so vulnerable to power.

In the eleventh and twelfth centuries, Scotland was thinly settled and deeply rural, the total population being estimated at something well under half a million people (Dodgshon 1980: 47). However, this was no open, frontier society, with land and resources free for the taking by any intrepid settler, but already a fiercely contested, increasingly feudal realm. Sea resources were seen as an extension of land rights and not as common property, as modern Americans often perceive them "naturally" – though problematically – to be (McGoodwin 1990: 97; McCay 1989: 207). Rights to fishing in rivers and from the coast, along with access to pasturage, arable land, and forest, were eagerly sought for political and economic ends, and laws were drawn early to restrict access.

Salmon were particularly prized because they were so popular on continental European tables. Rights in salmon fishing from river, estuary and sea were, even at that early date, owned by the Crown or by the Crown's feudal vassals and were inherited along with an estate. Legislation regulating their catch and possession was introduced in 1318 and then again in 1449. Poachers were vigorously prosecuted (Association of Scottish District Fishery Boards 1977).

The people who worked farm, field and coast formed an essential part of the property and power-making process that supported the rise of Scotland's landed elites. Like farm workers, most fishing people lived as tenants on large estates. And like the farmfolk, they had fixed obligations of work and rent to their landlords.

Holders of Crown charters held possession of "Fishings, hawkings and huntings" and we know that many fishermen were obliged to hand over part of their catch to their overlord. A feudal due of one night's fishing a week was common. The court book of the Barony of Urie in Kincardineshire tells us fishermen in the seventeenth century were obliged to pay a yearly custom to the laird's lady of a hundred haddock and a pint of oil. (Lockhart 1997: 3)

In some places, fishers as well as farm workers were essentially enserfed, though not yet entirely dependent upon the sea. Following a common

North European pattern, they had access to a little common ground for growing root crops and rights to graze animals and gather firewood (Byron 1994; Coull 1969; 1971; Lofgren 1972, 1976). Fishing provided a crucial supplement to their meager land income. Thus there was little to distinguish these unspecialized crofter fishermen from the poorest of the subtenants in their conditions of work or dependence (Coull 1969). All starved equally during times of famine, when grain became unavailable. Thus we can read that in 1696, white fishers in Kincardine sought relief from the Poll Tax, "for they are beggin through the countrey this winter and spring and have not to cover their nakedness" (Flinn 1977: 167).

Some of what these fishing tenants caught went from net to household table, or was exchanged locally. The rest of the catch went to pay their rent in kind and found its way into a much larger nexus of trade. This nexus involved both the Crown and its feudal vassals, including barons and religious houses; the Scottish monarchy's control over the countryside was still relatively weak and its authority was continually challenged by the various rivalrous barons who built fortified houses to assert and protect their domains. Thus, beginning in the twelfth century, kings adopted a strategy of seeking out or creating allies in the countryside – more particularly, in the Lowlands – whose own vested interests would encourage them to resist the power of the nobility (Webster 1975: 12).

Among these allies were the monastic houses that had obtained Royal charters granting them land and fishing rights in return for their support against the nobles. The monks formed a powerful presence in the countryside and "possessed various exclusive privileges of trade and fisheries" from the twelfth century, if not earlier (Taylor 1859: 219). In the East Neuk of Fife on the Firth of Forth, for example, "the lands of Pittenweem and Inverin [St Monans] were given . . . to the monks of the Isle of May . . . in about 1143" (Martin 1991).

A Crown grant to an abbey or baron, however, did not ensure that all parties would assent peacefully to the division of the land in question. Access to the coast was often a contentious issue. For instance, in the following, rather picturesque account, we read about a conflict waged with both brute force and supernatural threat between landowner and monks in the thirteenth century:

. . . the Lord of Dundas, on the south side of the Firth of Forth, having asserted a right in his own person to certain rocks along the shore convenient for the landing of boats, interfered with the servants and boats of the Abbot of Dunfermline when attempting to use them. The abbot maintained that the rocks were the exclusive property of his monastery, and launched a sentence of excommunication against his opponent, who finding himself compelled to yield, "humbly supplicated the abbot, sitting along with some of his council on these rocks as being in possession of them, that he would absolve him from the sentence of excommunication, and he should abstain from molesting the men and boats in future . . ." (Taylor 1859: 175)

Near the English border, in the southeast region of Eyemouth, Benedictine monks owned the rights to sea fishing from that coast by the end of the thirteenth century (Anson 1930: 51). Northwards, in Auchmithie, in the fifteenth century:

> the fishermen were bound to the Abbey of Aberbrothock [Arbroath], providing a regular supply of fish for the monks, their guests and the cluster of habitations outside the Abbey Precinct. (King: n.d.: 4)

Of even wider significance for the Scottish economic landscape than contesting lairds and monks were the chartered market towns known as Royal Burghs. Beginning with King Alexander I (1107–24) and his son, David I (1124–53), Scottish kings attempted to consolidate control over rural resources by giving special trading status and rights to a number of these fortified centers. As legally privileged sites, they became pivotal nodes in organizing rural development, including both agriculture and fisheries. Their charters entitled them to monopolize trade over a wide hinterland. Within Burgh domain, only Burgesses – that is, only tradesmen who were recognized by the Burgh as members of the Merchant Guild – could buy and sell commodities.

Burgh control over the fish trade provided a source of revenue for the Royal purse through a series of taxes imposed from the thirteenth through the fifteenth centuries.

> The fact that a tax had been imposed on fish indicating [sic] that it must have been carried on to quite a large extent, and could provide a substantial source of revenue to the perpetually impoverished Scottish kings . . . (Sutherland n.d.: 13).

Given the increasing profitability of fishing, it is not surprising to learn of efforts to encourage more shipbuilding during the fifteenth century: ". . . Lordes, Barrones, and burrowes gar mak schippis, busches [large boats] and great pink boats with nettes . . ." (Sutherland n.d.: 13).

Many of the early Burghs, such as the North Sea ports of Aberdeen, Fraserburgh and Montrose, had their own fisher districts (Coull 1996: 35). However, few separate fishing villages existed at the time. In fact, before the eighteenth century, according to a survey of British fishing history, relatively few "small independent fishing communities proper, of the village type" had as yet appeared anywhere in Britain (Coull 1983: 13; see also Coull 1969). "There is evidence . . . that fishermen had settled along the coast in huddles of earth and thatch houses by the mid-seventeenth century, about a century before the first planned fishing villages appeared" (Millman 1975: 166).

Every foot of coastal ground in Scotland was owned or controlled by Crown, Burgh, religious house, or laird, so rural development was stymied. According to Millman (1975: 153), "until the sixteenth century [the Burghs] were largely responsible for the lack of village communities until the second half of the eighteenth century."

Later on, between the fifteenth and the seventeenth centuries, a number of smaller market centers, chartered by nobles as Burghs of Barony, arose to compete with the Royal Burghs. All in all, seventy Royal Burghs and some two hundred others were eventually established, mostly in the Lowlands (Lenman 1981: 3). The merchants of these Burghs not only dominated local trade, but also carried on a substantial long-distance business with English and European ports, exporting such goods as grain, hides and skins, wool and coal, as well as fish (Lenman 1977). It was not until the latter part of the fifteenth century that fish became increasingly important to the Scottish economy, in part because trade in wool and hides declined. This trend continued in the sixteenth and seventeenth centuries, if by fits and starts (Lynch 1992: 71).

The growth of Scottish fisheries was also prompted by envy of more successful European fleets. But it was also hampered by inconsistent laws, uncommitted investors, the dominance of lairds, an unskilled labor force, slowly developing technology and burdensome taxes. In the late fifteenth century, cod fishing efforts by Portuguese and English sailors off the Grand Banks of Newfoundland were spectacularly successful. North Atlantic fisheries in many places quickly became big business and, increasingly, the subject of governmental regulation. In a prelude to modern debates over coastal domain and territorial waters, fifteenth- and sixteenth-century monarchs worried that Scotland was losing out to foreign competition. The Dutch, in particular, who maintained a monopoly over the herring shoals and the Continental market, maddeningly sailed unchallenged into Scottish waters off Shetland, Aberdeen, and Fife.[2]

In the fifteenth century, James IV's answer to this threat was to promote the building of harbors and ships on the Firth of Forth. Along the way, he made use of what were widely seen as the "surplus" poor:

Among various laws that were passed in his reign was one ordering that "all maritime burghs should build busses, or vessels of at least twenty tons burden, to be employed in fishing, and all idle persons should be pressed into that service". (Anson 1930: 1)

Small-time fishermen on many coastlines found themselves being coerced or enticed (or both) to fish more and to venture further offshore (Lofgren 1972). Such efforts to coerce "idle persons" were vigorously pursued:

"In ilke [each] Burgh of the Royaltie, that officares of the burgh make all starke, idel men within their boundes to pass with the said schippes for their wages, and gif [if] the said idle men refuses to passe, that they banish them the burgh" . . . and if the officers of the burgh omitted to banish reluctant fishermen, then they in their turn could be fined 20 pounds . . . for neglect of their duties. (Sutherland n.d. 15)

Despite such pursuit, Scottish fisheries in the sixteenth and seventeenth centuries continued to remain relatively undeveloped. It was not that fishermen were recalcitrant, but that such development was not under their control. Though serfdom as an institution had generally died out in Scotland by the middle of the fourteenth century, the system of land tenure, labor and residance remained staunchly feudal. Moreover, certain classes of workers were re-claimed as serfs in 1606 when Parliament passed laws creating a "system of life binding for coal and salt workers" (Whatley 1988: 237; see also Wallerstein 1980: 93).

In some places, fishermen were similarly bound. King, for example, notes that those Auchmithie fishermen enserfed to the Abbey at Arbroath were not released at the formal and final abolition of serfdom in Scotland in 1799 (King n.d.). Summers (1995: 39) says that "in Northeast Scotland . . . It was also an offence for anyone to resettle, harbor, or entertain the fishers and boatmen who belong to another". Hay and Walker (1985: 18) provide an example where the spirit of the law apparently outlasted its letter:

An earlier migration into Arbroath at the beginning of the eighteenth century "clandestinely and under a cloud of night" by a family named Cargill, had led to a judicial decision in 1805, granting in favour of the Earl of Northesk, the right to look upon his white fishers as serfs or thralls. [and note that the date follows the act of 1799]

Smout (1969: 170), on the other hand, argues that efforts to enserf fishermen in the northeast failed because the fishermen simply "sailed away." He contrasts fishers with colliers and salters who were enserfed in part because the localized nature of their work made such bondage easy to impose (1969: 170). Whether enserfed or not, however, medieval fishers were tied to the domain of a landed proprietor and subject to strong control. The lairds of many coastal estates claimed "exclusive rights to land fish, beach boats, and gather bait . . . on their respective foreshores (Summers 1995: 39). Thus, the popular image of the fishermen roaming the seas (like the fish they pursue) is a rather misleading one. True, they might sail where they wished, but where could they land, and what would await them there?

## The New Fishing Specialists: Objects of Improvement

Scottish fishing can be said to have entered its second phase in the eighteenth century with the rise of specialized communities. It took a remarkable complex of ecological and economic developments to organize coastal society on an entrepreneurial basis and to create specialist fishers. Chief among these were: migrations of herring away from their old Baltic haunts into North Sea waters; infusions of Royal and mercantile capital into boat building, fish catching and marketing; and a new ethos of agrarian commercialism that transformed the entire countryside from a post-feudal economic torpor to a new, aggressive capitalist search for profit. This new ethos was strongly stimulated by a crucial political development, namely, the Union of 1707, in which the Scots relinquished their rights to a separate Parliament, essentially ceding sovereignty to England. This led to the lowering of trade barriers and to new opportunities for foreign investments that inspired a rising generation of entrepreneurs.

In their efforts to develop the fisheries, landowners thus had help both from organized capital and government. An important turning point was the recognition by George I in 1718 that the lingering "shadow of the Dutch" (Gray 1978: 5) might be lifted by stimulating fishing through a new set of institutionalized incentives. These, including bounties to fishermen and curers and subsidies to build fishing boats, as well as "detailed regulations as to the time and season when fishing was to be carried on" (Anson 1930: 2), proved somewhat more successful than the earlier efforts of James IV to build harbors and boats. In 1750, more bounties were introduced, specifically targeted at increasing the herring catch. Yet, these still met with limited success. As Scottish economic historian Malcolm Gray (1978: 5) points out, few merchants were yet seriously committed to the fishery:

The merchants who took the financial risks were men for whom herring fishing was but one of many interests; the vessels were designed for more than one purpose and were turned into trading ships for a large part of the year; and the labour force was created by attracting, for a season, men from different districts and occupations. When profits failed the whole enterprise was threatened with extinction, leaving no solid interest or community. But, at the end of the century, public money still brought the annual creation of a fishing fleet, artificial and rootless as it might be.

The opening of the Baltic market in the middle of the eighteenth century finally turned the tide (Fraser 1971: 70). After this, fishing became an organized industry. Indeed, in 1786, the British Fisheries Society was founded, "promoted by men of the landlord and merchant classes with an over-riding interest in social development, particularly of the western Highlands" (Gray 1977: 5). In 1809, the British Board of Manufactures established an adjunct Fishery Board to promote the herring trade (Coull 1992: 117). By the 1830s, fisheries on the east coast were well established and the bounties were discontinued.

But progress tended to exact a price. Governmental efforts to develop the fisheries operated at the expense of local autonomy and the poorer participants. From the outset, small-scale, part-time fishermen, those using small boats, were marginalized. Laws prohibited them from selling their herring catch to the large-boat fleet that had been produced by the bounty incentives. In addition, the salt laws mandated the use of expensive foreign salt that was available duty-free only to fish-curers, or middlemen. By and large, "ordinary fishermen were hampered rather than helped by legislation" (Gray 1978: 6).

All over rural Scotland, the poor were becoming marginalized in other ways as well. After all, changes in the fishing industry were but one part of a much larger set of changes being set in motion during the late eighteenth and early nineteenth centuries. Historians refer to this period as the Improving Movement or Era, which was intimately linked both to new economic ambitions and to the philosophical, scientific and social development of the Scottish Enlightenment or Renaissance (Phillipson and Mitchison 1970). Writing in the middle of the nineteenth century, historian Thomas Buckle (1970: 150) saw the new, progressive spirit of entrepreneurship and systematic inquiry resulting in "two powerful and active classes, whose aim was essentially secular; the intellectual class, and the industrious class". Membership in these classes overlapped and included philosophers, inventors, and scientists such as Adam Smith, Adam Ferguson, David Hume, Joseph Black, Frances Hutcheson, Lord

Kames, and James Hutton, to name just a few of the well-known luminaries. Benjamin Franklin, who visited Scotland several times, found it to be much in sympathy with his own ideals (Sher 1993).

The entire country seemed caught up in the social philosophy and capitalist goals of the Improvers. These men believed that rural life in particular, and Scottish life more generally, would be greatly enhanced by reorganizing the rural population. In so doing, new sets of distinctions between laborers and landowners were also introduced. Mitchison notes a growing emphasis at this time on domestic cleanliness, for example, as well as more demands upon farm tenants to provide labor and service. Master and servant now kept their distance from one another, instead of mixing freely and even eating together as had formerly been common practice. "So we get social divisions, temporary or permanent, sharpening into class" (Mitchison 1978: 84–5).

Moreover, what amounted to an agricultural revolution began to excise "excess population" from the countryside and draw it to the coasts. "However rational the basis of the change, as it came about it involved in many cases the compulsory movement of unwilling population to a place and type of life they had no experience of and to a new system of hard and regular work" (Mitchison 1978: 110). People from both Highland and Lowland regions were moved into planned villages dedicated to particular occupations. Many of these places were laid out according to principles of hygiene and efficiency on privately owned land, thus providing local labor reserves, particularly for agriculture and fisheries, but also textile manufacture (spinning and weaving), salt and sea-coal production (Houston 1948; Gray 1984: 19). Smout (1969) estimates that about 130 communities were established in this manner, most of them east of the Highland line.

Many landowners were also convinced that by establishing villages, they were providing a moral service to the nation in civilizing the rude and uncouth denizens of the countryside. After all, as Carter (1981: 9) has said:

> Until the end of the eighteenth century ruling class attitudes to the Scots peasantry were universally hostile. Peasants were sub-human, mere beasts of burden who produced rents upon which a gentleman might live in comfort. When, under the influence of the Scottish Enlightenment's brief efflorescence, ideas of scientific agriculture began to circulate in genteel circles, then the peasantry moved from being simply irrelevant to being positively awkward . . . they represented a major obstacle to the rational – and for landlords and proto-capitalist farmers, highly profitable – reorganisation of agriculture.

In Smout's (1970: 79) view:

> [Landowners believed] that a village community, properly conducted, offered the ideal moral environment in which to keep a working population virtuous and respectful, the perfect mean between the indolence of the deep rural peasantry and the profligacy of unregulated life in the big towns.

Such settlements were thus meant to produce a new class of worthy and industrious – and, of course, profitable – poor. The surpluses extracted from their labor would feed the trading appetites of the lairds, who would reinvest back into rural industries. Eventually, Scotland's share of international trade would grow. The whole nation would thus be "Improved," or modernized.

> The eighteenth century village was developed in response to and also to assist a revolution in the economy of the estate and of the nation: it was expected to provide a completely new framework for human life in the countryside. (Smout 1970: 75)

This framework entailed a radical reconfiguration of the working landscape.

> In both the Lowlands and the Highlands the old clachans [hamlets] and run-rig farming were swept away and replaced in the broad straths and Lowland vales by a more or less regular pattern of large square fields in individual holdings. Hedges, sporting coverts, ornamental woodlands and shelter belts were laid out by Improving Lairds who often vied with each other in their planting activities. (Millman 1975: 103)

In a rather anodyne summary of a process that must have caused the pain of dislocation to many working men and women, Phillipson and Mitchison (1970: 4) write that:

> A whole ruling class, the great nobility, country gentlemen, lawyers, ministers, educationalists, philosophers and men of letters singly, but more often collectively, can be seen trying to adapt a given social, economic, political and ideological infrastructure to promote economic growth and social progress.

In addition to the planned settlements, many others were simply "planted," that is, established for similar purposes but with less investment. Coull (1969: 17) summarizes the process as it played out in the lives of the fisherfolk:

In the rise of the fisheries, the lairds of coastal estates were the prime movers as organizers and entrepreneurs, and the fisherfolk on their part eventually developed into distinctive communities separate from their farming neighbors, and in them the work was organized on a family basis (Coull 1969: 17).

The east coast saw the greatest proliferation of new fishing villages. According to Gray, efforts to found west-coast fishing settlements were generally less successful, despite the best efforts of the British Fisheries Society.[3] Few west-coast landlords took much interest in developing the fisheries, perhaps because herring shoals appeared less "reliably" in western waters (Coull 1971: 4). West-coast fishers were generally spread out on widely spaced smallholdings and they continued to mix fishing with farming. Thus the radical division of fisherfolk from farmfolk never took hold there, though Czerkawska indicates that some fishing villages on the Ayrshire coast were once "isolated from the agricultural community" (Czerkawska 1975: 1).[4]

Thus the Improvers were crucial to giving Scottish fishing industry a vital injection of capital and attention. During the Improving Era, fishing, like agriculture, became increasingly commoditized and many households were reorganized in its service. By the end of the eighteenth century, the days of mixing farming with fishing were over for east-coast communities. By this time, few fishers there had even the meagerest access to land for gardens. Indeed, that was the point. People with no land would fish and fish hard. "With his very existence depending on regular and reasonable returns from his fishing, the drive to find the best system of fishing was correspondingly more intense" (Gray 1978: 7). Like early Newfoundland fishermen who were prohibited by law from owning land, lest they divert their energies in unprofitable ways, Scottish fishermen could – and did – provide a new resource for landowners and merchants eager to participate in the rise of European capitalism (Sider 1988: 112).

It thus became common in the eighteenth century for a laird to own a "fish-toun," as he might a "ferm-toun." In the Moray Firth region, for example, we find that, in 1716, Findochty "was built by one John Ord for thirteen fishermen and eleven boys" (Wood 1991: 26); Portgordon "was founded in 1797 by the 4th Duke of Gordon" (Wood 1991: 44); "William Young . . . in 1806 founded Hopeman as a fishing port" (Seton 1985: 7); and Portessie was founded as a fishing station in 1727 by the local laird, Hay of Rannes" (Seton 1987: 20), and

. . . by the 1790s an entire seatown, home to "ninety-three families", presumably mostly fishers, had grown up [in Avoch], the families moving in from other parts of the Moray Firth coast. Macduff grew from a small place in 1732 with only a few fisher houses to a large village of 1000 people by 1790, with well-laid-out streets and a harbour on which the laird, Lord Fife, had already spent 15000 . . . Eight fishermen in Elie were granted rent-free houses on the condition that they supply the town with fish at least three times a week. (Millar 1999: 8)

Lairds also owned the very boats in which the fishermen sailed. Summers (1995: 39) notes, for example, that

in Buchan [the northeast] in the late eighteenth century, the laird let the rights of the fishings to a 'tacksman' who then purchased boats and contracted a crew to fish in each boat for a specified numbers of years for rent . . . fishermen were only free agents when their contract expired, at which time they could enter a new contract or move elsewhere.

Over time, new lairds built new fisher settlements, sometimes recruiting fishermen with incentives advertised in local newspapers (Summers 1995: 41). Fisherfolk began to migrate from one village to the next, looking for better harbors and working conditions. Talking about the recruitment techniques that landowners employed, Lockhart (1982: 38) says that they or their agents

travelled to existing villages to bargain with boat crews. The system of tenure in older maritime villages favoured such visits. Leases were granted for a period of seven years, the expected life of a boat hull supplied by the proprietor to each crew. In return, a combined rent was paid for the boat and cottages occupied by the fishermen. At the end of each period the crew was free to re-engage or alternatively leave in search of lower rental terms or better harbour facilities.

Lockhart's analysis of migrations to planned villages shows that the fishers seldom moved very far, usually less than twenty miles: "it seems probable that a desire to remain in personal contact with friends and relatives and to continue fishing in familiar waters influence migration decisions" (Lockhart 1982: 42). There were some exceptions. The fisherfolk of Ferryden, for example, claim that their forebears came from much farther away. They emigrated from the Black Isle, on the Cromarty Firth, enticed by the landlord with promises of good fishing and financial support.

From the late eighteenth century through the early nineteenth century, however, there was another source of labor for the fisheries of the northeast, particularly along the coasts of Sutherland and Caithness. These were the evicted clansmen from the Highland glens, the victims of the Clearances. Taking place at a time when a "mercantile and money-making spirit was diffused to an extent formerly unknown" (Buckle 1970: 144), the Clearances were really the last gasp of the centuries-old enclosure movements depriving peasants of access to land in both Britain and the European continent.

Beginning in the 1780s, encouraged by the prospects for profits to be made from the wool trade, Highland clan chiefs, lairds and aristocrats began the process of ejecting entire communities to free up land for grazing. Landlords drove sheep onto land that had been used for cattle pasture and crops. Thousands of people in communities from Sutherland to Skye felt the scourge of the eviction notice. The process was often violent, always brutal. Prebble (1963) records that landowners' agents, called factors, did not hesitate to pull recalcitrant tenants from their cottages or even to burn them out (see also Hunter 1976).

Although many of those displaced made their way to Glasgow, or sailed for Canada or the United States, the outflow could not be entirely absorbed by urban or overseas emigration. Something had to be done with those left over. Luckily for the lairds, a precedent was available: James IV's decree that "idle persons" should be pressed into the service of the fishery. Some of the population for the new fisher settlements, particularly in the regions north of Inverness – Caithness, Sutherland, and Ross and Cromarty – were thus drawn from inland areas of the Highlands:

> . . . in Sutherland in the early nineteenth century it was largely the erroneous belief that the population could find employment as fishermen, within the estate but on the coast, that led the Countess to allow the clearance of several thousand tenants from potential sheep farms lying inland. (Flinn 1977: 32)

Families who had known only subsistence agriculture and cattle droving were forced, virtually overnight, to learn the rigors of fishing. Green (1936: 111) refers to some places along the Moray Firth as having been settled by "squatting" on land that was of no use for farming (1936: 111). Many died in this attempt. Others adapted, in a struggle which has been compellingly recounted in Neil Gunn's romantic novel of the northeast coast, *The Silver Darlings*:

> They had come from beyond the mountain which rose up behind them, from inland valleys and swelling pastures, where they and their people before them had lived from time immemorial. The landlord had driven them from these

valleys and pastures, and burned their houses, and set them here against the sea-shore to live if they could and, if not, to die. (Gunn 1941: 12)

Once settled into a fishing village, fishers, whether there voluntarily or not, found themselves bound up in a set of obligations to the laird. As already seen, the laird generally owned or held mortgages on the boats, which were rented or sold to the fishermen in shares. The fisherfolk paid their rent in kind. But by virtue of the debt they had incurred, they were not free to leave. They also had little control over the conditions of their work and could be forced to face dangers for which they were ill prepared:

This persisted into the latter part of the eighteenth century, as is instanced at Fraserburgh, where the fisherman was bound to serve for a fixed period in a boat . . . and at Buckie it is reported that the laird Dunbar drove his men to sea when they were reluctant to go out in adverse weather. (Coull 1969: 24)

Also, in Buckie, "fishermen who did not go to sea often enough to please the laird were put in the 'joogs,' or manacled with irons" (Hutcheson 1888). The laird, of course, had his eye on the profits to be made from the fishermen's risk.

Whether the new residents were novices or experienced fishers, the creation of the Scottish fishery entailed a radical separation of fisherfolk from land people. Many of modern Scotland's fishing communities thus originated as occupational enclaves, surrounded by farms, perhaps abutting towns, but always as distinct places. Their inhabitants were, moreover, usually derived from the poorest segments of the agrarian population (Byron 1994).

Now wholly dedicated to fishing, by the beginning of the nineteenth century, the villages of Scotland's east coast had taken on a distinct character and rhythm of work. First the white fish, and later the herring, dominated their economies. Some northern communities also sent lobsters and crabs to the London market. Dogfish, a generic term for small sharks used for oil and fertilizer, were also valued (Coull 1969: 26–7).

Whatever they pursued, fishermen had to be highly skilled. Their basic technique was hand-lining, which took two forms. Most common was the inshore, or sma' [small] line fishing, which used a lighter weight line to catch fish found relatively close to shore. For these, men made daily trips five to 10 miles offshore. Some communities, notably Buckie and Peterhead, also had a spring "great-line" season that took men much farther away for days at a time in their sail-powered, wooden vessels to pursue larger species (Elliott 1978).

Like their peers elsewhere around the North Atlantic, crews often comprised brothers and their sons. This generally made for good working relationships but, of course, it also meant that the loss of a boat could mean the loss of an entire family (see Britain 1974; Lofgren 1972; Nemec 1972). (This was an occupational hazard rarely visited upon farmers.) As coastal-dwellers, they faced danger from yet another source: this was the threat of the press gang. During the Napoleonic Wars, boats at sea might be boarded and the young men essentially kidnapped for Navy service (P. Smith 1985). Many of these, of course, never returned.

> Fishermen were lifted from the beach as well as being forced from their homes and sobbing families to be put in irons until taken aboard the man o' war needing their services. Horrible as that was, one's fury rises more when it is learned a favourite trick of the press-gang was to wait in hiding for a boat returning from the fishing grounds and grab the crew in their exhausted condition. No wonder the spies who would secretly mark the house of a good seaman were so detested. No wonder secret warning signs were put up by wives when the presence of press-gang was noted. Many a fisherman had a secret recess or bolthole he would make for when there was an unknown knock at the door. (Lockhart 1997: 8)

Along with risk, fishermen shared whatever profits there might be. Typically, the catch was divided on what was called the Scottish share system. Details of this varied around the coast, but in general meant that each fisherman received an equal share of the profits, if any, after allocating two-thirds of the catch to the boat and gear. No distinctions were made according to the success of each man's line, or to his seniority, with the exception of boys just starting out. This practice ensured continuing equality both on board and on shore – even though this might be an equality of dearth:

> This plan was sufficiently flexible to allow a man to become a crew member although he had no fishing gear; usually it was the skipper who would put in an extra deal and the share-out would be adjusted accordingly . . . The other side of this system was that poor fishing could mean weeks of work with no earnings, and even being in debt at the end of a season, with the fishermen having to "pay-in" to cover the main expenses. (Murray 1986: 5)

By the end of the eighteenth century, the laird's power began to give way to that of the fish curer. The rise of entrepreneurial capitalism meant the erosion of feudal control as fishers came to rely upon the cash subsidies and advances the curers offered in exchange for exclusive rights to the catch, sometimes for an entire fishing season. Reportedly, curers favored village ale shops as places to make these transactions because a befuddled fisherman might be a less-than-shrewd bargainer.

Curers, it seems, were everywhere. Thompson estimates some 400 of them along the east coast by the 1830s. A few of these became powerful merchants, eventually founding dynastic family firms such as Joseph Johnston & Sons of Montrose. However, many were quite short lived, suffering the usual fate of undercapitalized small ventures.

> Indeed, a typical firm lasted less than five years. A curer needed little fixed capital: a cooperage, barrel and a salt store, a farlin (trough) and an open space – which could be hired – for the gutters to work; and sufficient work for just one full-time cooper making barrels through the year, and a dozen fishgirls and labourers for the season . . . (Thompson, Wailey and Lummis 1983: 152–3)

According to Thompson, Wailey and Lummis (1983: 152) herring fishermen from the north-east had

> already secured ownership of their boats and gear by the 1820s. Instead of working for landlords, they engaged themselves seasonally to curers, fishing for pre-arranged prices, provided certain quantities were reached. Settlement was at the end of each season . . . After an unsuccessful season a fisherman would be in debt to the curer, and after a run of bad seasons could lose his boat to him. But while this happened in individual cases, the rising prosperity of the industry meant that it was not the general pattern.

It must be said, however, the for the white fishermen further down the coast, boat-ownership was still highly elusive.

As they penetrated deeper and deeper into the lives of fishing communities, curers developed a widespread reputation for rapacity and sharp dealing. "The fish-curer is the enemy of the fisherman," was the phrase repeated to me often in Ferryden. But there is an irony here. From a longer, historical perspective, curers were the advance guard of modernity. They were indispensable in generating the capital without which the herring fishery and the many villages supporting this fishery along the east coast would not have arisen or grown (Gray 1978: 29). These communities, still visible today, have come to constitute "real" or archetypal fishing communities in the contemporary popular imagination. Thus, as we shall explore later on, without the lairds, the Improvers, and the curers, there would now be no villages for tourists to visit. But I am ahead of myself here. Chapter 6 takes up this more recent development.

For now, it suffices to reiterate the chronic poverty and hardship that fishers endured during these early days. What we have seen up to this point is that fisher people and fisher communities, right from medieval times, were subject, first, to feudal and then to mercantile control. In addition, the special conditions of their work and its localized encapsulation on land also left them vulnerable to stigmatizing ideologies of difference and inferiority, ideologies already implicit with the Improving movement, but made increasingly explicit later on.

## Putting Fishers in their Place: Stigma

By the end of the eighteenth century, fishing specialists lived in clearly identifiable settlements with sharply marked boundaries. These were occupational communities, or single-industry places that were small and homogeneous. Within them, virtually every member of the community, male and female, relied directly upon the success of the catch. Villagers' neighbors knew the details of each others' lives inside and out. Everyone shared the same standard of living and everyone's life chances were roughly the same. More often than not, co-workers were kin. More than just accidental concentrations of workers, villages were solidary, multi-generational enclaves of fishery specialists. People lived their lives within dense social webs that could sometimes extend outward to include fishers from other villages, but that were otherwise tightly contained.

Among the many aspects of life they all shared, regardless of which village they inhabited, was the stigma attached to their way of life. Fishing enclaves were held in very low esteem by most non-fishing people. Fishers were marked as a peculiar kind of "other," an alien breed of people inhabiting the coast. At first glance, this seems curious. After all, no part of Scotland is more than 60 miles from the coast. The mainland can be regarded as a large, heavily indented peninsula continually dampened by the cold and turbulent waters of the North Sea and the North Atlantic. Scotland's economic history has been perforce a largely maritime one: coastal and long-distance trade, shipbuilding, and, of course, fishing, have been of paramount importance in building the Scottish economy. Nonetheless, a saying that I heard in Ferryden has also been reported for other fishing villages going back many generations: "The corn and the cod dinna mix" (Coull 1969: 23).

Many studies of Scottish fishing communities (Baks and Postel-Coster 1977; Byron 1986; Gray 1978; Knipe 1984; Postel-Coster and Heijmarin 1973) have tended to ignore or underplay the role that social exclusion has played in the ways fisherfolk see, and have seen, themselves in relation to the rest of Scottish society. This omission is all the more curious because the wider literature on fishing peoples suggests that identifying fisherfolk as different and strange is remarkably common throughout Europe and elsewhere in the world. Coull (1972), for example, claims that in many parts of Europe, fishing "has been regarded as an occupation of the lowest social classes". Smith (1977: 8) notes that fisherfolk often appear to be "a denigrated, if not despised segment" of the societies in which they live. Ward points out that the sea-fishermen of Kwangtung (Hong Kong) "have been despised, placed at the bottom of local systems of social stratification" and even believed to be physiologically peculiar (1965: 117). In some, though not all, parts of Japan, people are reported to have regarded fishermen as "unclean" (Norbeck 1967; Kalland 1995: 19). Fishing stigma has also been reported for parts of Korea (Brandt 1971). Moerman says that fishers are often aggressive and individualistic as a way of keeping their communities tightly bounded and that outsiders interpret this as "bad manners" (1984: 53).

In Scotland, explicit references to fishers as different and undesirable emerged in the eighteenth century along with the rise of specialization (Coull 1969; Dorian 1981). The relationship between fishing and non-fishing people varied considerably from region to region, so that not all communities experienced the same degree or intensity of social rejection (Gray 1978: 7). We saw, for example, that west-coast fishers were rarely denigrated to the same degree as those of the east coast. However, the status of most fishing people throughout the east and northeast of Scotland was sufficiently low that one might add them to Barth's list of European pariah groups, a set that includes "executioners, dealers in horseflesh and leather, collectors of nightsoil, gypsies, etc." (Barth 1969: 31).

Coull (1969: 23) ascribes the social separation of fishers and farm people to the striking differences between their ways of life, as well as to fisher endogamy. However, for social differences to become boundary markers, people must invest value in them. The mere existence of differences does not explain how or why they are ranked or even remarked upon. How, then, have these differences been evaluated? One way to approach this is through the peculiar notion of race, an idea that conflates body, language, locality and custom in effort to construct hierarchy.

While their Scottish neighbors may have been content with seeing fisherfolk as merely peculiar or dirty, outside observers of the nineteenth and early twentieth centuries often attempted to place them within contemporary racialist understandings of difference. Victorian scholars were quick to rank peoples and to discern "types," racial and otherwise. Their theories became popular ways of explaining and justifying inequalities between the English and their various subject peoples, both abroad and at home. Ideas that physically observable differences were tied to character and behavior widely prevailed. Racialist list making assumed that hereditary characteristics were important in many different kinds of communities, including those defined by occupation.

Science used race to construct internal or domestic "others." Exotic, colonized peoples were not the only ones to have their skulls measured and their habits observed. Urry tells us that plans for an exhaustive anthropometric survey of Great Britain were launched early in the twentieth century. While such a survey was never completed, some attempts were made to carry out such investigations, including "the work of the Scottish Committee studying the pigmentation of school children" (Urry 1984: 99). Photographic technology was also employed. Hundreds of photographs from Wales, Scotland and Cornwall were taken between 1875 and 1883 in an effort by the British Association for the Advancement of Science "to investigate . . . the 'national or local types of race prevailing in different parts of the United Kingdom'" (Taylor 1994: 22).

We can instructively compare the classification of fishers as backward with similar views of Celtic peoples as "barbarians." Chapman asserts that from the perspective of many Europeans, Celts occupy a disturbing terrain in which order is challenged and upset (Chapman 1992: 161–4). Surveying classical historical texts, he finds the Celts associated with themes of violence, sexual promiscuity, inebriation and superstition. This, despite the fact that, as Stocking (1987: 235) says, Celts were included among white Indo-Europeans:

> all manifestations of otherness within British society were contained within the bounds of what had long been regarded as a single large linguistic-cum-racial group – the Celts, the Anglo-Saxons and the Normans being all white-skinned members of the Indo-European family.

However, Celts occupied a distinctly lower stratum than the others within this group and, in fact, were not always thought to be entirely "white." In Chapman's words, they were a group that "represented, and still represent, in the European order, manners and habits which are 'old-fashioned,'" or even primitive (Chapman 1992: 3). The Irish Celts were commonly evicted from this "family" altogether, as Stocking (1987: 229) himself notes. Popular nineteenth-century cartoons in *Punch* magazine depicted them as grotesque, shambling and swarthy figures, and claimed that in evolutionary terms they ranked somewhere "between the gorilla and the Negro" (Lebow 1976: 40). Solomos (1993: 43) makes the important point that

Images of the racial or cultural inferiority of the Irish were based not only on particularly ideological constructions of the Irish but on a self-definition of Englishness or Anglo-Saxon culture in terms of particular racial and cultural attributes.

It is clear from some remarkably similar comments on fishers' "natural" character that the British, like other Europeans, were willing to find other internal groups to characterize in a comparable vein. Miles links this to the project of nation-building, which, he says

> is a history of a multiplicity of *interior* processes, including those of *racial-isation* and *civilisation* . . . In the interstices of this articulation . . . the "backwardness" and "insularity" of rural peasants, and the "savagery" of the urbanised working class were often interpreted as biological attributes which obstructed their incorporation as "races" into membership of the nation. (Miles 1993: 47)

We can find a compelling example in the Swedish middle class of the Oscarian period (roughly contemporaneous with the Victorian). According to Frykman (1987), they constructed boundaries between themselves and the peasants who formed their significant Other. In the bourgeois view, peasants led polluted lives by engaging directly with dirt and disorder. Lacking manners, cleanliness and propriety, these rude specimens served to remind people of what civilization should *not* include. In Scotland, fisherfolk were cast in the same light.

Historical accounts, novels, poems, memoirs and modern reminiscences, as well as recent conversations all richly attest to the attitudes that set fishers apart. These show clearly that the fisherpeople have had to contend with condescension, at best, and hostility, at worst. To pick from a couple of well-known Scottish novelists, we find John Buchan referring to "yon queer folk from Pittenweem" (*The Free Fishers* 1936: 23) and Lewis Grassic Gibbon speaking of the "coarse fisher brutes" of Gourdon in *Sunset Song* (1971: 99).

Outsiders branded fishers as backward, dirty, inbred, superstitious and intrinsically disreputable. Their villages were cast as dangerous places that strangers would do well to avoid. With this ambiguous, but generally seamy reputation, fisherfolk found their engagements with others – particularly with fish dealers, employers, landowners, social workers and bureaucrats of all stripes – to be fraught with difficulty (Nadel 1984; see also Coull 1969; Dorian 1981). In Ferryden, for example, a nineteenth century schoolmaster wrote that "I did not think I could endure their society" (Douglas 1857: 5).

Not surprisingly, people thought to be of such alien character must also be given alien origin. Like the Traveller-Gypsies of England, fisherfolk were widely assumed to be of foreign descent (Okely 1983). Popular stories of how fishers somehow appeared *de novo*, as it were, confirmed local people's convictions that fishers were inherently other, perhaps not even fully British. An eighteenth-century minister insisted that some Fife fishers were descended from stranded Dutch sailors from the time of Philip II (Anson 1974 [1930]: 86). A report of the International Fisheries Exhibition of 1883 claimed Scandinavian blood for the fishermen of northeastern Scotland and Phoenician [!] blood for those of Cornwall (Levi 1883: 27).[5]

> Newhaven was reputed to be Flemish in Character. Mrs George Cupples, who wrote an account of Newhaven's history and origins in 1888, identified the people of Newhaven as descended from the Flemings who had fled from religious persecution Her argument was based on a cheerfully romantic view of the village, rather than on historical evidence: "To any one who is personally acquainted with their village ways, customs, idioms, family names, and costumes, it is often noticeable how much they resemble Flemish and Dutch fisherfolk . . ." (Stevenson 1991: 19)

Green says that "the fishers appear to have been long regarded as foreigners by the inhabitants of the 'landward areas'" (1936: 110). The favored explanation for the arrival of these putative Dutch, Scandinavian, Flemish, Spanish, and even Phoenician ancestors on Scottish and English coasts was, not surprisingly, shipwreck (Mather 1969: 3).

In fact, the genealogies of Scottish and English fishers cannot be extricated from those of farm workers and townspeople. Like the *pescadores* of northwest Portugal, who also form a subordinate class, Scottish fishers' genealogies intertwine with those who work on the land (Cole 1991). Even in the most closed-in villages, fisher intermarriage is generally no more than 200 to 300 years old, despite the myth's insistence that fishers' inferior or degenerate nature has been due to generations of inbreeding. Implications of incest are but thinly veiled, if at all. One social worker insisted to me that many fisherfolk have been genetically damaged by in-marriage. Modern villagers often hasten, defensively, it would seem, to assert that while they share a common surname with their affines, they are not, in fact, "related."

Language has sometimes played a role in differentiating fishers from their neighbors. Dorian details the importance of Gaelic as a marker for fisher identity in eastern Sutherland in her book, *Language Death*. These fishermen, she says, suffered a double stigma since Gaelic was widely regarded as inferior to English (Dorian 1981: 62). However, most fishers in eastern Scotland, like the rural and town-based people, have long spoken various dialects of Lowland Scots, a heavily Germanicized dialect of English. Nonetheless, in 1922, Barclay stressed both dialect and intermarriage as evidence that fisherfolk were "a race apart. Their difference of dialect has already been noticed. Remarkable, too, is the way their communities have maintained a continuity of family names . . ." (Barclay 1922: 66).

Fishers were seen as different not only for their way of life but for their general appearance, including physiognomy, dress, and facial expressions. Erving Goffman helps us to understand why this was so with his discussion of stigma as "spoiled identity": those with such identity are less able than others to participate in the negotiations of everyday life (Goffman 1963). Their "face value" has been lessened. As Goffman is looking here at people with various physical infirmities, his approach tends to stress the visible and this suggests the circular logic of stigma. After all, if physical differences are the mark of social inferiority, then those who are socially inferior must have some distinct physical trait one can see.

More than one writer has described the fishermen in what sound to modern ears as racially suggestive terms, stressing physiognomy as well as dress, facial expression and supposed character. Descriptions of Scottish fishers that refer to dark features are intriguing given the widespread belief that skin color was a particularly important marker of a group's evolutionary status. Observing the fishermen and women who attended the 1883 International Fisheries Exhibition in London, Levi (1883: 27) claimed to notice

> several characteristics of their character and peculiarities. Many of the men had a face which seemed to have defied a thousand storms – a *dark, sallow* countenance, yet bold and firm features, indicating daring and adventure. Whilst the women, whether Scotch, French or Dutch, had evidently a taste for all that is gaudy, showy and gay. Go a little deeper into their nationalities and you find them everywhere a peculiar people. [italics mine]

The following year, Hugh Miller sounded a similar essentializing note when he wrote that fishing villagers were "stationary . . . sluggish, inert," and their actions "appear rather automatical than efforts of volition . . ." (Miller 1884: 30, cited in Mather 1969: 2). All that is missing from such comments is an anthropometric assessment relating these traits to anatomical peculiarities or perhaps to an overabundance of phlegm (cf. Gould

1996; Urry 1984). In all cases, these descriptions mark fishers as innately separate from the "normal" population.

The highly subjective and culturally constructed process of racial typing is most popularly thought of in such contexts as apartheid in South Africa or segregation and the "one-drop rule" in the United States. Whether one is "black" may have less to do with skin tone than with what is known or surmised about one's genealogy. The category precedes the ascription. Similarly, if members of a group behave differently in terms of occupation, belief, language or dress, and particularly if they are also poor and powerless, how easy it is to fit a lens over the eye and see them as differently "colored." Berreman (1972), in analysing caste systems in wider context, notes that "societies with birth-ascribed status hierarchies dramatize and legitimize these crucial differences by attributing to them innate biological, hence 'racial' differences". In other words, descent is often seen as a necessary explanation for cultural difference.

Such lines of thought did not, alas, die out with the Victorians. Significantly, a postwar travel narrative of Scotland echoes earlier accounts concerning the inhabitants of the east coast fishing villages:

> Apparently of a different race from the other people of the country, with separate traditions and customs of their own, they have kept by themselves and intermarried among themselves for many centuries . . . Possibly these stalwart, tan-skinned dwellers by the deep are Danish in origin, and represent, by pure and direct descent, early settlements of Scandinavian sea-rovers. (Eyre-Todd 1947: 46)

Interestingly, however, in this last comment we see that denigration is not the only form that the vision of fisherfolk as "other" may take. In the nineteenth century, fishers also fulfilled, for some, a vision of the noble savage, standing as an icon of primitive, if domestic, "otherness" that contrasted favorably to the demoralizing effects of industrialization. In this way, they were not so different from other internal primitives constructed by British society.

Chapman (1992: 122) points to "an apparent counter-current" in depictions of the previously mentioned Celts; with the rise of romanticism, they were also described as a people of ancient lore and wisdom. Furthermore, as James (1999) argues, canonical historical and archaeological assumptions also drew upon romantic ideas of Celtic unity. Claims that bearers of ancient Celtic culture came from "elsewhere" and spread by invasion throughout Western Europe have supported a monolithic belief in a singular Celtic culture of foreign origin.

Such essentializing romanticism has indeed been applied to people from small villages throughout Britain, who have often been stereotyped. Stripped to their foundation, they become simple local "yokels" assumed to be lost in history's slipstream: to be uncorrupted, unmaterialistic incarnations of humans close to nature. And so it has been with fishers. Some writers, in fact, portrayed them as seaborne hunters of undoubted courage, though of simple character. Sir Walter Scott, that great purveyor of a romanticized Scotland, sets fishers in a place he calls "Mussel Crag" (based upon the actual village of Auchmithie, 10 miles south of Montrose), in *The Antiquary*. In the Mucklebackit family, we see not only a comic rendition of fishers as "clarty" (dirty) and uncouth. We also see an appreciation of what they must bear when sea and rocks become murderers of men. "It's no fish ye're buyin', it's men's lives" (1907: 107). Reportedly, Scott was so fascinated by coastal life that he planned to set another novel there.

> During the brief residence of Sir Walter at the fishing village of Auchmithie, on the Forfarshire coast, he had many opportunities of studying the daily round of fisher life. Twenty years ago there were persons in Auchmithie who remembered the illustrious visitor, and who took note of his anxiety to make himself acquainted with the eccentric people who formed the little community . . . In the rude fishing village, the fisher folk were unchanged from the days of a far back period and even at this day they are still much as they were then – a peculiar people. (Bertram 1883: 2)

The romanticized fisher also provided a compelling visual subject. As early as the 1840s, photographers Hill and Adamson memorialized the fishers of Newhaven (on the Firth of Forth) in a series of pictures that depicts them as stalwart, pensive and industrious (Stevenson 1991). George Washington Wilson, a noted Scottish photographer of the late nineteenth and early twentieth century, found fishing villages and fisherfolk aptly picturesque subjects that appealed to his growing tourist clientele (Durie and Ingram 1994). Winslow Homer spent 20 months in Cullercoats, a village in northern England, where he painted the fisherfolk in a simple, naturalist style (Cooper 1986). Painters from the Glasgow School of Art could be found on the Fife shore rendering images of the fishers there in deep rich colors. Their faces and figures bespeak endurance, strength, and often, beauty. As we shall see in the next chapter, painters lavished particular attention upon fisher women.

Fisher culture, much of it labeled superstition, could be portrayed in either romantic or derisory fashion. An entry in the *Dundee Courier* dated 31 July 1907 remarks on the peculiarity of fishers and talks about how fishers assign blame for a transgression within their community by opening the Bible to a page at random. After placing keys that faced in different directions on the page, a culprit's initials could be identified by observing the letters to which the keys pointed. To render an account of northeast fishing villages more colorful, a postwar travel writer said "We are delighted to find queer superstitions persisting, men refusing to say 'rabbit,' or to refer to salmon as other than 'red fish'" (Scott-Moncrieff 1949).

Even writers deeply concerned for fishing communities cannot resist such engaging and colorful detail. A modern case in point was Peter Anson. Anson (1889–1973), was a monk, an artist and an ardent chronicler of fisher life. He spent years living in various fishing villages in Scotland, including Ferryden and Buckie, and lovingly portrayed them in beautiful, meticulous line drawings and watercolors, as well as in numerous books (Anson 1974 [30]; 1975 [32]; 1965; 1969). Yet he also devoted many pages to magical practices and ways of warding off harm.

Thus, fisherfolk apparently have long both repelled and intrigued. They have stood as an exemplar for popular beliefs about ancient folk survivals lingering in out-of-the-way corners of the British isles. Regarded as more primitive than urban Britons, and thus preserving what had otherwise been lost, they were enfolded into the lower rungs of a hierarchy of rationality and truth.

I will say more about this subject in Chapter 6, when I take up the subject of fishing people as tourist attractions. For now, it is enough to note that whether the commentary is harsh or kind, being stereotyped as exotic is seldom a benign condition. Gypsies and Travelers (in Scotland, known as Tinks), are the quintessential example of this (Okeley 1983). Renowned as fortune tellers and dancers, they are also reviled as thieves, seducers and despoilers. They are will o' the wisps, here one day, gone the next. Like them, fishers also have seemed suspiciously detached from land and property, with limited commitment to such presumably agrarian and industrial values as prudence, reliability and piety leavened with reason.

## Conclusion

This chapter has taken a primarily historical look at the period in which fishers emerged as occupational specialists. It has laid the background necessary to understand fishers' vulnerability as well as the irony of their position. Their very livelihood was rooted in Enlightenment values of industry and rationality. Yet, fishers themselves have experienced a public image that depicts them as backward and prerational.

The next two chapters take us into the nineteenth and early twentieth centuries to explore how stigma, stereotype and marginality continued to affect fisherfolk identity as fishing became industrialized. In the pages that follow, we shall see how gender and localism became crucial factors in isolating fishers from "mainstream" society.

# Notes

1. A comment about this number is in order. To reach it, I counted up the communities specifically referred to in Anson's *Fishing Boats and Fisher Folk on the east Coast of Scotland* (1974 [1930]), because this appears to be the most comprehensive account available. It was not possible simply to count the settlements identified on any map, as I have found no map of the east coast that agrees with any other in naming fishing communities. There are several reasons for this. One is that several fishing communities are attached to larger towns, and are only locally distinguished as having a separate identity. An example is Cellardyke, which looks like part of Anstruther, but which any local person can tell you is a separate community. Some communities are basically extinct, or derelict. And another reason is that authors are selective about the communities they consider significant for their history of fishing. Ferryden, for example, appears on very few maps of the fishing coast.
2. Wallerstein (1980: 39) attributes Dutch success to "the invention, around 1400, of the *haringbuis*, or buss, a fishing boat whose high length-to-breadth ratio" gave it greater speed and maneuverability.
3. Exceptions include Ullapool and Tobermory, built by the British Fisheries Society. Tobermory, however, did not thrive as a fishing port.
4. In Scotland, this economic mix continues in the west and in the northern islands. In the Western Isles, the complex rules of crofting legislation (see Parman) have sustained this marginal economy since the 1880s. In the north, it is sometimes remarked that Orcadians are farmers with fishing boats, while Shetlanders are fishers with farms.
5. The myth of foreign origin for east coast fishermen does not stop at the Border. Clark (1982: 23) reports that the fisherfolk of Staithes, in Yorkshire, are regarded as "strange and slightly different" and that some believe that the village has Scandinavian roots (1982: 21).

# –3–

# Fisher Lassies: Gender, Stereotypes and Marginality

Wha'll buy my caller [fresh] herrin'?
Oh ye may call them vulgar farin;
Wives and mithers maist desparin'
Ca' them lives o' men

Lady Nairne

In the previous chapter I examined the rise of fishing communities as stigmatized, as stereotyped and as marginalized occupational enclaves. This chapter explores the gendered face of stereotype, stigma and marginality. In effect, women's prominent, public roles in the fishing industry helped to brand them and their families as odd, indeed, as less respectable than most other Scots.

During the nineteenth and much of the twentieth centuries, respectability had been a core bourgeois value. It was determined, in part, by adherence to gender-appropriate social convention: sober industriousness (for both sexes) and the expectation that women be the exemplars of domestic virtue in their roles as caretakers of the home. Of course, many working-class women outside the fishing communities had to labor outside the home during the eighteenth and nineteenth centuries. They could be found in a number of industries, including mining, spinning and factory work, as well as agricultural labor (Devine 1984; Houston 1989). And Whatley (1988: 240) notes that

> Many females in Scotland, as elsewhere, made (and continued to make) "hidden" contributions to production within the context of the family economy, acting as carriers, sellers, organizers and wheelers and dealers in occupations which were apparently male preserves, but which in fact were wholly dependent upon the female contribution.

However, the work of fisherwomen was anything but "hidden." Rather, women were seen as very different because of their roles in the marketing and processing of fish. In fact, outsiders often saw them as matriarchal, which meant that they were too bold and assertive, too dominant to be "proper" women. Their husbands, by implication, could hardly be proper men, no matter how hardy and daring their exploits on the sea. Thus, as we shall see, fisherwomen's anomalous gender behavior became one of the key points around which outsiders' ideas of fisher disreputability were organized. Before I explore these outsiders' ideas, I must elucidate the significance of women's work from the fishers' point of view.

## Home is Where You Bait the Lines

When I began my fieldwork, I did not immediately recognize the importance of women in the fishery and certainly had not yet thought about what the role they played there meant. Nor had I considered how stereotypes of women contributed to fisher stigma. I held the usual stereotypes of fishing as a purely masculine occupation, an image reinforced by much of the existing literature, including romantic poems such as this one by Robert Louis Stevenson (from Lockhart 1997):

> Some think of the fisher skipper
> beyond the Inchcape stone
> But I of the fisher woman
> That lies at home alone . . .
> The foolish fisher woman!
> Her heart is on the deep.

For many years, scholars writing about fishermen of the North Atlantic had, apparently, also assumed that women were restricted to domesticity and prone to worrying, while the fishery itself was run only by men (Davis and Nadel-Klein 1988). Certainly, many in Scottish universities held this view. When Margaret Buchan, a student from a Peterhead fishing family, set out to research women in Scottish fishing, she found that

> . . . a Reader at the University said to me that he thought that no one had ever considered talking to a humble fishwife. Most academics were more interested in the men and the fishing methods which they used and the contribution which they made to the national Economy. (Buchan 1977)

In fact, in the 1970s, little had yet been written about women in the wider Scottish workforce. As Hendry points out:

In Scotland, the anthropologist/historian has come in with his notebook, right enough, but being a male person, he will unthinkingly record what is important according to masculine values: the affairs of state, "intellectual" discourse, great inventions – the things obviously of the public domain . . . The female expression of a national character is vital, indeed indispensable: O gentle dames, Scotland hath need of thee. (Hendry 1992: 136)

By the early 1990s, when Hendry wrote this, some female anthropologists had, in fact, anticipated her call and had already arrived on the Scottish scene (Armstrong 1976, 1977, 1978; Dorian 1981; Ennew 1980; Forsythe 1974, 1980; Macdonald 1987; Nadel-Klein 1988; Neville 1979; Parman 1990; Renwanz 1981). Some of these specifically focused on women; others did not but were nonetheless sensitive to gender issues.

Indeed, some folklorists had even earlier "seen" women, perhaps because they had a tradition of strong interest in the material and the symbolic details of domestic life. However, being folklorists, they tended to receive rather short shrift from many academic departments – particularly those in Britain (see Buchan 1984: 9) – concerned with national and international agendas. Evidence for this can be seen in the relative paucity of citations from their work (see Aitken 1973; Grant 1961; King 1992–3) by other students of Scottish life.

Nonetheless, Hendry's point remains valid. Historical, sociological and economic studies of work and community have, until very recently, tended to elaborate male roles, relegating women's labor and lives to secondary positions (Gray 1978; Payne 1967; Carter 1979). Today, studies of women as weavers, textile mill workers, domestic servants and farm laborers have done much to rectify the gender skew, though there is still a long way to go (Breitenbach, Brown and Myers 1998; Devine 1984; Gordon 1990; Gordon and Breitenbach 1990).

During my initial research, my concern with identity, power and politics had not yet led me to explore women's lives and the significance of gendered cultural constructions. I should have known better. My training in graduate school had already taught me to look at women's roles in agricultural change around the world (see especially Boserup 1970; Mencher 1982). But fisheries seemed such an obviously masculine domain, more like hunting than horticulture. In other words, my consciousness, as we used to say, had not yet been "raised."

The fisherfolk themselves convinced me that this androcentric bias simply would not do. Not that they did this in any conscious or deliberate way. They, like most other Scots of the 1970s, were scarcely in the vanguard of the women's movement. Scottish society is typically, and, I think, fairly, characterized as quite male dominated. McIvor (1992: 138), for example, sees Scotland overall as "an intensely patriarchal society [with] . . . Deep-rooted patriarchal concepts of the 'lesser value' of female labour". Indeed, Scots may have held on even longer, and more closely, to the ideal of women's domestic duties than the English. According to McCrone (1996: 109), "Until well after 1945, the economic activity rate for married women in Scotland was only two-thirds that of the rest of Britain . . ."

However, when explaining to me what the fishing life had been like in their childhoods or in their parents' youths, fisherfolk talked often and proudly about women's work: what their mothers and grandmothers had done and how their labor, strengths and skills had sustained both family and fishery. Their emphasis forced me to re-evaluate my own assumptions, as ethnographers must so often do. Women's tasks could not be regarded in a merely functional or utilitarian way that ignored their meaning within the fishing communities; nor could they be submerged as mere "curiosities" (see Nadel-Klein 1988).

As we saw in the previous chapter, east coast fishers of the eighteenth and nineteenth centuries pursued both white fish and herring from small boats. Like peasants, classically defined, they harvested natural resources within a subsistence as well as a cash nexus. They also relied heavily upon kin-based labor (Wolf 1969). This mode of subsistence shaped the complementary division of labor characteristic of fisher households, an arrangement well summed up by the phrase, "a fisher laddie needs a fisher lassie." So this is where I will begin.

It must be made clear at the outset that gendered ideas pervaded the fishery. The sea itself was female, as is common throughout the North Atlantic. So were the fishing boats. These, however, could only be inhabited by males, perfectly illustrating Ardener's insight that spatial arrangements of people and objects may express cultural notions of gendered spheres (S. Ardener 1993).[1] Even more than in the House of Parliament, which Rodgers wittily dissects as a Western version of a New Guinea men's house, fishermen at sea were – and are – very uneasy at the thought of women's presence among them (Rodgers 1993).

Fisher folklore is replete with taboos concerning women's contact with boats or with fishermen on their way to the shore. Thompson says that "in the past fishermen might take it as a bad omen, and perhaps even turn back home, if they met with particular women [some of these were said to be witches] on their way to the harbour. Sea work was men's work and for women to have any place in it would be a pollution" (Thompson et al. 1983: 173). Women did not even have to go on board, in fact, to damage the outcome of a trip. Livingstone, in a comment that suggests a resemblance to menstrual taboo or "blood pollution," says that "No woman, especially a bare-footed one, should step over the nets or they could not be used" (1996: 107; and see Anson 1975). Anson (who, as we shall see in Chapter 6, took a great interest in fisher "superstitions") reports a number of other beliefs concerning women's power to affect men's chances of a good catch, or even survival. A woman had magical power when her husband was out to sea and could, wittingly or unwittingly, keep him from returning. For example, it was said that a fishwife must never comb her hair after nightfall while her husband's boat was out to sea, for if she did, he would surely drown.

These gender-focused anxieties notwithstanding, women made essential contributions to the economic and technological requirements of white fishing. Each household needed a man to catch the fish and a woman to undertake shore-based tasks before, during and after the voyage. Thus a wife and mother had two full-time jobs: one in the fishery, one in the household. She raised the children and managed the domestic economy; she also made it possible for her man to fish. So now, let us take a closer look at how this work was organized.

In both the *sma'* and the great-line fishing for white fish, described in the previous chapter, a man would take on board a woven basket or "scull" packed with coiled fishing lines. Each line could run up to a mile in length and carry from 600 to 1200 baited hooks. The hooks hung from *snoods* (variously spelled *snids* or *snuids*), which were short lines made from horsehair, spaced a few feet apart. Each member of a four to six man crew "shot" at least one line in every voyage (for more detail, see Adams 1991; Hay and Walker 1985: 53–4).

But first, women had to prepare these lines: a complex, dirty, smelly and time-consuming process involving many steps. Fishermen preferred to use mussels for bait. However, these did not grow on every shore. Nor, as we shall see in the next chapter, were they a free resource, for curers or lairds usually owned the mussel beds. In Ferryden, where the mussels were near at hand, women raked them up from the mucky sands. Every few days, small groups of women left the village at low tide. Working in hymn-singing groups of two or three, they hauled thousands of the black, shiny shellfish up the bank to the village. They then dumped them into *scaups*, shallow pits dug on the foreshore to keep them fresh.

Then the women began their long and monotonous labor of shelling the mussels and baiting the lines. This often began at dawn and continued till nightfall. We read that in Broughty Ferry, near Dundee:

After gathering the bait, the women then went for 'bent' (dune grass) which was used to layer the lines. After they arrived home they then had to bait lines, sometimes to twelve o'clock at night . . . The women did three times the work of the men, and yet it could come to nothing if wind and tide kept the fishermen ashore. (McMillan, n.d.)

Old Mrs. Potter of Ferryden remembered her mother's endless work and said to me, "It took oors and oors tae sheil the mussels and bait the lines, and if it came away bad weather and they couldna' use the lines for a few days, ye had to undae the hale thing."

Children were also expected to help, regardless of all other obligations, including school (Coull 1989: 38). Older daughters often had to take over such household tasks as cooking and child minding. Always, the fishing came first. Boys typically went to sea with their fathers by the age of 14, but before that, would also be expected to help their mothers.

William Smith of Cellardyke, Fife, as the oldest child in the family, would rise with his mother about four o'clock on winter mornings to do the shelling. "I have seen her," he wrote, "when she had a baby in the cradle, with the cradle-string tied to her foot rocking the cradle and with her hands baiting the line". (Martin 1995: 17)

Christian Watt (1833–1923), a woman from Broadsea, by Fraserburgh, left a memoir of her life as a fisherwoman that is rich with detail concerning women's work. She remembered how such work had looked to her as a small child:

I hated the small lines for this meant so much more work for the adults, shelling the mussels, baiting the lines . . . My parents' day began at three in the morning and often ended at midnight . . . I have seen both of my parents fall down with exhaustion at the end of a day, after my father had come in from the sea. (Fraser 1983)

Christian Watt's granddaughter, Christian Watt Marshall, also from Broadsea, was born in 1896. In her own memoirs, she counted herself lucky that she "didn't have to suffer the poverty of the 1880s when folk were no more than galley slaves in every walk of working class life" (Sutherland 1994: 2). Still, she had to bait the lines and liked it no more than had her grandmother.

Nobody liked doing the small lines in winter. It was a messy job shelling mussels and baiting lines, but it was our living . . . We had to be careful – a lot of folk got blood poisoning by catching their fingers on the barbs of the hooks.

It was hard and weary work with little reward. The drudgery was relentless. (Sutherland 1994: 9)

While each woman was responsible for her family's boat and gear, women often worked in groups, preferably of female kin (thus paralleling the fishing crews). In this way, they kept each other company through the long hours of painstaking labor. Margaret Buchan quotes an old woman from the Peterhead area:

She said if the weather was fine we all sat outside and baited lines on the pavement, my mother, my sisters and myself. If the weather was bad, we then had to work in the kitchen, and then the place was in a right "steer." However, she said if anyone needed help it was given gladly. (Buchan 1977)

Line fishing also provided some women with their own source of income. Writing about the coastal stretch between Arbroath (12 miles south of Montrose) and Gourdon (7 miles north), Hay and Walker tell us that many fisherwomen became quite entrepreneurial; they also note the unusual degree of autonomy that fishwives possessed.

Fishermen's wives were often in business for themselves as fish merchants and would purchase fish from the local market and prepare them for sale. This could simply be a small quantity prepared each day and taken to Dundee, or some other town, in rips or creels to be sold. The "rounds" were often in the suburbs and landward areas where there were no established fish shops, but some families also prepared fish for established fish shops. This activity resulted in the wives being much more independent of their husbands than in most types of community and in times of low quayside fish prices the fishermen's wives often made considerably more money than their husbands. (Hay and Walker 1985: 82)

Gourdon, on the Kincardineshire coast, became the last Scottish community to use the old hand-line method. Undoubtedly, the line fishing survived there because it could provide a special market niche: line-caught fish were always in better condition than those brought in by the net, and therefore "were particularly prized for the manufacture of smoked fish along the east coast" (Hay and Walker 1985: 81). The Gourdon women could be found baiting the lines in the old way into the 1980s and there "the men freely admitted that they owed their prosperity to their women-folk, who each day baited 1200 hooks with mussels" (R. Smith 1991: 10).

However time-consuming, baiting lines was only one portion of women's obligations to the household fishery. They were often expected to take ballast (frequently in the form of heavy rocks) and lines out to the boats; then, they might have to help launch the boats and later drag them back to shore. "Fishing used to be very hard. There were no engines. Women had to haul the boats up river over the rocks," I was told in Ferryden. "Women had to be marvelous workers," said an old lady from Cellardyke. Later, when drift-netting for herring became part of the fishermen's routine, women took part in net-mending, as well.

Fishermen's houses were always work-places as well as homes, and it was usually the woman's job to do the actual mending of . . . the easily torn nets . . . The end of a herring season away from home, when each man brought home twenty or more nets to be mended, left little free time for anybody; one net, measuring sixty yards by about twenty yards, could take three hours or three days to mend, and there were no short-cuts. (Murray 1986: 5)

Murray lists still more tasks in which women were involved: preserving the nets by a technique called "barking," in which nets were dipped in a hot resin or an alum solution; water-proofing the oilskin clothing and boots; and, of course, washing huge amounts of clothing.

Most of the older villages at that time had no piers from which the men could walk dry-shod to their boats. This gave rise to what was, at least from an outsider's perspective, women's most unusual job: they carried men piggy-back to, and often from, the boats. To do so, they waded through waist-high water to protect their men's feet, subjecting themselves to the biting waters of the cold North Sea. The cover of *To Work and To Weep: Women in Fishing Economies*, which Dona Davis and I co-edited in 1988, shows an old drawing of fisherwomen standing in the tide. The muscular fishwives, skirts tucked immodestly up to their waists carry relatively small, but heavily clothed fishermen hoisted on their backs like creels. This practice struck many outsiders as bizarre, gender-defiant behavior that provided further evidence of fisher peculiarity. Bertram describes the scene for the neighboring village of Auchmithie, along the south Angus coast:

I have seen the women of Auchmithie 'kilt their coats' and rush into the water in order to aid in shoving off the boats, and on the return of the fleet carry the men ashore on their brawny shoulders with the greatest ease and all the nonchalance imaginable, no matter who might be looking at them. (Bertram 1869: 444)

Informants generally agreed that the practice was clearly meant to keep the men's feet, encased in heavy leather sea-boots, dry before setting out on a long sea voyage. Before the first half of the nineteenth century, east-coast fishing boats were undecked, so that fishermen had no shelter from the constant wash of the chilling, salt spray. Even with the later intro-duction of decked boats, fishing was always cold, wet work. Pneumonia was a common way for a fisherman to die. Yet, explaining this practice in an exclusively instrumental manner would be partial. For, as we have seen, women sometimes carried the men back to shore again when they returned, which makes the dry-feet rationale a bit suspect (King, n.d.: 5; see also Anson 1975 [1932]: 212).

A structuralist interpretation that unifies opposites might suggest itself here. By carrying them from the dry land of the foreshore to the boats, the women raised the men above the liminal tidal zone, the ambiguous beach (sometimes land and sometimes water) to the safety of the land that floats on the sea – namely the boats. Thus women kept the men out of the water which the men feared to enter, lest they never leave it again. Just as they gave birth to children, delivering them to safety, so too did women bear their men, delivering them onto their boats. The fishermen's wives both literally and figuratively negotiated their passage between land and sea.

Regardless of how we explain the custom, one thing is clear: women certainly had to be strong. They carried both the fishermen and the fishery. Even after childbirth, a woman had scant time to rest. The grandmother of one of my elderly informants, herself an octogenarian Ferryden woman, had told her that "women would go out to rake mussels less than a week after giving birth. The water was red around them." And in a novel written about nineteenth century northeast fisherfolk, a fishwife continues to work and refuses to see a doctor, despite the agonizing pain of a mysterious and ultimately fatal disease, because "in the Fishertown you had the doctor only when you died" (Patterson 1950: 37).[2]

Idle hands were regarded with disdain and work did not stop even when the boats had sailed away. For one thing, there were the family's clothes to make and mend, including the heavy, knitted ganseys (jerseys), stock-ings and long underwear the men required. Many informants said that women knitted endlessly, needles flashing even as they walked. To this end they wore *wiskers*, small leather pouches strapped around their waists that were pierced with holes to stabilize the needles (Bochel 1979: 18).

When the boats returned after grueling, 12 to 14-hour trips, the exhausted men would unload the catch and then head straight home to sleep. People in Ferryden remembered how, as children, they were turned out of their beds in the small, crowded houses to make room for their fathers and older brothers when they returned before dawn.

If all had gone well, the sailing boats could bring back huge catches. Anson claims that, as early as 1840, "in the summer months it was not an uncommon event for fifteen or sixteen boats at Ferryden to come in . . . with a thousand haddocks each," and that these would sell for roughly a farthing per pound (Anson 1974 [1930]: 117). Not that the fishermen saw much of this. Obligations to laird or curer came first. Then the fishermen's wives took the rest of the fresh catch to sell in the countryside or towns.

What remained became women's preserve – literally so, since they smoked or pickled much of it. In all the villages, women were responsible for transforming the slippery, raw resource into a saleable commodity. For example, in Auchmithie,

> There followed intense activity by the whole family around each fisherman's cottage. One woman would decapitate and gut the haddocks, another would slit and clean them, another put them in salt in a tub and yet another tied them by the tails in pairs on a pole. The fish were then hung on a scaffolding to dry before being sent for sale . . . (Gray 1978)

Further north,

> The fish were taken from the small market by the fisherwives themselves and then they smoked some of them over fir-cones ready for the creel. There were no fish shops round Golspie at that time. It was just the women trudging round. (Blair 1987: 129)

Some women carried heavy loads of fresh or preserved fish for miles, straight to rural households; stories of their stamina appear in many accounts. For example, fishwives from Dunbar, near Edinburgh, were reported to have "trotted" with a full creel, twenty-six miles in five hours (Bertram 1883).

Each fishwife had a regular clientele among the farm workers of her territory. These, too, were poor people and, with some of them, she might develop close and affectionate relationships (see Fraser 1983). Usually, they paid her in kind with butter, eggs, cheese, turnips and grain. "The creel was often carried home heavier than it was carried out" (Anson 1965: 139). One observer of the fishwives, succumbing to the stereotype we saw in Chapter 2 of fishers as mentally limited, believed that the women irrationally added to their own burdens:

> These poor drudges will thus travel fifteen miles before breakfast . . . such is the force of habit, that they would think it a punishment to be obliged to return home without a load in their baskets, equal in weight to a third of their outward-

bound cargo. If so they have neither goods nor provisions to carry home, they generally take in ballast of stones . . . (Knox [1784] in Anson 1965: 141).

This seems singularly unlikely. However, it is true that inland journeys were not always profitable. "Towards the end of the six-monthly period after payment of their wages, rural laborers' incomes were insufficient to buy fish regularly and the fishwife would have a walk to the nearest town in an attempt to sell off surplus stocks" (Hay and Walker 1985: 37). There, the remainder could be sold to itinerant cadgers for cash or hawked directly to customers on the street. The return for this labor was usually quite poor – a hundredweight of fish fetched only a few shillings. Importantly, the fishwives' street cries ("buy my caller [fresh] herring," made the Newhaven fishwives famous, for example) earned them a reputation for aggressive verbal ability. In fact, the stereotype of being loud, shrill women, as in the phrase, "shrieking like a fish-wife," remains alive today.

Women setting off to market fish often preferred to travel in groups, for these expeditions could be dangerous as well as exhausting. "Fishwives were often attacked both for money and carnal knowledge. All carried sharp gutting knives," recalled Christian Watt (Fraser 1983). Children of both sexes occasionally went along, and "by fourteen a daughter was able to cover the round on her own" (Hay and Walker 1985: 37).

Before the railways penetrated the Scottish coast, beginning in the 1840s, all these marketing expeditions had to be made on foot. Trains enabled the fishwives to extend their range and made an enormous difference to the fishery. "The Great North of Scotland Railway had special fish-wife concession fares which allowed the women to reach considerable greater distances from home" (Coull 1989: 41). However, although the trains broadened women's vending opportunities, they did not eliminate their pedestrian burdens.

My grandmother walked the two mile from home, got the train at Macduff at six o'clock in the morning, got off at King Edward and then went to a' the different farms, walking all the time. Then she'd come back with the train at night. Sometimes instead of money she'd get fresh butter and bring that home to salt down for the winter. She enjoyed that life. She was a big strong woman, my granny. (Blair 1987: 129)

The itinerant fishwife became a "kenspeckle [well-recognized] figure in traditional Scottish life" (Coull 1989: 41). She continued to be a noted symbol of the fishing community, even after the fisher communities had begun their inexorable decline and fishers began to mix more freely with townsfolk.

There was a time, said a policeman, when the fisher folk rarely mixed much with the townspeople, but now many a pretty fisher girl who bears a creel on her back during the day appears in the evening in silk stockings and a smart costume. "But," he said, lowering his voice, "ye can aye tell her because of her walk. She bends forward, ye ken, from bearin' the creel." (Morton 1933: 339)

Others may have been able to recognize Scottish fishwives for bearing the creel, in addition to their fortitude and willingness to sacrifice themselves for the good of their husbands and families. But how did they view themselves? What were the women's own vulnerabilities and fears. Although they may often have appeared to be stoical, surely they had their preferences, their likes and dislikes, even if they seldom had choices about the lives they would lead. It is to explore these preferences that I turn in the next section to songs, poems, memoirs, and historical accounts, as well as to the stories of my informants.

## "Work and Wait and Dree Your Weird [Dread Your Fate]"

A newly married fisher couple would have had no illusions of a secure, stress-free existence. To the contrary, their childhoods would have prepared them well for a future filled with danger and unpredictability. But no amount of preparation could inure them to the emotional costs of "living from the sea" (Smith 1977). Doubtless, men bore the greater risks to life and limb. However, women were forced to endure dangers of their own, as well as continual anxiety and stress with little relief. In those days before ship-to-shore communication, women would have had no way of knowing how their men were faring.

In matter-of-fact voices, the older women I spoke to talked about the uncertainties of life on shore. They never dramatized their fears, but said that, of course, they had watched the weather and worried. They had to face the ever-present threat of losing their husbands, brothers and sons to the menacing sea. The lifeboat was often busy; sometimes, a boat would sink in sight of land. Even after a rescue, a man might still succumb. The Ferryden lifeboat records, for example, make stark reading: "Alexander Paton died of exposure and shock after being thrown overboard. Left widow and two children" (Duncan n.d.: 25).

The words of Christian Watt, who lived from 1833 to 1923, bear eloquent witness to the toll these experiences could take. She spent the last 45 years of her life in Aberdeen's Cornhill Asylum, a victim of what would probably now be called depression. Reading her criticisms of power and oppression, however, I have to wonder if she was labeled mentally ill in part because she was so outspoken. I have, of course, no way of knowing. Like Nisa, the independent-minded !Kung woman of the Kalahari desert described by Shostak (1983), Christian did not get along with everyone around her and had her own ideas of how to live her life. Like Nisa, she watched the familiar conditions of her life be transformed by powerful outsiders. And, like Nisa, she resisted marriage. Indeed, Christian most especially did not want to be a fisherman's wife:

I dreaded being landed with a fisherman for (I will tell no lies) I hated the chave [work] from morning to beyond night, and I dreaded marriage like the plague, but unfortunately I fell head over heels in love, and knew it was the right one whenever I set eyes upon him, so all my own plans for the future came to nought. (Fraser 1983: 67)

Her fears were realized. Christian's life was filled with poverty and loss. Her husband died at sea 18 years after they were married. Of her ten children, seven predeceased her, as did numerous grandchildren, nieces and nephews. In her often rambling but sharply observant account she provides us with an intimate, critical view of a Scottish fisherwoman's world that is unparalleled by any other source:

The Congregational Minister came to the door. I asked him which one of my folk was lost, he said, "It is the husband" . . . It was the 21st August, exactly three years and two weeks to the day since my son Peter was drowned and in that time I had lost five of my nearest . . . My son James was 17, so Maritime laws would not allow him to skipper the boat, which meant I would have to pay somebody to do so. Shortly afterwards I was to lose another son and daughter . . . I had my trust in Christ the Man of sorrow, and knew what he felt as he stood before Pontius Pilate the Procurator of Judea. (Fraser 1983: 101)

Many songs have been written to express fisherwomen's fears of bereavement. I quote from three here: the first is a traditional song, voiced by a fisherman's daughter; the second is a modern interpretation, this time sung by the fisherman's wife; the third, also modern, emphasizes how tragically a marriage based upon romantic love could end. The latter two, in particular, make it clear that fisher marriage could be more than a merely utilitarian arrangement, as it has sometimes been depicted: "A bride had to be selected in much the same manner as a new boat, a net, or any other kind of fishing gear. She was regarded not only as a breeder of children, but also as a human 'tool'" (Anson 1965: 145).

"When father's out upon the sea
We're out upon the pier,
For we must dread in terror
And we must dread in fear,
Lest he should meet a watery grave
And be snatched from our grasp,
And we'd wander broken-hearted,"
Said the bonnie fisher lass.

(*The Bonnie Fisher Lass*, traditional, from Buchan and Hall 1973: 78)

Work and wait and dree your weird [suffer your fate],
Pin your faith in herrin' sales,
And oftimes lie awake at nicht
In fear and dread o' winter gales.
But men maun wark tae earn their breid,
And men maun sweat tae gain their fee,
And fishermen will aye gang oot
As lang as fish swim in the sea.

(*Fisherman's Wife* by Ewan MacColl, from Buchan and Hall 1973: 33).

By the storm-torn shoreline a woman is standing,
The spray strung like jewels in her hair.
And the sea tore the rocks near the desolate landing,
As though it had known she stood there.
(Chorus): For she has come down to condemn that wild ocean,
For the murderous loss of her man.
His boat sailed out on a Wednesday morning,
And it's feared she's gone down wi' all hands

(*The Fisherman's Song* by Andy Stewart 1981).[3]

Elaborating a similar theme in a poem entitled, *To Suffie, Last of the Buchan Fishwives*, a girl from the countryside pens her sympathy for the burdens of a fishwerwoman's life:

We nivver hid to flee demintit
Tull [to] the pier-heid,
Nor harken tull the heerican at midnicht,
Caul' wi dreid.
Spring efter Spring, or the teuchat's storm [wintry March weather] wis past
Ye wannert [wandered] the road,
Heid tull the sleety win' an boo't twa-faal [bent over]
Shoodrin [shouldering] yer load. (Garry 1988)

These songs, poems and stories (and many others quite similar) tell us several things about the preferences – the likes and dislikes, vulnerabilities and fears – of fisherwomen: they longed for security, but found the sea unpredictable and unforgiving; they acceded to hard work, but desired more leisure and less loneliness; they would be stoic and stolid, but never safe. These songs, poems and stories also attest to another important aspect of the lived experiences of fisherwomen, namely their full partnership in productive labor. They were not skippers, but they were not subordinate. Their work mattered, and they knew it did, even if they had too much of it to do and with too little security to show for it.

## A Fisher Laddie needs A Fisher Lassie

During the eighteenth, nineteenth, and the early twentieth century, and in sharp contrast to modern times, fishermen and their wives relied directly upon each other. Marriage was a significant factor within the economy of fishing. And most fishers married other fishers, often within the same village.

The usual explanation given for in-marriage among fishers from the same village was that "a fisher laddie needs a fisher lassie." Indeed, this was not merely a euphonious aphorism or romantic ideal. Fishermen consciously sought wives who would be effective helpmates. As one man said to me, "Ye had to marry wi'in the fisherfolk. Ye needed a wife who knew the wark."

> A fisher-girl had, in addition to innumerable household tasks, to mend the nets, bait the hooks, gut the fish, wash the offal from the street, and, after marriage, run the family single-handed while the man was away from home for long periods at sea. It bred great independence of character, and it was not thought that a farmworker's daughter could ever learn what was required . . . inter-marriage between country families and Buckie fishing families was practically unknown before the Second World War; nine-tenths of those interviewed in Buckie had found their wives either from within the town itself or from similar villages along the coast. There was such a sense of apartness that farm children were held by fisher children to smell bad. (Smout 1986: 176)

Intriguingly, this quote reveals an instance where stigma was reversed, the "bad smell" coming from the farmers, rather than the fishers. But I digress.

The fisher laddie formulation sees marriage only from the male point of view and cannot be taken solely at face value. To do so would be to accept, without further thought, a purely male model. It would be akin to viewing alliance-making as "the exchange of women" or of women depicted as "zeroes" on the kinship charts (Porter ). It can just as well be said, in fact, that a fisher lassie needed a fisher lassie, for, as we have seen, female work groups were also organized around core groups of kin. Like men, women said that they felt more comfortable working with family members. They also relied on each other for moral and emotional support. Mother-daughter ties were particular strong. Ferryden's parish records showed that many women delivered their first and even their second children in their mothers' houses, even if they had married away from the village. Some even returned from North America to do so. "When the men were away, as they often were, for eight to ten weeks at a time [during the herring fishing] then the women and children had each other for company and protection" (Buchan 1977: 4).

Such bonds made women understandably reluctant to marry out of the village. The only way to resolve the tension between agnatic and uterine bonds would have been to keep marriage within the village as much as possible. Endogamy was not a hard and fast rule, of course, and many a fisherman or woman found a spouse from another fishing community, particularly after herring curing took women away to work (as we shall see shortly). But in general, people preferred to avoid the conflict and to remain close to their natal families. As one author says, "none of the communities would easily absorb outsiders, whether male or female" (Gray 1978). Buchan further suggests that an out-marrying woman might have been less than keen to work with her mother-in-law: "If a fisherman married from outside the community, then usually his mother took over and instructed the outsider in her duties. Sometimes this situation worked very well, at other times it led to bitterness and rancour" (Buchan 1977: 5). Indeed, the fishing community of Peterhead was known for women's insistence on remaining, forcing "foreign" fisher husbands to move in.

So village endogamy provided the ideal solution: men and women were assured of mates whose skills and values were compatible with their own while intra-sex solidarity could persist unchallenged. Furthermore, as we shall see, it reinforced local solidarity in the face of social stigma. Ironically, stigmatizing notions drew upon these practices to find further evidence of fisher difference from everyone else. The strength of women's kinship bonds no doubt contributed to these communities' reputation for matriarchy, a subject I take up later in this chapter, just as endogamy helped to brand them as inbred.

Scotland is a small country, but kinship practices are not identical everywhere within it. For example, Hebridean Gaelic kinship involves different terms for maternal and paternal kin, even though clan member-ship was acquired ambilineally (Parman 1990) and people take these distinctions seriously (see Ennew 1980). Among Lowland Scots, on the other hand, mothers' and fathers' sides of the family are generally assumed to be equivalent, in a manner quite similar to that of American kinship (Schneider 1968). Most Lowlanders see themselves as living within a bounded group of relatives whose importance varies with personal close-ness. This also applies to fishers, but a distinct tendency for women to be closer to their mothers' kin, men their fathers' relatives, is clearly visible. Take, for example, the business of naming.

Fishing villagers knew each other lineally as their mothers' daughters or fathers' sons: one might be Mary's Catherine's Betty, for example, or Williamina's Rose's Elizabeth (and see Wilson 1980). This genealogical reiteration stressed the continuity of same-sex lines and encoded life history narratives in a way that outsiders could never comprehend. For women, it helped to counteract their submersion in patrilineally acquired surnames. Married surname use also allowed a woman's natal identity to persist. Women retained their maiden names for all but official purposes, or for dealing with outsiders. When I first went to Ferryden I found this quite confusing. A woman would be introduced to me as, say, Mrs James Watt, but from then on would be referred to as Agnes Coull.

There is one further point concerning kinship and community: in addition to endogamy, fishers might use inheritance to ensure that children stayed close by. Sons were not the only heirs. A woman might inherit not only a house, but also a boat, even though she could not sail in it herself. An early example comes from a 1792 will from the northern village of Broadsea, where an ancestor of Christian Watt, the fisherman James Lascelles, left

> all my worldly goods and chattels whatsoever and wherever situate to my great grand daughter Helen Noble or Lascelles widow of Andrew Noble a White fisher and to her eldest child . . . to be left in fee in her Mother's lifetime in time to be her own absolute property. (Fraser 1983)

This property included not only household goods, but fishing gear: "my great lines and my small lines." Clearly, the hope would have been that his widowed descendant would remarry a local fisherman who could make use of them.

Female solidarity persisted as the fishery itself began to change. As we have seen, by the middle of the nineteenth century, the emphasis in Scottish fishing had begun to shift from white fish to herring, and from small family-based boats to larger craft in which most men were employed by boat owners. The transition did not take place all at once; nor did all abandon white fishing. However, many men now made longer voyages, sometimes lasting months at a time. The impact upon the small communities was severe. "By the second half of the 19th century, when the fisheries expanded, the family as an autonomous economic entity was untenable" (Telford 1998: 2).

Women also found themselves with new roles to play. With the rise of the herring fleets, a host of shoreside workers was needed to process and pack the highly perishable fish for transport and sale. Thousands of women responded to this new opportunity to earn money. This did not mean, however, that they deserted their home villages for good. Rather, like the fishermen and coopers (male fishing barrel makers), they became seasonal, migrant laborers. Often, groups of related women traveled and stayed together. In this new setting, they became known as herring lassies. It is to this new activity, one crucial to understanding the relationship between gender and stigma, that I turn now.

## Herring Quines and Gutting Lassies

> There's coopers here and curers there and buyers, canny chiels,
> And lassies at the pickling and others at the creels,
> And you'll wish the fish had been a' left in the sea
> By the time you finish guttin' herrin' on the Yarmouth quay.
>
> (*Song of the Fish-Gutters* by Ewan MacColl, from Buchan and Hall 1973: 99).

As I have already indicated, herring were not a new species to all Scottish fishermen. For many years, particularly in the northeast, men had been pursued them from small boats.

> Herring fishing . . . had been spreading over several sectors of the east coast since the late eighteenth century . . . Through the eighty years up to 1870 it was carried on by men drawn from more than a hundred fishing communities . . . Line fishing, mainly for cod and haddock, had been the occupation of their ancestors from a much earlier time and, when they turned to herring fishing in the nineteenth century, the more traditional line fishing still continued to occupy a good part of the year. Herring fishing, then, was a nineteenth century innovation in communities which had long depended on other forms of fishing. (Gray n.d.: 1).

The big curing firms began to change the rhythm of work by hiring fishermen to spend several months a year in large fleets, following the shoals around the British coast. Fueled by demand from Germany and the Baltic, and encouraged by changes in the terms of trade, the herring industry grew exponentially, reaching its zenith in the 1880s and declining slowly until the First World War, when many of the boats were commandeered for battle. Markets, too, became inaccessible. At first, only a few places had the large boats and enough investment capital to make herring fishing the primary activity (Coull 1969: 27), and most communities continued to include white fish in their yearly rounds. Following the end of the war, some men went back to fishing, but the boom was over. The consequences of this decline are still unfolding, as Chapters 5 and 6 will explain.

During this period, however, women added herring curing to their already full work loads. As the fleets went further and further offshore, the herring fishery made periodic and increasingly significant interruptions to the village-based labor patterns that had been based on short trips. Herring shoals are migratory and not always predictable. Maturing in northern waters, they swim southward to breed. They could be caught at many places along the coast, but the richest waters were those off Great Yarmouth, in England, Scotland's Western Isles, and the Shetlands. Thus men would join herring crews on a seasonal basis. Along the Fife coast, for example, men went out to the late summer herring (known as "the Lammas Drave") and to the winter herring (Smith 1985). Boats left for weeks or even months at a time to join the "great and mobile herring fleet which by 1870 amounted to over 4000 boats" (Gray n.d.: 1).

Curers owned much of the fleet, and drew their crews from all around the coast.

> This practice meant that the price of herring per cran [a standardized measure of fish: roughly 700-1000 cured fish] was fixed and the quantity to be landed agreed on. Once the complement of crans were landed, the fishermen were free to go home, or stay and fish at a much less price. Being engaged to a curer had the advantage that money was received in advance, this was commonly called Bounty, and was sufficient to keep the wives and children alive while the boats were away fishing. If herring were scarce it meant boats in some cases would be away for as long as twenty weeks from home before catching their complement. (Stewart n.d.: 11).

Gray further estimates that when east coast fishing was at its height in the 1870s, "some 30,000 fishermen and about the same number of shore workers were thus employed" (1967: 187). By this time, the herring industry was a very different, capital intensive "kettle of fish" than the small-scale efforts that had preceded it.

The profits now generated for curers firmly ensconced many in the solid middle class; fishermen did not do so well. Thus emerged a radically new, more proletarianized, and increasingly class-conscious division of labor. Christian Watt, whose political views, as we have seen, were more radicalized than many, reflected bitterly on the disparity between curers' and fishers' profits from the trade.

> We now had to work terribly hard, for herring prices were so poor. Fisherman chaved [worked] their guts out for nothing but to line the curers' pouch. The herring boom hit the Broch [Fraserburgh] like a thunderbolt. They were gutting and packing on the streets . . . It was a scandal folk were so poorly paid; we managed to give our bairns a pair of shoes and rig out for Sunday, but they had to go barefoot to school through the week.
>
> The 1870s were a bad time for the working class. The industrial upheaval was well under way. As fishers we felt the pinch, for most folk had gone over to herring fishing completely. You could not barter herring for dairy produce the same way as you could do with white fish . . . We certainly were very poor in my childhood, but my own children had far less to eat than we had for times were now geared to put all the profit into the curer's pocket . . . In truth we had been robbed of our independence . . . (Fraser 1983: 88)

In this next passage, she embeds her observations in a critique that mixes class inequity with religious consequence:

> whatever is said of the Victorians in the future, be they Empire builders or what have you, they were certainly not champions of humanity, as so many shall one day have to stand before an angry God and testify. It seemed hordes of bullies had been rounded up to take on foremen's jobs in gutting yards, to drive the women as hard as they could. (Fraser 1983: 89)

Thousands of women were recruited to cure the "silver darlings," as herring were commonly called in the northeast. Labor demands were so great, in fact, that men and women from the Highlands also sought work on the coast. The women became variously known as fishgirls, herring girls, herring lassies, or gutting *quines* (women). This new work had significant domestic consequences: traveling to distant places away from village confines, men and women encountered attractive strangers, and the strong tendency to marry only from within the village began to weaken. The new spouses were usually fisherfolk, however, so occupational endogamy, at least, still prevailed.

However, not all curing operations were done in far-away places. Joseph Johnston's of Montrose, a curing firm about which we will learn more Chapter 4, was said to have originally sent several Ferryden women to Sweden to learn Scandinavian herring curing methods so that they could teach others in the village. The firm then began to hire Ferryden village women directly as wage-earners. "My mother stayed guttin' herrin' till two or three A.M.," recalled one Ferryden woman. During the summer months, Johnston's sent coopers around the village to gather the women for work, crying out, "A'body! A'body!" Another Ferryden woman recalled that her mother would return home, exhausted, at two or three in the morning. "A woman was finished at fifty in those days."

A former herring lassie from Peterhead remembered working hungry in her home town during her teenage years, before the post-War unions brought some improvement in working conditions:

> When I was a girl in Peterhead, in the old days before the First War, a man would come round tae the house and tell ye that the herrin' would be in the yard at nine o'clock, and sometimes we didna stop till three or four o'clock the next morning. Gutting all the time. Ye got nothing tae eat unless someone brought it. (Butcher 1987: 12).

For most, however, being a herring lassie meant leaving home, village and family boat for long periods of time. For the first time, significant numbers of women from the fishing communities were working outside of the domestic economy.

> Herring fishing's demand for ancillary labour was not contained within the framework of the family group . . . during the fishing itself the crew would operate without the direct aid of their women-folk. Nets had to be spread for drying but it was done either by the crew or by laborers hired for the purpose. The transport of fish from boat to yard was the responsibility of the curer and he would engage specialized carters for the purpose. The women, on the other hand, finding employment within the yards as gutters and packers, did not directly support the crews in which their men-folk were organized. Rather, they were hired as wage-earners by the curers to share impersonally in the work of a yard into which the catches of many boats might be discharged. (Gray 1978)

To reach the herring stations, women journeyed by train or boat, most commonly south to the East Anglian ports of Great Yarmouth and Lowestoft, west to the Hebrides or Ireland and north to Lerwick, in the Shetlands. Reaching Lerwick involved a long, often fearsome crossing by ship.

The voyage to Lerwick was feared: the overnight crossing of sixteen hours from Aberdeen could make many sick, the ship was too crowded for everyone to have a bunk and many lay on deck under tarpaulins. Some women might have some whisky but many of the fisher girls came from temperance communities and refused this solace. (Miller 1999: 109)

One of my Ferryden informants remembered that when her mother had gone to cure herring in Shetland, "the boats were filthy and people were pushed in among the cattle." Another told me that the women were sent out in small open boats, lashed in to protect them from being washed overboard in heavy seas.

With their belongings packed in heavy wooden *kists* (chests or trunks) that could double as tables or chairs, they went to live in rude, unfurnished huts near the quays. Their communal lodgings were spartan and even unhealthy. "The huts were overcrowded and the women were overworked so if disease struck it took a terrible toll" (Buchan 1977)

Girls could start in the gutting as early as the age of 10, although they usually waited until they left school at 14. "They were often taught their trade by their mothers who ensured their daughters carried on the family line of work" (Taylor, n.d.: 63). Both unmarried and married women went, and Telford (1998: 3) tells us that "It was common to have sexagenarian grandmothers at the gutting".

They were always referred to as fisher girls regardless of age, but as the Jenkins collection of photographs shows a high proportion of them were goodlooking young women. It is not surprising that quite a number of today's Norfolk and Suffolk grandmothers first came south after the herring and stayed to marry. (Elliott 1979: 50)

Some women followed the fishing virtually year round. Bochel, a woman from the fisher community of Nairn, writes that others

whose homes were well supported by menfolk owning a fishing vessel, did not work all the year round and usually chose to go to Lerwick in the summer and Yarmouth in the winter. For the remainder of the year they were busily occupied with their mothers at home on the never ending tasks of knitting, washing and repairing clothes, mending nets and generally helping to sustain, at a distance, the trade by which their families lived. (1979: 2–3)

Some of the older women along the east coast today remember those days with a mixture of pride and pain. They recall being wakened to the cry of "get up and tie your fingers!" (Miller 1999: 110). For the long hours working in barrels of brine, they wrapped their fingers in cotton rags, called *cloots* or *clooties*, because gutting made sores and the brine inflamed them. The salt alone cut holes between their fingers and they remember hands cracked, raw, and bleeding. "Even in the late autumn they were expected to continue working in the open 'exposed to rain, sleet and wind,' standing into the night ankle-deep in quagmires of mud, sand and fish refuse" (Thompson et al. 1983: 172).

With their razor sharp knives flashing at lightning speed they could deal with as many as 50 herring a minute. The fish were first sprinkled with salt otherwise they would have been too slippery to handle at such speed. (Elliott 1979)

To protect their clothes, they wore heavy oilskin aprons, wellington boots, headscarves or caps, and rolled their sleeves back to the elbow.

They typically worked in groups of threes, two gutters and one packer to a barrel. The gutters stood over the troughs, or *farlans*, of fish, eviscerating them at lightning speed. The packer filled the barrels with layers of fish graded by size and condition. Each layer of fish was then covered with a layer of salt. The packer was also responsible for keeping track of all financial transactions. (Buchan 1977)

At the time of hiring, curers advanced a small sum, called *arles,* which bound a girl to stay for the entire season. This was never more than £1 and usually less. Curers also paid gutters' travel expenses plus a small, subsistence wage (Elliott 1979: 50). Pay rates were poor. One writer described their work as "slave labour as workers on the quay were not protected by the factory Act" (Wood 1998: 53).

In the early years of this century the women received 8d. between the crew [in other words, to be divided three ways] for each barrel of herring packed and gutted [from 850 to 1000 fish]. Later it rose to 10d., then to 1/-. The most anyone ever remembers receiving was 2/6d. per barrel. My mother says when she received L40 for working at the summer fishing she thought that she had made a fortune. (Buchan 1977)

As indeed, she had. "Before 1914 the average wage for a herring girl was 25s a week . . . But by 1924 the girls were only earning 20s a week wages [which went for food and lodging], plus one shilling between three girls for each barrel filled . . . a crew filling about 30 barrels a day" (Telford 1998: 5).

Some women remembered their days as members of gutting crews as a time of adventure and camaraderie.

Crews remained intact for many fishings and only illness or marriage broke up a partnership. Close friendships were made, and the unselfish devotion of crew members to each other endured through all the changing fortunes of their future lives. (Bochel 1979: 13)

Others, however, recalled great hardship, belying claims – usually by people who were not there – that gutters were always cheerful (the way African-American field hands were supposed to be, perhaps). In an example of how representations can be deceiving, Lockhart (1997: 17) interprets group photographs of the lassies' smiling faces to mean that the gutters were always happy. Given their conditions of work, this seems rather unlikely, and becomes even more suspect when we read that "Dressing up to be photographed was one of the first things they did after settling in for the season," suggesting that many of these illustrations were less than candid (Bochel 1979: 5). The lassies were not exactly "shucking and jiving," but the smiling photographs might well have been taken at least partly to convince family back home of their daughters' wellbeing. In any case, fisherfolk bairns were raised not to "greet" (cry or complain) overmuch.

Other evidence suggests significant suffering. Given the speed at which they worked, cuts and infections were commonplace, sometimes forcing them to leave the herring stations and return home with nothing to show for their efforts. The cold and wet could be a major source of misery, as the following account from a Shetland girl (in Shetland dialect) reveals:

When we wir in Yarmouth we hed dat 'black frost'. Whan we gied oot da lapels a wir coast wis frozen stiff . . . Sometimes, da ice wis on da top a da barrels an we hed to staand wi wir hands ida barrels ta get wir hands osed to do cold. Da tears wir streaming doon wir faces fir we got osed to da cold in wir hands. (Telford 1998: 24)

An oral history of fishing in the Aberdeen region gives us a clear example of the risks involved in working under such conditions. (Note: R.R., C.O'C. and S.M are women; B.W., a man):

R.R.    '. . . Jessie got her finger caed aff . . . Ye didna get peyed if ye didna work, an if the herrin didna come in ye'd nae pey. Ye'd maybe aboot five shillins guaranteed . . .

D.A.    [interviewer] So if you were choppin fish and you chopped your finger off you didn't get paid?

B.W.    No, it was your fault. Compensation? Never heard of compensation.

*C.O'C.*  Ye did get sick pey, but it wisna hell of a much. Jessie jist come doon, she didna ken, she was spikkin [speaking] . . .
*S.M.*  Ay, her hands had been that caul [cold].
*C.O'C.*  Knifes were that sharp that ye didna ken ye'd cut yersel . . . (Atherton 1992: 30)

As "slaves to short-arsed curers," as the poet Derick Thomson put it, women faced hardship together, doubtless putting a bold face on poverty whenever they could (Thomson 1997: 18). Nonetheless, some rebelled and even took collective action. A short-lived class-conscious rhetoric was beginning to penetrate the proletarianized ranks of both sexes.

Protests were stimulated not only by poor wages on the quayside but by a growing sense that fishing communities generally were in peril. One source was the threat to the small-scale white fishery posed by the large, new steam drifters coming out of large ports like Aberdeen. Fishermen immediately perceived the threat these posed to fish stocks. In some places, fishers even threw stones at the trawlers and refused to sail in them. They also saw, correctly as it has turned out, that this new marriage of technology and capital presaged trouble for community-based fishing.

Signs of decline had already begun. As early as the 1890s, demand for herring lassies began to slacken, in part because trains became more and more effective transport for fresh fish packed in ice, obviating the need for pickling the fish in brine (Sutherland n.d.). A few years later, many such chilly cargoes from the southeast coast were being sent by ship to Baltic ports. The steam vessels that made these trips were nicknamed the Klondykers (after the Yukon gold rush), because of their owners' aggressive entrepreneurial behavior in buying fish and because of the fortunes their owners made (Gibson 1994: 47).

Meanwhile, steam drifters with their vast nets were finding shrinking catches. The decline did not happen all at once. In 1912, one author says that 21,749 fishermen and 10,818 gutters and packers were still working from Shetland to Yarmouth (Miller 1999: 108). In 1913, a fishermen's union organizer spoke of

The grip of the capitalist . . . Capitalism has no sentiment about villages and no attachments to any place . . . It is only a question of time before the centralisation is more complete and the depopulation of the herring fishing villages as mournful as that of the villages of the white fish . . . (Thompson et al. 1983: 157)

The women were listening. Thompson argues that they were often quicker to adopt a combative outlook than the men:

In fact the strike wave which was to sweep through the fishing industry in 1913–14 was heralded by the Aberdeen women fishworkers who struck for increased wages in April 1913, parading the streets "singing and shouting lustily . . ." (1983: 169)

Among the songs they sang, some undoubtedly stressed the difficulties of getting by on a gutter's pay. Here is one example:

I'm a fish gutting lassie gutting herring's my trade,
But I'll never be wealthy no fortunes are made.
For ten-pence a barrel is all we are paid,
Life is hard with the herring shoals.
(Ian Sinclair, in Bochel 1982: 39)

The words bear a strong (though less poetic) resemblance to another working class women's song, this one from the weaving mills, whose refrain goes: "Oh dear me, the warld's ill-divided . . . Them that work's the hardest is aye wi' least provided."

The First World War was a catalyst for radical action throughout Scotland.

The pressures and circumstances of wartime thus strengthened independence, confidence, morale and class consciousness amongst working women. At one level, this advanced awareness was illustrated in rapidly rising female membership of trade unions, with Scottish women contributing disproportionately to the doubling of trade union membership between 1914 and 1920. Perhaps the most tangible expressions of this heightened class awareness amongst working women occurred on Clydeside. Witness, for example, the spate of female workers strikes and spiraling demands for inflation-matching wage rises . . . (McIvor 1992: 145)

The radicalizing climate of labor that intensified during the years following Britain's General Strike of 1926 clearly reached the northern coasts. In the late 1920s, demand for gutters had fallen sharply; nonetheless, some of them protested poor wages and living conditions by refusing to work. In 1931, gutters in Yarmouth, Peterhead, Shetland and Stornoway struck for better wages.

At that time we were getting tenpence a barrel between three of us. You had a lot of herring to gut before you got that. We were paid fourpence an hour when we were doing other work . . . We were on strike for a week anyway and we won. I think our pay went up to one shilling a barrel. (Miller 1999: 113)

Further strikes occurred in 1936, 1946, 1949 and 1953, by which time the herring yards were all but gone (Telford 1998: 6).

In considering the fish lassies' willingness to strike, Thompson et al. (1983: 172) argue that the women "had less to lose" than the men, being young and working to provide "a family extra." They go further to say that "they were in a sense the unspoken voice of the men in the depression years". This perspective misses the mark for it presupposes that, no matter what women did, men were still the "real" providers, and, moreover, that women did not speak out for their own interests. On the contrary: poverty and exploitation affected men and women equally. And, if we have seen anything from the foregoing descriptions of women's work in the fishery, it is that women regarded themselves and their work as no less important than that of their men.

During this period of proletarian labor and workers' consciousness, Scottish fisher women began to move closer in spirit to other working-class women than they had been previously. Like other women of the rural working class between the wars who found themselves unemployed or forced into domestic service, the slump in the fisheries meant that many herring and fisherlassies also had to find other kinds of work. However, unlike the farm workers, most continued to live within the fishing community.[4]

"Guttin' herrin' on the Yarmouth quay" proved to be a relatively short-lived way of life, the victim of a boom-and-bust cycle in fishing that has never recovered. Both economics and technology were responsible. A combination of foreign competition and the severe depletion of herring stocks by the big steam drifters led to a long-lasting slump. By the middle of the 1920s, the industry was in bad shape. At the larger ports, fishermen continued to land herring with varying success, but for the smaller villages, the era was already ending. One Fife coast historian reports that 1926 was "the last time I saw gutters at work in Anstruther" (Smith 1985: 109).

Today, only a few women work in fishery-related occupations, chiefly in fish-processing factories, where hot, steamy conditions have replaced the cold, wet ones. How one interprets the historical evidence regarding this development is open to debate. Byron suggests that women left the fishery largely by choice. Indeed, if one were to look only at modern fisherwomen's perceptions of their mothers' hardships, that might be a logical conclusion. Writing of changes in the northern European (primarily Scandinavian and Scottish) maritime household, Byron sees modernity, in the form of alternative labor, as enabling women to "disengage themselves from their former obligations, doing so largely in order to realise their aspirations for domestic independence" (1994: 271). This statement also implies that women have wanted to remove themselves from the "relationships of kinship, affinity, and neighbourhood as economic and social resources" that continue, in Byron's view, to characterize fishermen's activities.

Certainly many women have, as the songs, poems and stories to which I earlier referred make clear, longed for freedom from their hard work and insecure futures. As another example, Carter discusses the dramatic drain of female labor from the peasant farms of northeast Scotland at the end of the nineteenth century:

> The first group to leave peasant agriculture in large numbers from choice was, as always, young women – for whom there was no hope of ever replacing domestic servitude with the independence of the peasant farmer. By the 1890s the trickle of young women . . . become a flood: "They seem to be running away from the land," "Our girls about the country are all getting an education and finding their ways into shops as cashiers, and bookkeepers, and into business." (Carter 1979: 95)

During this same era, some fisher girls also sought other occupations (Gray 1978: 81). Mrs Potter, a nonagenarian in Ferryden at the time of my first fieldwork there, told me that when she saw how hard her mother worked shelling mussels and baiting lines, "I used to think to myself, I wouldna like to spend my whole life deein that." And she didn't. She went out to domestic service, married the son of a railwayman, and only returned to live in the village when he retired.

However, as we have seen, many Scottish fisherwomen remained intensely involved in the industry. Clearly, Byron's claim that women left the fishery by choice must therefore be modified and contextualized. We must ask what they lost, as well as what they gained. One thing is clear, Scottish fishwives had their own cash income as well as considerable domestic authority. They did not, in other words, have to wait for their husbands to dole out part of a wage packet, as many do today. Thus, the loss of their jobs as shoreside partners may well have meant less independence for them, not more.[5]

But the real answer to this question is to be found in women's relationships to their communities. Most Scottish fisherwomen left the fishery only when the fishery, in effect, left them: that is, when its community basis began to erode and when the herring curing collapsed (see Armstrong 1986). In fact, had women left the fishery in droves before this point they would have damaged it severely, perhaps beyond repair. But this was not really an option. Not only income, but home and family, as well as bonds with other women were on the line. Thus, "choice" may be a misleading word, and certainly an ambiguous one.

It would also be misleading, however, to assume that before the fishery failed, all Scottish fisherwomen were like Mrs Mucklebackit in *The Antiquary* (about which I will have more to say below). Although they may have been equal partners in a domestic mode of production, they did not rule the roost. Yet, there is no doubt that this image of Scottish fishwives as all-powerful matriarchs is quite ubiquitous. Indeed, many modern fishermen describe their female ancestors in these terms. Just why and with what implications, I explore below.

## Exoticizing Women, Emasculating Men: Matriarchs in a Patriarchal Society

As I said at the beginning of this chapter, my fisherfolk acquaintances saw to it that I learned about women's former importance in the fishery, emphasizing their physical and social strength. For example, one fisherman from Fife said to me that

> The women were right in at the heart of it; they were harder than the men. My grandmother was a matriarch. She was ninety when I was 16. My father, myself and three cousins who all owned boats, we all went to her house on Saturday to smoke cigarettes and talk about the fishing. My grandfather was a placid man who did what his wife told him.

Even Peter Anson, whom I mentioned earlier, stated flatly that "it was the women who ruled over most fisher families" (1965: 27). Adams concurred: ". . . in the old days they held the purse strings and doled out pocket money to their menfolk and were usually boss in the house" (Adams 1991: 9). Certainly, such a vision of women has come to dominate the heritage industry. Thus, an exhibit text in the tourist-oriented Buckie Drifter Project heritage center punctuates its comment with an exclamation point: "the head of the family was a matriarch with a multiplicity of roles!"

There are some dissenters, of course, King, for example, emphasize equality over matriarchy.

> Unlike some women of this period the fisherman's wife was not treated as a delicate ornament. The fisherwomen had a confidence and liberty which few other women could enjoy. The man and wife relationship was a partnership of equals, sometimes with the woman playing the dominant role. (King n.d.: 5)

So, too, does an extract from the Aberdeenshire oral history to which I earlier referred. In it shared responsibility is highlighted over dominance. The male informant is talking about the 1930s:

> I look at it this wye . . . your wife is yer partner, and it was your job to earn the money, and her to organise the spendin' o' it. I gave my wife the money and she would give me back 5 bob for my pocket money . . . If you were at sea, ye didn't need onything in yer pooch, there was nowhere to spend it! Yer whole world was 110 feet long, by 22 feet broad. (Atherton 1992: 63)

Finally, one of the "Memory Lane" columns devoted to industrial history in *Scottish Fishing Monthly* declares that "Fishing is often considered to be a trade run by men. However, certain aspects of it owe their success to woman as much as men, for example, the herring fishery off the east coast of Britain" (Harrison 1995: 13).

Yet, within the historical documents at least, it is the image of fishwives as matriarchs that wins out. It is, perhaps, not surprising that onlookers would conclude from fishwives' public behavior that women ruled the domestic roost. Through the middle of the twentieth century (and in many cases, beyond), it was generally assumed that the breadwinner (normally the man) was head of the house. And everything about the fisherwomen – their voices, their muscles, their assertiveness – ran counter to middle-class beliefs that women were by nature passive and best suited to stay within domestic confines. They were far too "masculine." For many nineteenth century commentators, steeped in patriarchal, middle class notions of the ideal female, equality was such an unthinkable idea that translating it to "matriarchy" was an easy step to take.

> The cult of domesticity which gathered momentum through the Victorian period dictated that by 1900 the inalienable cultural norm in Scotland was that the primary role of women in life was the servicing of a male "breadwinner" within the home and family. (McIvor 1996: 189)

The meaning of matriarchy, for these commentators, was clearly far different than it was for my twentieth-century Fife informant, who spoke of his grandmother in almost reverential tones. Beliefs that matriarchy revealed a state of social backwardness or even savagery permeated the intellectual classes. Indeed, in scholarly circles dedicated to notions of unilineal evolution (Bachofen 1861; McLennan 1865; Morgan 1877; Tylor 1899), civilization was believed to have arisen with patriarchy. Importantly, as Stocking points out, one could find pockets of savagery alive and well within societies that had achieved civilization. Thus, McLennan could label deviant behavior in his own society as savage behavior (Stocking 1987: 202). Although McLennan dwelled on the deviant sexual behavior of city dwellers, others clearly applied the idea of savages within the civilized world to the inhabitants of rural areas, as well.

Thus, envisioning fishwives as matriarchs could only have contributed to the widespread stigmatization of fishers as a separate caste or race and as a throwback to earlier times, as Chapter 2 has shown. In the spirit of Victorian ethnology, observers often made their remarks about fisher-women as law-like generalizations, voiced in a distanced, scientific tone.

> It may not, perhaps, be generally known to those who are not in possession of special sources of information, that in all fishing communities, the woman is head of the house . . . She is ruler over her household and chancellor of her husband's exchequer. (Bertram 1883: 4)

Emphasizing men's degradation even more strongly, Bertram else-where declares:

> Just now there are many fishermen who will not go to sea as long as they imagine their wives have got a penny left from the last hawking excursion. The women enslave the men to their will, and keep them enchained under petticoat government. Did the women remain at home in their domestic sphere, looking after the children and their husbands' comforts, the men would pluck up spirit and exert themselves to make money in order to keep their families at home comfortable and respectable. (cited in Anson 1965: 142)

Similarly, Andrew Douglas (1857: 53), a nineteenth-century Ferryden schoolmaster, noted in his memoirs that "Among fisher people in general the women rule supreme". And in the nineteenth century novel, *Christie Johnstone*, a middle-class woman enjoins her infatuated son to break off his liason with a fisher woman, saying that "It is a Newhaven idea that the female is the natural protector of the male . . ." (Reade 1855: 78).

These were shocking commentaries, indeed, during the height of the Victorian era, when, as I have said, the ideal woman was supposed to be the modest and retiring keeper of the household flame. The fishwives moving about the countryside so freely, arguing with curers and with customers, and the herring lassies, covered in fish guts and surrounded by strange men, struck many as degraded examples of the "fair sex."

It must be said, however, that gendered notions of middle-class propriety affected women in other outdoor occupations, such as field labor:

> I must here make some allusion to those females engaged in outwork; surely their lot is far from desirable and their far from effeminate. Many of the are hired at very low wages to pull turnips during the winter. Conceive a female

having to work in the open air all day . . . Is this fit and proper work for a woman? (Smout and Wood 1991: 96)

Female farm workers also attracted notice as emblems of Britain's living peasant past. Gordon remarks, for example, that "Nineteenth-century photographer loved taking pictures of women doing their domestic work outdoors" (Gordon 1990: 210).

A number of nineteenth century observers seem to have subscribed to the idea that extra-domestic, heavy labor led directly to women's bodily, as well as spiritual degradation, perhaps even to evolutionary backsliding. Women employed in coal mining were believed to have acquired "a peculiar type of mouth, wide, open, thick-lipped, projecting equally above and below [like] savages in their lowest and most degraded state" (Miller 1856, cited in Mitchison 1978).

Thus, fisherwomen were not the only ones singled out for such remark. However, identified as matriarchs and coming from communities already stigmatized, the fisherwomen possibly seemed the strangest, most exotic and least "evolved" of all.

Literature provides us with an example of how exaggerated the image of the matriarch could be. In a passage from *The Antiquary*, whose setting was modeled on the Angus village of Auchmithie, the stalwart Luckie Mucklebackit describes her husband's fear of her in response to a customer's disdain for the hard lives of fisherwomen.

. . . Thae's your landward and burrows-town notions . . . Fisher-wives ken better – they keep the man, and keep the house, and keep the siller too, lass . . . Show me a word my Saunders daur speak, or a turn he daur do about the house, without it be just to tak his meat, and his drink, and his diversion, like ony o' the weans. He has mair sense than to ca' onything about the bigging [house] his ain, frae the rooftree down to a crackit trencher on the bink [drain alongside the house]. He kens well eneugh wha' feeds him, and cleeds [clothes] him, and keeps a' tight, thack and rape [thatched], when his coble [boat] is jowing awa [rolling] in the Firth, puir fallow. Na, na lass – them that sells the goods guide the purse – them that guide the purse rule the house. Show me ane o' your bits o' farmer-bodies that wad let their wife drive the stock to the market, and ca' in the debts. (Scott 1923 [1816]: 247; also cited in Stevenson 1991: 20)

Scott's fishwife expresses contempt for her man's abilities to take care of himself. In effect, she emasculates him and thus exemplifies the matriarchal stereotype.

A milder, still humorous version comes from the memoirs of Fanny Kemble, the noted actress. She visited Newhaven (south of Edinburgh) in the late 1820s. Wishing to go out on the Forth, she stopped at a fisher cottage to find someone to take her. There met the fishwife, Sandie Flockhart, for whom she developed a kind of fascinated fondness. Nonetheless, it is clear that Kemble regarded her as a creature very different from herself:

Ay, my man and boy shall gang wi' ye'. A few lusty screams brought her husband and son forth, and at her bidding they got a boat ready . . . The husband was a comparatively small man, with dark eyes, hair and complexion; but her 'boy,' the eldest, who had come with him to take care of me, was a fair-haired fresh-faced young giant, of his mother's strain, and, like her, looked as if he had come of the Northern Vikings, or some of the *Niebelungen Lied* heroes. (Stevenson 1991: 17)

Both depictions use humor to paint an exaggerated picture of fishwife matriarchy. But herring girls were often even further denigrated, in fact, they were sometimes rendered in animal-like terms, as akin to the birds and fish among which they worked.[6] In Weld's description, for example, one could even infer his belief that if Darwin's theory of evolution were correct, the primitive fishwife was working her way back down the evolutionary ladder.

Wick harbour is surrounded on the land side by hundreds of . . . gutting troughs. Round them stood rows of what close inspection led you to conclude were women, though at first sight you might be excused for having some doubts respecting their sex. They all wore strange-shaped canvas garments, so bespattered with blood and the entrails and scales of fish as to cause them to resemble *animals of the ichthyological kingdom* [italics mine], recently divested of their skin, undergoing perhaps one of those transitions set forth in Mr. Darwin's speculative book, "On the Origin of Species." And if a man may become a monkey, or has been a whale, why should not a Caithness damsel become a herring?

The author continues his analogy in this next passage and reinforces the view that fish gutters are not proper women. This time, he does it by noting the exceptions among them, girls who were inappropriately employed because they were too pretty.

. . . the women, familiar called gutters, pounce upon the herrings like *a bird of prey* [italics mine], seize their victims, and, with a rapidity of motion which baffles your eye, deprive the fish of their viscera . . . At this rapid rate you no longer wonder at the silence that prevails while the bloody work is going on, nor at the incarnadined condition of the women. How habit deadens feeling!

Who would imagine that a delicate looking girl could be tempted by even a high wage to spend long days at this work? Such, however, is the fact; for although the majority of the 2,500 women employed in gutting herrings are certainly not lovely nor delicate limbed, still I observed several pretty and modest-looking girls *who would apparently have made better shepherdesses than fish-gutters* [italics mine] . . . the love of gain overcomes repugnance. The damsel who kindly inducted me into the mysteries of the art of evisceration told me that she had sometimes made £8, in a good fishing season, a large and welcome addition to her annual wage as a domestic servant . . . (Weld 1860, quoted in Smout and Wood 1991: 87)

If literature describing fishwives as matriarchs implied that they were less civilized than decent (read docile) Scottish women, then the new art of photography stereotyped them in manners that, while seemingly different, were fundamentally the same. Indeed many early photographers found fisherwomen to be apt subjects, both at the fishcuring and in the village setting. Some photographs were taken for artistic reasons; others for sale to the growing tourist market. Herring lassies were shown to be, if not matriarchs, then strong women with powerful arm and shoulder muscles. A few flashed rather cheeky grins, though most looked shy or somber, intent on their work. Often, they were depicted standing close together on the crowded quays, in settings that can only be described as industrial. Always, they lacked the demeanor and accouterments of Victorian femininity. Village fishwives, on the other hand, were portrayed as, healthy, hardworking and either nubile or maternal. They were earthy (or should I say maritime) examples of a life spent close to nature's bounty, archetypal visions of humanity's connections to the source of life.

These images were, to the Victorian eye, of women as primitive as those that Weld described. We can better understand them if we consider Lutz and Collins' (1993: 3) claim that "representations . . . are never irrelevant, never unconnected to the world of actual social relations". Thus, images that connected women to the world of fish also served to isolate them from the world of town and city. Rarely were they depicted in conjunction with people from outside the fisher community. This photographic practice reinforced the view that fishers constituted a separate people, a backward race, as we saw in the previous chapter. As Lutz and Collins (1993: 158) have noted for images of Third World people that appear in *National Geographic*, such separation of peoples into separate race-like categories of the developed and the undeveloped in photographic images is not unusual (see also Nadel-Klein 1991b on postcard images of Australian Aboriginal peoples). Such a separation homogenizes and simplifies and, thereby, stereotypes.

If exceptions prove the rule, then the picture captioned "Buyers and onlookers at Cockenzie market" is very revealing (Gibson 1994: 48). Here we see separation working through a different medium. The picture shows a group of woman standing on the quayside. But wait, is this one group or two? The answer comes quickly, told by clothing. Looking into the camera are five women dressed in long skirts and heavy shawls; three others standing among them wear much shorter skirts, white shirtwaist blouses and brimmed hats. Clearly, the first are the fishwives and the second are the "onlookers." The two groups do not look at each other, but at the camera; they occupy different social worlds, one seemingly premodern, the other up to date. Their proximity is temporary.

Painters from the nineteenth and early twentieth century also stereotyped fishers as backward, but they often placed a different spin on this evaluation. Their painting tended to evoke the theme of nature and a world unsullied by industrialization. As we shall see in Chapter 6 many northern Europeans at this time were discovering the peasant world as a source of spiritual rejuvenation. Nature might be savage, but it could also be rejuvenating and full of fruitful promise. Comely lasses, from farm or fishing village, became widely used symbols of this ideal:

> Sea genre had come into prominence in the late 1850's [sic] . Although the English had practiced marine painting for some time, it was not until James Clarke Hook, followed by Colin Hunter, Stanhope Forbes, and others, that the picturesque aspects of the English seafaring population – rugged fishermen in jerseys and sou'westers, and sturdy barefooted fisherwomen with tucked-up skirts and ruddy faces – became the principal subjects of a picture. (Cooper 1986: 82–3)

In these portraits, young women emerged as figures of fecund sexuality: of nature only partially modified by culture. Often, however, they were shown as incomplete without their men. A favorite picture was the worried, yearning woman standing on a beach, a cliff or a quayside, looking out at a gathering storm with no boat in view. Such a lassie needed her laddie. Her life was dominated by worrying and waiting.

In the 1880s, Winslow Homer, the American painter, also began to immortalize the fisherwomen, concentrating on the Scottish lassies' northern English counterparts across the Border in the village of Cullercoats. Nearly 150 watercolors, drawings, and oils resulted from his twenty-month stay:

> The inhabitants of the small fishing port, particularly the women at their daily tasks, gradually became archetypes for him, like ancient sculpture, imbued

with a sober and noble simplicity. They seemed to Homer *indivisible from nature* [emphasis mine] and, hence, became his connection to nature's power. (Cooper 1986: 92)

Between 1881 and 1883, Homer produced watercolors with such titles as *Fishergirls on the Beach* (1881), *Four Fisherwives* (1881) *Mending the Nets* (1882), *Girl with Red Stockings* (1882), and *Inside the Bar* (1883). Previously, according to Cooper, Homer had depicted women in close, confined settings. The fisherwomen provided a striking contrast:

> At Cullercoats, the women are often alone or in smaller groups of two or three, confronting the elements full face – standing on cliffs, walking on beaches, climbing on rocks . . . Silhouetted against the broad sky, they are at risk in a nature that is uncontrollable and inscrutable . . . This shift in thematic and psychological perspective suggests Homer's growing willingness to confront the *primitive elements in nature*, [emphasis mine] and perhaps in himself, more directly. (Cooper 1986: 118)

Returning to verbal fiction, for the moment, Reade's (1855: 22) comment in *Christie Johnstone* on fisherwomen's figures is worth noting here as it reinforces that contrast between confinement and freedom, artifice and nature: "These women had a grand corporeal trait: they had never known a corset! So they were straight as javelins; they could lift their hands above their heads actually!" As Davies (1982) has made clear, debilitating, tight-laced corsets were the defining effort of middle-class Victorians to mold women into ornamental objects. Such women would have born little resemblance – in outline, at least – to the unbound, "natural" fisher lassies.

Glasgow artist John McGhie spent a number of summers in the Fife village of Pittenweem before the First World War. Older residents today recall stories of how he would stand in the tide, sketching intently as the water rose about his knees. One of his favorite subjects, a beautiful young woman named Jeannie Meldrum, whom a few of my older informants remembered, was portrayed straining against the shore wind, hair escaping from her head scarf as she rested a heavy basket of fish against her hip.

The problem of all such imagery, of course, is that the degree to which fishwives were seen as one with nature was the degree to which they were seen as outside of culture. The Victorians believed that you could learn *from* nature, but they believed as well that being *of* nature was being a lesser kind of person. The civilized could learn from the savage, but not vice versa (Bloch and Bloch 1980). Indeed, Stevenson (1991: 25) tells us that the photographer David Hill explicitly sought in his photographs of

Newhaven fisherfolk to capture that which was "the ideal, the heroic, the poetic". She also points to the above-mentioned *Christie Johnstone* (Reade 1855), in which a young nobleman finds spiritual salvation by going to live among the fisherfolk of Newhaven.

> The village acts not merely as a model but as a source of practical inspiration and knowledge – by listening to and by joining in the activities of the fishermen and women, he [the Viscount Ipsden] acquires the understanding which makes him a man. Reade described the village, and especially the fishwife, Christie Johnstone, as a model of vigorous life, morality and culture in contrast to the emasculating dependency of the rich. (Stevenson 1991: 25)

Fishwives themselves could be put on display, for example, much as zoo animals were. I am referring here to sporting exhibitions. Here women were shown in ways that traded upon their obvious femininity, but hinted at their masculine side as well. For example, in the nineteenth century, the worthy burgesses of Musselburgh, near Edinburgh, held special foot races and golf tournaments for the fisherwomen of Fisherrow, awarding a shawl and creel "to the best golfer amongst the fishwives" (Meikle 1947: 245). Anson (1965: 140) records that the Musselburgh fisherwomen also played an annual football match. All this activity brought not only painters and photographers, but tourists.

Consider the following descriptions from those who those who wished wish to see Scottish fishwives in their local habitat and what they saw:

> By the 1840s, the rush of summer visitors from Edinburgh down to the seaside . . . found the activities of the village of Newhaven a natural tourist entertainment. The more numerous visitors to the city encountered the fishwives, famous for their beauty and their picturesque dress, as a distinct and engaging feature of the Edinburgh scene. This mild interest in the fishermen and women is reflected in paintings, engravings, pottery figures and songs about fishing life (Stevenson 1991: 17)

> They were a hardworking and industrious class of women, a great assistance to their equally hardworking husbands, and most surely an interest and a pleasure to all who looked on their sonsy [comely, cheerful] faces and fascinating costume, with the wide sleeve showing their strong round arms, and the snowy cap that often surmounted a weather-beaten but still handsome countenance. (Story 1911, quoted in Smout and Wood 1991: 89)

Even Royalty could be smitten:

> . . . The Newhaven fishwife has become a celebrity, and she is indebted to King George the Fourth for much of her fame. That monarch during his memorable

visit to Edinburgh, in the year 1822, said to Sir Walter Scott, that some of the Newhaven women were the handsomest he had ever seen, and her present gracious Majesty has been likewise pleased to admire them. Indeed, since the Queen's first visit to Edinburgh, the Newhaven fishwife, with her picturesque peculiarities and the dulcet notes with she charms the public ear . . . has been painted in oil, modeled in card board, made up as a whisky bottle, given to children as a doll, printed in numerous Cartes de visite, and generally has been made much more public all over the world than other honest women. She is a familiar figure in the Cafe Greco at Rome, as well as in the print shops of Berlin and Venice . . . (Bertram 1883: 4)

In all of these portrayals – literary, photographic and painterly – fisherwomen were cast in exotic terms: whether as matriarchs, as scaly and unfeminine herring gutters or as fertile fisher lassies, they provided a contrast between urban, middle-class modernity and its Other, the primitive at home (see Nadel-Klein 1995). They were emblems of the fisherfolk's intrinsic difference. In other words, women were stereotyped and, even when portrayed in flattering terms, that stereotype contributed to fisher marginalization.

## A Man's World Now

What many saw as fisher oddity and difference was, as have seen, relative equality and solidarity between men and women. With the demise of the family boat and the curing yard, however, fishing communities have changed dramatically from the days when women were full, complementary partners in the industry. Fisherfolk now have become much like other Scottish working-class families, where men's and women's spheres are sharply divided and where neither sex seems to have much admiration for the other.

Among the fisherfolk of my acquaintance, discussions about the fishery were usually a distinctly gendered and hierarchical affair. The men tended to be outgoing and talkative, but I found many of their wives to be more reserved, certainly in their husbands' presence, but out of it as well. In fact, women's attempts to participate in general discussions of the past were often met with impatient corrections. One man, for example, consistently reprimanded his wife for using local dialect in front of me, rather than the more anglicized version of Lowland Scots generally adopted for strangers. Some men simply interrupted their wives, amending details or even changing the subject.

Yet, retired fishermen, affluent skippers, and even younger crew members speak proudly about the importance of women in the days when they mended nets, knitted clothes, and gutted herring. They know that women's shore-based skills and labor had once been essential and often contrast the supposedly easy and less important work their wives perform with the arduous and crucial tasks of their maternal ancestors. It seems now to be an unspoken assumption that men are the authorities on fisher life and that women, who may be homemakers, office-workers, shopkeepers, or teachers, are simply prone to trivial, domestic chatter. When I asked a skipper what his wife did when he was away at sea, he responded by saying: "she takes aerobics classes. Women have a soft life now. They don't have to do anything."

When modern fishermen extol the virtues of their grandmothers, their wives fare ill by the implied invidious comparison. "A fisherwoman's doorstep *was* always clean" (emphasis mine); "In those days, the wives had the hardest job. There was nae a feminist movement." Women are also remembered as very resourceful. A widow facing poverty would "put up a counter [open a shop], no matter how small." However, the same informants who describe their mothers as stalwart household rulers have no qualms about telling their wives to provide tea for the guest.

After dispatching his wife to the kitchen, one retired northeast skipper told me of his plans to take a fishing holiday in the Canaries with some friends. "It'll be a woman-free zone," he said, clearly relishing the thought. He then went on to say that "my wife has never seen anything of the fishing except the money I brought home. I always tell her she's had an easy life, just taking care of the house and kids, though she wouldn't agree with that. I suppose you bein' a woman would agree wi' her."

Being a canny ethnographer who wanted to preserve a good working relationship I did not argue the point but I wondered to myself what his wife's response might have been. Unfortunately, I did not get the chance to ask her. But other wives with whom I raised the subject agreed with men that women years ago had a very tough time. However, they also quickly dismissed the idea that they themselves had it easy. To borrow the language of Dona Davis's Newfoundlanders, they saw themselves as the equivalents of "shore skippers," or managers as well as worriers (Davis 1983, 1988). They had to run the household and make all decisions when men were away, even while holding jobs outside the home. Even if they had never handled fish, they still had plenty of work to do. Like their predecessors, they also had to wait and wonder whether their husbands would return each time they sailed away.

Indeed, women's former positions as complementary workers in processing and selling fish have all but vanished. Women still make up the bulk of the shrinking fish-plant labor force, but are not necessarily recruited from fishing families. Successful skippers' wives do not need to work outside the home and have become housewives, the Scottish equivalent of Cole's (1991) *donas de casa* of northwest Portugal. Less affluent fishermen's wives may work in offices, shops, or schools – in jobs generally considered subordinate and unrelated to their husband's occupation. King (1992–3: 33) reports that some fishermen's wives in Fife "still have a dominant role in the handling of family finances and travel to various places buying parts for the fishing boat", but their number is undoubtedly small.

Ironically, despite losing their central position in the fishery, Scottish fishermen's wives today may well experience marginalization less acutely than their husbands and sons and may, in fact, be seen as more flexible and adaptive to changing circumstances. Certainly, in their conversations with me, they were far less inclined than men to dwell on the past. They were far less nostalgic for the days when partnership meant sharing poverty as well as grueling labor.

Nor has the political engagement of their fish-gutting ancestresses survived. Unlike the fishermen's wives of Gloucester, Massachusetts, who assert themselves in fisheries politics, lobbying intensively to protect their families' livelihood against such threats as offshore oil drilling or foreign fleets in coastal waters, Scottish fishermen's wives tend to leave such activism to the men (Clark 1988). While the Gloucester Fishermen's Wives Association has, as of this writing, just erected a public statue of a fisherman's wife looking out to sea with her children by her side, such depictions of Scottish fishwives have generally been small scale and part of male projects.

By definition, no modern woman can ever approach the idealized image of the fisherman's mother or grandmother because she no longer works within his world. This is not to say that I agree with Knipe's (1984: 141) claim that "the fishwife may never have existed." However, I take Knipe's point that "the *notion* [italics mine] of the fishwife does represent an idealized type". It may even approach the status of myth, and a myth is not an "objectively" historical report, no matter how much factual detail is embedded in it; it is a story with a message, a device to explain and legitimate cultural expectations. Modern fishermen's wives are caught between cultural expectations derived from recent memory, and a way of life that does not permit them to fulfil these expectations. This way of life is much closer to the bourgeois standards of other Scots, particularly for those of the middle class.

In stark contrast to the old days, the Scottish fishing industry today has become a man's world. Not only have women's former roles all but vanished, but the catching side remains virtually closed to them, despite Western women's progress in infiltrating formerly male-dominated occupations (including, in some places, the fishing industry: see Allison, Jacobs and Porter 1989; Greenlaw 1999). It would be unthinkable for Scotland's premier fishing magazine, *Fishing Monthly*, to run a cover titled, "Girls Just Wanna Catch Fish!" as appeared recently in the United States publication, *National Fisherman* (June, 2001). As we saw earlier, excluding women from the boats was never questioned. Attempts to include them today draw much invidious speculation about sexual promiscuity. Why else would a woman wish to spend her working life in such an intimately and publicly male setting? Indeed, when I asked a fisheries training specialist in Buckie whether any women had entered his program he said dismissively that one had, but "she got pregnant." End of story.

## Conclusion

As many authors have noted, the segregation of the sexes and the devaluation of women tend to be quite strong in much of Britain (Whitehead 1976; Bell and Newby 1976; Jackson 1968). Work and endogamy helped to give fisher women a higher status vis à vis men than that enjoyed by women in most other sectors of Scottish society. However, fisherwomen were not matriarchs; they were simply explained as such. As such they came to stand for fisher difference in the eyes of the outside world.

Today, the gendered differences that once were stigmatized have been transformed into identity-affirming stereotypes within fishing communities. While women's direct participation in the fishery has all but vanished, women – in their former incarnations – remain prominent as present-day emblems of how important fishing once was.

These emblems are, moreover, being appropriated by the tourist industry. As we shall see more fully in Chapter 6, they are being used to announce the presence of a culturally distinctive, even mysterious location. When one enters the coastal area of Fife known as the East Neuk, for example, one will find that road signs ("Welcome to the East Neuk") are marked with a colorful drawing of a woman in traditional fisher garb, including an apron, striped petticoat and creel. Thus the traveler learns that this new, "secret" cultural arena is a gendered one.[7]

In effect, the fishwife has come to stand as an icon of the fisherfolk. She remains exotic, even if her granddaughters do not. When fishermen talk about her, they reassert the centrality of their occupation and deny their continuing marginalization. They leave stigma behind.

## Notes

1. An analogy within the farmers' world was men's total control over anything to do with horses. While women worked in many parts of agriculture, a ploughman was always male.
2. Doctors were not only expensive: they were not always trusted. Some Ferrydeners recalled a sense of mistrust, for doctors came from the middle classes who looked down on them. Certainly they mistrusted medicine. Birth records from the earlier part of the twentieth century, for example, reveal widespread refusal to accept vaccinations for their infants.
3. Andy Stewart, of the folk group *Silly Wizard*, wrote this song after living in Buckie. "This song is a tribute to the courage of the fishermen and their families, though it is primarily a condemnation of the circumstances and pressures that force them into such a hazardous profession."
4. Agricultural laborers in Scotland typically had six-month contracts. At the end of this time, they might move to another farm. They did not, therefore, have such strong attachments to particular villages, having grown up under semi-nomadic conditions.
5. We might look to South America for an instructive comparison on this point. As Murphy and Murphy (1974) argued for the Mundurucu, replacing a foraging and horticultural subsistence base with the "modern" mode of male wage work (tapping rubber) left women with less domestic autonomy, not more. As herring fishing gradually came to predominate in the east coast communities, the power of middlemen and fishcurers grew, threatening the women's domestic control over the purse strings. As Ester Boserup (1970) pointed out and others have continued to document, women's status may decline dramatically with the transition from subsistence to commercial agriculture (Linares 1985).
6. This metaphorical strategy puts me in mind of similar analogies made between colonial subjects and local fauna. Consider, for example, Camus' *The Stranger*, whose protagonist likens Arabs to lizards.
7. The Scottish tourist industry may be highlighting women's roles in fishing, but they continue to be obscured elsewhere. On a holiday in 1998, I stopped in to the Lunenberg, Nova Scotia, Fisheries Museum. I was curious to see how it compared with the many Scottish fisheries museums in which women's roles feature prominently. To my surprise, its otherwise excellent displays omitted women entirely. When I asked museum staff and local people why women were not represented, I received a polite, but surprised response: "Why should there be women in the exhibits? Women never had anything to do with the fishery. They had to stay at home and raise the families."

# –4–

# Ferryden: Place, Power and Identity

From Ferryden- (ane place of housen vile,
Where Fishermen and fisherwives abide . . .)
Bowick et al, 1880: 35

Now we will look close-up at Ferryden, a place where "they used to be fishers." This chapter addresses the question of how villagers' identity articulates with place, as well as with occupation. As we shall see, place is something Ferrydeners can no longer take for granted, any more than they can take for granted the occupation of fishing. They have become among the most marginalized fishers of all. This is so because of the direct economic power that the town of Montrose has long held over them. Most recently, Montrosians were even instrumental in making drastic changes to the village landscape. Thus, the relationship between town and village provides an excellent venue in which to see how people from outside, as well as from inside, re-imagine community under circumstances in which traditional connections to people, work and location have been undermined (Macdonald 1997; Rodman 1992).

This re-imagining began to become necessary in the 1970s, when North Sea oil emerged on the Scottish scene. An elite group of town-based entrepreneurs was largely responsible for wooing the offshore industry to the area. The result of that wooing was an offshore support base that was built not in Montrose itself but on Ferryden's foreshore. This set the stage for an unfolding drama in which Ferryden was either the star or an understudy, depending upon one's perspective.

This drama highlighted the opposing possibilities of how a place could be re-defined. In fact, it raised the question whether Ferryden even had a separate existence or was merely an extension of Montrose. As we shall see as this chapter unfolds, this was not merely an abstract issue for mapmakers, but one that cut to the heart of Ferrydeners' concerns about being able to claim that they lived in a fishing village, and therefore, to see themselves as fisherfolk.

Many villagers saw the development of an offshore support base as unsightly, a recapitulation of past injustices and yet another example of how the people "in charge" would get their way no matter what the fisherfolk wanted. Meanwhile, Montrosians saw villagers' objections as an awkward and irrational impediment to the inevitable march of progress. For them, Ferryden's separate identity was a thing of the past, to be consigned to the category of the quaint, the timeless, and the dispensable. Each of these perspectives has had a long, dialectically constructed history which this chapter will elucidate.

First, however, a word on "identity." Identity is one of those slippery concepts that everyone uses but seldom defines. I use here it in its two linked senses of self-reference and ascription. These two senses of identity face each other and "converse." That is, the way people refer to themselves as belonging to a group is produced in part by the ways in which others see them.

Identity – whether collective or individual – is never simply received. It is learned, lived, transmuted and always contextualized. Thus it should be regarded neither as a rigid blueprint nor as an imprisoning constraint. In this sense, of identity-in-progress, "Ferrydenness" continues to evolve in response to contemporary conditions. Local ideas of what the past was like and what the future might become engage with those of others who have different objectives. Thus identity is, by necessity, inventive. The mutual subjectivities that produce it are malleable and porous; they may be strategically, even combatively, deployed.

As we saw in the previous chapter, people talk about fishers in different ways, but almost always in ways that stereotype and stigmatize. Fishers themselves, however, deploy local knowledge to assert their special importance. What Herzfeld (1987: 43) says about nationality or ethnicity applies thus equally well to local identity claims, namely that the "language of . . . identity is indeed a language of morality. It is an encoded discourse about inclusion and exclusion."

It is clear that, in Ferryden, the viewpoints of insider and outsider have reinforced each other over the years like a tennis match of labels and claims. We will never know who lobbed the original serve, but in this chapter we will see how accusations of insularity have been met by proclamations of solidarity. In short, identity has been manipulated to serve a variety of ends, not least of which has been the claim to place. Indeed, my informants were clearly preoccupied with "belonging" (see Cohen 1987). In their view, they belonged to Ferryden and Ferryden belonged to them. For years, the outside world had been content to leave this formulation alone but with the advent the oil base, Ferrydeners were forced to confront the reality of what Tolkein's wise Elf, Gildor, said to the still-naive hobbit, Frodo of the Shire: "the wide world is all about you; you can fence yourselves in, but you cannot forever fence it out".

Indeed, Tolkein's Shire is a wonderfully idealized example of how a place can bind one to it. It is cozy, familiar and pleasant to look at. Trees, hedgerows, streams and valleys all have a special, comforting significance. Even the smallest feature of the landscape has a name (see Gaffin 1996 on the Faroe Islands for a real-world example). People (or hobbits) feel safe there. Ferryden was not so lovely, nor were its people so content or so parochial. However, they cherished the place itself: the streets and closes, houses and sheds, and most of all, the sea-lapped shore. There, one could meet relatives and friends, work companions, lovers and enemies.

I do not mean to romanticize. The place could also be confining, the poverty oppressive, the work smelly, cold and dangerous. There were fights and feuds. Nonetheless, beyond the village, across the bridge or over the fields, lay Montrose, a less welcoming environment. Previously, the village had contained the predictable and the known. With the advent of the oil base, villagers were forced to confront the increasing presence of new inhabitants who were not part of this intimate realm. Ferryden's boundaries were blurring.

As I have argued elsewhere, village history can be read as a particularly explicit and problematic demonstration of how a locality can be *both* built *and* destroyed by forces of capital and power. Capitalism does not only destroy locality, as contemporary observations of rural devastation or depopulation might suggest. It also produces it (Nadel-Klein 1991a). To put it in Marxian terms, localities themselves become commoditized in the process of generating exchange-values. Ferryden has been no exception. Its inhabitants have experienced it as home; its exploiters have seen it as a source of revenue. The two perspectives have coexisted in a fragile relationship that has now become undone.

There are those in Ferryden for whom localism remains significant. They still define themselves as a group with a sense of commitment to a particular place and to a set of cultural practices that are self-consciously articulated and to some degree separated and directed away from the surrounding social world. But they are living in a time of rupture. Before I elaborate, one proviso is necessary. However "local" or attached to place Ferrydeners might be, they have never been isolated. Ferryden, like any locality in Scotland, has always been deeply embedded within many interdigitating layers of social practice, its boundaries more elastic, permeable and arbitrary than the villagers themselves might acknowledge. A host of national-level institutions have been forceful players in their lives. To interpret their experience of identity and place requires an extra-local and an historical perspective, as well as an ethnographic focus.

## Ferryden: an Introduction

Like many villages discussed in the second chapter, Ferryden owed its start to an Improver. According to Adams (1993: 228), Robert Scott, the laird of Craig, "was among the earliest agricultural enclosers and improvers in Angus in the early eighteenth century". Ferryden was not a planned village. Scott simply built a row of small cottages on the side of a hill overlooking Montrose Harbor. He then induced a small group of experienced fisher families to settle there by providing them with boats and gear.

The village was thus established as an occupational enclave. Over the succeeding two centuries, its fortunes, along with its population, waxed and waned according to the vagaries of fish, technology, and outsiders' investment strategies. For a time, Ferryden became one of the most active and important fishing ports in the greater Montrose region (Adams 1993).[1] By 1777, according to the *Old Statistical Account*, the population had grown to include 38 families, with six boats (four men to each boat). By 1815, the village held 500 people. And by 1885, at the height of the herring boom, Anson tells us that the village had 156 boats, manned by 350 fishermen (Anson 1930: 118). Following the First World War, however, the number of boats shrank rapidly and by the end of the 1920s numbered scarcely more than two dozen. Today, there are none. But before I can relate how these changes have been interpreted and experienced, let me walk you through the village, as I first did in 1975, to a get a sense of the place.

Ferryden's 800-odd people inhabit a mile-long line of houses near the northern end of what used to be called the County of Angus (in 1975, the county system was abolished, so Angus is now a district). This is about 30 miles south of Aberdeen, one mile south of Montrose, or 90 miles north of Edinburgh. The land of northern Angus is well watered, drained by the streams and rivers that flow out of the upland lochs. The South Esk River rises in the Grampians above Loch Esk. Fed by numerous small streams that empty into it on its way down from the Highlands, the South Esk flows through Glen Clova, angling down to the town of Brechin, some 15 miles west of Montrose. After leaving Brechin, the river broadens, taking a slower and smoother course to its North Sea destination at the Basin, or tidal estuary, of Montrose and Ferryden.

In the distance, a line of hills signals the edge of the Grampians, the mountains of the eastern Highlands. Rocky and barren, stripped of trees for many centuries past, their slopes are covered with gorse, heather and rough hill grasses. Sheep wear narrow trails along their sides. Piercing the edge of this bleak expanse are the glens, or narrow river valleys that lie like green arrows in the folds of the hills. In winter, deep snows may cut off the glens from the market towns and coastal villages for weeks at a time.

In contrast to the harsh, sparsely populated uplands, the coastal topography of Angus is varied and densely settled; the climate, mild. The rich farmland is painted with broad green fields of raspberries, strawberries, potatoes and the virulently yellow, EU-subsidized expanses of oilseed rape, delineated by dark-green hedgerows. The coast is an unforgiving one, notorious for its danger to sailors. However, the old, well-worn lava flows that formed the rocks here are rich in semi-precious stones, such as agates and carnelians, making the area popular with lapidaries and amateur jewelry makers.

As for the estuary at low tide, some call the Montrose Basin a mud flat, or, more poetically, "a barren expanse of glutinous glue" (Henderson 1990: 72). When filled with water, it is an gleaming, eddying expanse of blue-grey motion. The Basin is nationally famous for the varieties of waterfowl that gather there: eider ducks, pink-footed geese, mute swans, cormorants, among others. (It is also a place where one can witness the perverse sight of swans snaking their long necks up into the sewer pipes that end just below the water line. Their up-ended white bottoms look like agitated feather dusters.)

Of the three ways to enter Ferryden – from the sea, from the rural inland parish of Craig, or from the main coastal route – the last is the one most used today. But Ferryden does not get many visitors. From the main road, the village appears to be little more than a line of postwar, council-built cottages that face a bleak industrial site, making it look like a seedy, outflung suburb of Montrose. Neither charm nor quaintness (both major tourism desiderata) are immediately in view.

Nor does anything immediately suggest a distinctive character or history. Tourists usually give it a miss, as it is mentioned in few travelers' guidebooks and has even been left off the Scottish Tourist Board's map of "Scotland's Fishing Heritage Trail." (This trail is taken up in detail in Chapter 6.) A modern guidebook even refers (in passing) to the village's "demise" (Henderson 1990: 73), though, to paraphrase Mark Twain, such rumors are exaggerated. Even fisherfolk in other villages seem to have forgotten Ferryden.

As one ventures farther into the village, a different scene emerges. It seems as if there are two villages, one new and one old. Beyond the council houses on the south side of the road, a block of handsome and substantial-looking brown and gray stone houses signal modest prosperity. However, a few yards farther east, in the middle of the village, the houses become conspicuously smaller and older, examples of the type once known as "but and ben." But-and-ben houses have two rooms, one front and one back. In most, external stairways lead to identical layouts above, constructed for separate households.

Behind them runs a cluttered alleyway flanked by black-tarred sheds. From there it is an easy step down to the shingled beach. Occasionally, a pile of weathered lobster traps presents itself, or an old rowing boat. Washing hangs on lines that stretch out over the tideline, flapping noisily in the relentless wind.

Rossie Square, at the center of the village, holds the post office (a one-room affair, converted from the old village wash-house), the village store (which sells a little bit of everything, at high prices), and until recently, the village branch of the Scottish Cooperative Market. Across the street, two pubs sit side by side. One is large and shabby, its peeling grey paint testifying to the passing of better days. In 1975 it was known locally as *Diamond Lil's*, for its colorful proprietor. The other pub presented quite a contrast. It was then new and sparkling, a glass-and-concrete box that beckoned to the young, the affluent and the outsider. By 1995 however, it too had taken on an air of mild decrepitude. (When I stopped in for lunch one day the bar was occupied by a small group of youngish working men who were clearly curious about my presence there. I said that I was visiting and that I had stayed there 20 years earlier. "Well, we've got indoor toilets now," they offered, snickering. (Indeed, most people had them during my earlier stay, but many of the older folk could still remember the days of the village "lavs" and the communal wash house.)

Eastward from the Square, the village splits. One road leads along the shore (the Low Road) and the other (the High Road) winds "up the brae." At the village's far western end ("wast the toon", as Ferrydeners say), windows look directly across to the Montrose harbor mouth and thence to the North Sea. On a clear day, the St Cyrus cliffs (famous for nesting birds) are easily visible, five miles away to the north. But if the *haar*, the impenetrable, treacherous, North Sea fog comes rolling in, then the house next door can vanish almost instantly. Standing securely on land, this is merely rather disconcerting. At sea it can be deadly.

Hence the importance of the lighthouse for this rocky coast. It occupies a rocky promontory about a quarter mile past the last dwelling. The light

was built in 1870, after years of pleading from local shippers and fishermen (Adams 1993: 49), to warn unwary vessels away from the menace
of the rocks. My informants were very proud of the lighthouse and their
own part in building it:

> James's grandfather was skipper of a barge that brought the bricks to build the
> lighthouse over a hundred years ago. The light was visible twelve miles out to
> sea. They burnt an old boat on the high road to celebrate the installation of the
> lighthouse.

From Scurdyness, both Montrose and Ferryden are invisible and only
the cries of gulls can be heard over the constant wind. The occasional
visitor clambers around the rocks, perhaps looking for agates, which are
easily found by their glassy, bluish translucence when wet. But generally,
it is a lonely and forbidding spot. Once ensconced in these outer reaches,
it is easy to imagine that Ferryden occupies an isolated space and looks
only seaward. This, of course, is an illusion. Just across the river lies
Montrose.

In the middle of the 1970s, when I first visited Ferryden, the new
offshore oil and gas base already abutted the village, occupying a space
that had once been a tidal stream called the Inch Burn. The former water-
front had come to resemble a jungle of blocky office buildings, low-lying
warehouses, towering cranes, lengths of pipe and piles of other industrial
debris. A forbidding, chain-link fence encircled the whole, making if off-
limits to all villagers, except those few who had (very low-level) jobs
there.

This liminal space, neither in the village nor of it, but very much a
presence there, had become the site of an ongoing drama over Ferryden's
identity as a "fishing village." Before we can understand just what was at
stake, however, we must become acquainted with the people and their
history. In particular, we will look at three arenas that have informed
Ferrydeners' interpretation of and responses to power, as well as their
attachment to the place where they lived. These are their commitments to
kinship, their memories of living on parish relief, and their engagement
with dissenting religion.

## Finding True Ferrydeners

Offshore oil did not destroy Ferryden. In demographic and social terms,
Ferryden had already been utterly transformed by the 1960s, long before
the first wells were drilled in the North Sea. Most of the fishermen's

children had gone by this time, following the local dictum that "you have to get out to get on." They left behind a largely elderly population. Indeed, when I arrived in 1975, nearly one-third of the population was retired from active age-work and subsisted primarily on the old-age pension. Most of this group, along with the children and grandchildren still remaining, defined themselves explicitly as the "True Ferrydeners" in self-conscious distinction to the "incomers" among them.

Kinship is vital to understanding this critical division. Simply put, True Ferrydeners claimed direct lineal descent from one of the families that had settled the village in the eighteenth century. Here, as so often happens, the inhabitants' version of village origins diverges from academic history. According to Adams (1993: 228):

> The Perts and Patons probably came from Usan in the same parish. Records and family traditions show that the Coulls came from Buckie and the Wasts or Wests from Crovie in Banffshire just before 1700, while the Mearns and Findlays, two less common surnames, ordinate in the Mearns coast fishertouns south of Stonehaven.

My informants, on the other hand, while agreeing that the Coulls, Wests and Perts had all come from the Black Isle (a peninsula on the Cromarty Firth) sometime in the middle of the eighteenth century, said that the Patons had come from Usan shortly thereafter. Usan itself was said to have been settled by migrants from Orkney and Shetland. Regardless of the "truth" of the matter, what counted to my informants was their ability to demonstrate consanguineal connections to one of these four families. Thus, they could lay claim to the village by virtue of long association. One could say that this was the fisher version of the upper class idea of the "old family." That is, depth of descent lent a person both prestige and authority.

As I discussed in the previous chapter, generations of village endogamy, combined with occasional out-marriage to fishers from other communities made such claims to prestige and authority possible. Names were crucial to establishing them. A villager might say, "My name is Watt but my great-grannie was a Pert," or, "That woman is Annie Mearns Paton West."

Yet another naming mechanism underscored boundaries. This was the use of by- or tee-names (nicknames). This practice was not unique to Ferryden, being noted for fishers all along the coast (See Knipe 1984 on Gamrie (Gardenstown); Anson more generally). The usual explanation for this was that, given the limited stock of surnames within any village, as well as the common practice of naming children for parents and grandparents, several people in any given generation could be identically named, and thus needed another way to be distinguished. But it was also clear that by-names provided a kind of shorthand about personal histories for members of the community (they were often assigned on the basis of personal quirks, appearance or habits). Thus, outsiders did not have by-names, nor could they understand the significance of "Coddlin' Davie," "the Provost," "Young King," or "Skinem."

In order to comprehend the Ferrydeners' dense consanguineal system, I collected many genealogies. Older villagers generally already had these written down, keeping them in drawers or boxes along with old, faded photographs. Others, like Mrs. Potter, a nearly blind, nonagenarian woman, kept the names, birth dates, and places of residence of literally hundreds of relatives, both living and dead, stored in her capacious memory. This memory took us back to the latter part of the eighteenth century. (When I went to study the parish birth and death records, I found that her account matched them amazingly well.)

True Ferrydeners invoked kinship to explain their putatively instant-aneous network of gossip. "We're all forty-second cousins," True Ferry-deners often said. "Don't say anything about one of us that you don't want the rest of us to hear. If you tell one of us something in the morning, we'll all know it in the afternoon." They used this idea of consanguineal solid-arity to explain what they saw as their like-mindedness and preference for each other's company.

They also believed that most outsiders did not like or approve of them. "They don't speak to you in Montrose, even if you're standing in a bus queue," said one. "They all think they're toffs." I saw this belief confirmed when my Montrose landlady professed to know no one in the village. As her cleaning lady was a member of the Ferryden Old Age Pensioners' Lunch Club, I knew this could not possibly be true. However, such anecdotes were counterbalanced by the stories they told of their ancestors' perseverance, bravery, ingenuity and loyalty, stories that, in effect, inverted stigma. They went further, maintaining that fishers worked harder, had cleaner houses and were more pious than other folk.

Such lineal claims came loaded with heavy symbolic baggage and explicit social consequences. Villagers' claims of kinship were readily interpreted by others as evidence of their peculiar character. Often they were suspected of practicing incest and therefore of possibly being feeble minded. "True Ferrydeners are queer, shy. They peer from the door at strangers and hide," as one disgruntled incomer said to me. Mrs Black, who hailed originally from a more northerly fishing village, complained regularly about the way "true Ferrydeners" drew their boundaries. "My grandchildren were born in Ferryden, but when they were little, other schoolchildren told them, 'you don't belong to Ferryden.'" Other incomers claimed that they got along well enough with the Ferrydeners, but that "you never really get to know them." One of the village ministers commented to me that Ferrydeners would not easily accept outsiders, even from tiny Usan, a half-mile away.

> The Ferryden people are only interested in their own community. I'm kept at arm's length because I'm not from Ferryden. There's a mystique. The relationship between Ferrydeners is intense and you can't break into it. They're all in the know. They change dialect when they speak to me. Their kin from Canada and the US keep in touch more than other people's do.

Others confirmed that kin who had long since moved away, as well as their children or even grandchildren, still "belonged" to Ferryden. Exiles were expected to keep in touch, to write letters and pay visits. In Cohen's (1987: 21) terms, they were still seen as bound by "the ideology of close social association". Each summer would bring the return of kin on holiday for two weeks or more. Frequently, they would stay in the empty houses that their families still owned. Additionally, many retirees had come home to live; others were planning to do so. Nonetheless, Ferrydeners spoke of themselves as a dying breed. No wonder, then, that they kept such careful track of people.

No wonder, also, that changes in the physical nature of the village were such a threat. If Ferryden were to disappear or to be radically altered by new developments, there could be no point of focus for group cohesion, no place for sentiments to condense and coalesce. Indeed, some who had planned to retire back to the village changed their minds when they saw what the oil base looked like.

I first learned about this critical distinction from the members of the OAP's Lunch Club, a group that since 1973 (around the same time that work had begun at the oil base) had gathered each Wednesday at the village Primary School. A local social worker revealed that setting up the club had not been easy. For example, it been difficult at first to procure a van to transport the old people. The Montrose Soup Kitchen Committee refused to loan their Social Services minibus, saying tartly that "Ferryden is outwith the area of Montrose. It is unconstitutional." My informant suspected that the old antagonism between town and village was behind this answer because he had no difficulty getting a van from the inland town of Brechin. He also said that, when the OAPs first went to the Lunch Club, they were surprised, but pleased, to find that the meals were not free, but cost them 12 pence each. Free meals would have smacked of charity and they would have deeply resented that.

The 20 to 30 people attending ranged from their middle sixties to their early nineties. This routinized setting afforded me an excellent chance to get to know people in a non-intrusive manner. First came lunch, with eight people at each table. Then we all took chairs around the periphery of the room and chatted, played card games (the women) or dominoes (the men). Some napped. Others took turns entertaining the group by playing the fiddle, singing or reciting poetry.

Much of the music and many of the poems were strongly sentimental, evoking images of village life as warm and harmonious, even Edenic. A particular favorite was the *Ferryden Anthem*, with the following refrain:

> Don't let us be strangers,
> As long as we are together.
> Friends we'll be, we'll all agree,
> 'Tis far the better plan.
> Life is very short,
> So let us all remember,
> To be as good and kind to one another as we can.

The chorus of another cherished poem, written by Thomas Coull Pert, a Ferrydener who had died shortly before my arrival, echoed:

> We won't forget to tell our friends
> how kindly you have been.
> We're no awa' tae bide awa',
> we'll soon be back again.
> The summer breeze and sunlit seas of dear old Ferryden.

(In one of the more daring – or rash – moments of my fieldwork, I set the poem to music and, having brought my guitar along, sang it to them. Mercifully, they soon joined in.)

Few had actually spent their working lives at the fishing, but nearly all had been born into fisher families and had much to say about their childhoods and the lives their parents had led. In fact, a number of these supposedly insular people had spent much of their working lives elsewhere, only returning to the village upon retirement. Among them, they numbered a former railway engine driver in Motherwell; a joiner in Aberdeenshire; two dressmakers in Montrose; factory workers at the Montrose flax mill and then at the "jammie" (Chivers jam factory); a nurse in Aberdeen; and a widowed homemaker who had lived some years with her husband in Glasgow.

In general, people seemed quite happy to talk with me, though I am afraid most never quite understood what I was doing there. I first presented myself as a sociologist (knowing that the word "anthropology" would mean nothing to them). In their minds, this rapidly translated to social worker, for why else would I spend so much time listening to them talk? As one of my informants triumphantly announced, years later, "I ken what anthropology is. It's the study of auld men!" Finally, I simply announced that I was writing a book about the fisherfolk and the village. This appeared to satisfy them. Certainly, I had chosen an important topic. Also, the recently built oil base gave them much to discuss and criticize. So they kindly allowed me to participate in many revealing conversations, listen to their opinions and their stories, and generally learn what it meant to be a Ferrydener.

I must stress that their knowledge, although grounded in memory and the lore of many generations, did not represent a purely "oral" tradition. The old folk were literate, if not highly educated in a formal sense (most had left school by the age of 14). Some of what they related was derived, sometimes second- or even third-hand, from a variety of written sources. These included a popular column on local history in the weekly *Montrose Review* and the writings of Peter Anson, the aforementioned artist, monk and scholar of European fishing who had lived among them for several years. Of course, those writing about the village had mined these same memories, so the chicken-and-egg question of which came first can never be answered.

Like other fishers I came to know over the years, they were intensely interested in anything to do with fisher history and avidly collected all manner of pamphlets, books and poems. In fact, though they never used that word, they were deeply involved in "heritage." (At that time, "heritage" had not yet taken on its instant association with tourism and exhibit that Chapter 6 discusses.)

Not surprisingly, their accounts during Lunch Club meetings were sporadic, rambling, and often mutually constituted through a process of free association. In other words, they were rendered in a completely non-linear fashion. One incident would remind them of another one, so the connections would be made thematically rather than chronologically. Any specific question – about an individual, a boat, or an event – was likely to spark intense discussion or debate. My search for information set me in motion from one person to the next like a billiard ball.

Go see old Joe over there. He kens a' aboot the storm that kill't Jim's uncle William. His own uncle was ane o' the crew . . . Jim's grandfather's boat was

M.E. [Montrose] 555. She was the 'Alexandria' and she was caught in a storm in 1890. She was struck by lightning, and it killed Charley Coull when it ran down the mast.

For men, in particular, being a fishing villager meant being fairly obsessed with the sea. They recalled the names of fishing boats and fishing grounds, even though few of them had ever sailed:

> There was Shald water (Shallow Water), about 15 miles off the Lighthouse due east, and Castle Ness, southwest 10–12 miles. The Reef, 25 miles offshore, was a great herring ground once, but there are none left now; Kaillie, 6 or 7 miles out, was a bank formed when they dredged the river in 1905-6 and dumped the dredgings out to sea.

Hard times were another favorite topic. I heard about the great typhoid and cholera epidemics that had swept through the village in the 1870s, killing hundreds. "Every family kept what they called 'dead funds' to pay for funerals; otherwise the parish would have to bury them and that was a great shame."

In 1911, government reforms improved their lives to a degree. "Lloyd George established the National Health. You could get free medical care for men, but had to pay for the wife and bairns. In the thirties we got free milk for the under-fives." In 1918 gas street lights were introduced. The first public telephones at the post office and police station arrived in 1938. Still, no amount of modernization could erase their awareness of inferior status. "We used to have to touch our caps when the laird came by."

It was clear that, for these people, the past was hardly "a foreign country" (Lowenthal 1985), but a well-known, often visited, and some-times longed-for second home. When they recounted how, "in the old days," the young men would throw stones and fish refuse at Montrose boys who ventured over the bridge, little smiles would cross their faces. They smiled, too, when recalling how:

> As children Rossie Castle [where the laird lived; up the hill, about a quarter mile from the village] was a place we villagers went only on special occasions. We got a bun with our tea, ran races, and played games at all ages . . . Another highlight of summer was going to Lunan Bay [three miles down the coast] on the train. We would save up money for the jaunt. We collected rags and bones and scrap metal to sell to hawkers who came to the village on Saturdays . . . And there was a free breakfast on New Year's morning in the kirk hall . . . Captain Stansfield went around the primary schools in Ferryden and Craig and distributed an orange and an apple to each student.

What struck me as the conspicuous face of patronage was, for them, a fond memory of good times.

Of course, children had to work: their labor was a necessary source of household income. In addition to household and fishery-related chores, children supplied casual harvest labor for local farmers.

> Before the First War, we used to go tattie howking [potato lifting; in the 1970s, schoolchildren still got a two week autumn holiday so they could help with the harvest]. In 1912 I got a shilling a day. My mother got two shillings. In 1920s, the berries started, and we could go pick those.

A local historian who lived nearby in Craig showed me a picture of the Ferrydeners pulling "tatties" from that era and said that a van was sent around to collect villagers for this purpose. The driver was instructed not to go into the village, but to stop at the edge and make them walk out, because "Ferrydeners were funny folk."

But when none of these supplements sufficed, families would be forced to ask for credit, or "tick" from the shops. Some bakers and grocers are still remembered for their generosity in extending credit to destitute fisher households. Most people relied on this, and there seemed to be little shame involved. They were far more unhappy at being forced to accept parish relief. This institution, perhaps more than any other, undermined their sense of self-worth.

## The Burden of Relief

In 1976, a village man loaned me a set of the old parish relief records that he had unearthed from his attic. Their sepia-toned, hand-written pages chronicled the bare facts of poor relief from 1897 to 1912 in Ferryden – from the point of view, that is, of those administering assistance. These tantalizingly limited accounts invited Dickensian speculations about workhouses and sadistic applications of power. In fact, few hints of anything like this appeared. If Oliver Twist Coull lived in Ferryden, his misfortunes were not recalled in this chronicle.

The relief records did reveal that prominent landowners and officers of the fish curing company invariably chaired and dominated the proceedings of the committee that dispensed relief, though two or three fishermen also sat on it as village representatives. So relief applicants endured close personal scrutiny from those who already exerted significant control over their lives. Such scrutiny was, moreover, conditioned by a long legacy of ambivalence towards those applying for help.

Parish relief was not a nineteenth-century invention. It began much earlier and its history offers us as a way of viewing the impact of national institutions upon local experience. Scotland had begun to pass laws regulating (generally harassing, punishing and restricting) the poor during the fifteenth century. In 1574, an Act establishing a category of legal poor, that is, those who were allowed to beg, was passed (Cage 1981: 3). In 1597, the kirk session – the local ecclesiastical court of the Church of Scotland – was made responsible for administering relief in conjunction with the heritors, or property-owners, of the parish. "Besides their legal responsibilities towards the poor, the session also supervised the religious and moral character of the parishoners" (Cage 1981: 5).

Mitchison writes about the impact of an increasingly rigorous form of parish relief upon class relationships within rural parishes of the eighteenth century:

> Control by landowners of the money of a parish led to a basic change in the accepted poor law . . . By the 1780s a new interpretation of the law was gaining acceptance, that poor relief was only for those incapacitated permanently from earning their living and that even for these it should not be enough to live on . . . To a needy man the kirk session had become a 'them', a representative of civil government, allotting him, if he qualified under the new rigorous rules, a small sum from either rates or collections . . . Almost at the same time that the Scottish poor law became generally effective, it ceased to be the organ of a real sense of community. (Mitchinson 1978: 90)

Such attitudes would only increase the hostility and suspicion Ferrydeners already felt towards the landowners and the merchants of Montrose. From 1845 to 1894, poor relief was administered by parochial boards that comprised elected members, heritors, and representatives from the kirk sessions. From 1894 to 1929, these were superseded by parish councils, elected by the ratepayers (Kellas 1968: 159).

During the early part of the twentieth century, the Craig parish council, which administered Ferryden, appears to have been well-regarded by the General Superintendent of Poor, who stated that

> the Poor Law seems to be administered with much care and attention . . . that pauperism, as regards the number on the Roll, has been much the same for the last few years, that many of those in receipt of relief are upwards of forty years of age and that they seem to be well seen to and cared for. (13 May 1905)

Looking backward, of course, it seems curious that the numbers of paupers would have remained stable at this time, since the fishing was declining and unemployment generally was on the rise. One has to wonder whether criteria for relief were not simultaneously being made more rigorous.

Members of the Council examined the lives of the fisherfolk through their aptly titled agent, the Inspector of Poor, as well as through their personal connections to the community. Approvals depended not only upon physical need, but upon moral worthiness or being found "deserving," which required both disability and proper attitude. Administrators of the Scottish Poor Law had always taken a dim view of the poor, particularly of those deemed able-bodied. If the latter were destitute, it was due to their own shortcomings and moral failures.

Not all applications were granted. Members of the Council were clearly skeptical about a number of petitions. Orphans or those deemed the "sick poor" might be given such items as a flannel shift or a pair of boots. But in 1898, for example, we read of an application from a woman "for clothing for two of her children . . . Owing to her circumstances [which are not recorded], it was agreed to refuse her application." Sometimes a pauper's allotment was increased; at other times, it might be decreased or terminated.

Many of the councillors' deliberations seem to have centered on the details of what was then called "outdoor" relief, meaning a minimal subsistence afforded to non-institutionalized paupers. In addition, however, they were also responsible for Ferryden individuals institutionalized in Montrose, either in the asylum, as "lunatic paupers," or the House of Refuge (for children, the elderly, and the otherwise infirm). In the case of one man applying for outdoor relief, it was suggested that "the offer of indoor [asylum] relief should be made to him as a sort of test, and that [the councillor's] impression is that the offer would remove him from the roll."

Ian Levitt, writing about the Poor Law, remarks that the bourgeoisie "needed to create welfare institutions which, while offering assistance, did so in a way that bound the less fortunate to capitalism's predominant ethos" (Levitt 1988: 3). In Scotland, this implied the ethos of Calvinism – that hard work would save your soul and reveal your state of grace – and meant that the needy were bound to see themselves as suffering society's scorn. An intriguing entry in the parish minutes of 1906 revealed the attempt by two daughters of a pauper to discontinue their father's assistance, "they maintaining that such relief was not necessary".

Perhaps the most poignant example of the emotional legacy of parish relief for modern villagers was offered when I visited a very old woman who was spending her last days in the Montrose nursing home. Her niece brought me, thinking, rightly, that I would be interested in her aunt's reminiscences. Frail and wrinkled, her sparse white hair neatly combed, she lay propped up on pillows to receive her guests. "I never thought I'd end up in the House of Refuge," she said. "No, no, Auntie," her niece hastened to reassure her, "It's Dorward House, now."

While at any given time, no more than 10 per cent of the village was forced to accept relief, no family was untouched by its threat. Income from fishing was unreliable and they were, more often than not, deep in debt. As the next section will show, the uneasy and unequal relationship between themselves and the fishcurers, a relationship we have already probed in Chapter 2, played a large role in this. The family firm of Joseph Johnston's & Sons was especially important. Johnston's had established itself as the most powerful fishcuring company in the greater Montrose and, Ferrydeners said, effected much misery.

## "The Fishcurer is the Enemy of the Fisherman"

This next discussion takes us into the murky realms of myth, partial truths, and contested histories. If any single story in village lore could be said to have critical symbolic status, it is the tale of how Johnston's robbed the fisherfolk. As with the rendering of village origins, academics have their version and the fishers, another. In this case, the fishcurers have yet another still. The truths embedded in each reflect the different social positions of their tellers. It is not the ethnographer's task – nor, indeed, is it anyone's – to adjudicate among them. What matters for our purposes here is what the fishers' version tells us about their worldview.

When Ferrydeners spoke to me about Johnston's place in their history, their voices took on an edgy tone. They claimed that the company had stolen something precious from them long ago. They said that in the early years of the village, the laird had promised them that they would always be entitled, free of charge, to gather mussels from the "Back Sands" of the estuary to use to bait their lines.

But the laird's control over the Back Sands was, at some point in the early nineteenth century, transferred to the Montrose Town Council. According to village lore, Johnston's had bribed or talked the Town Council into giving them the rights over this vital resource. The firm already controlled salmon fishing throughout the area and so it was easy for it to extend its water patrols to guard the mussels, as well. Poachers would be fined or jailed. "Johnston's stole the mussel beds of the Back Sands from the fishermen. They gave a dinner for the Town Council, with a bottle of whisky for each member. The Council gave them the rights to the Back Sands." Another version was that Johnston's somehow got the fishermen themselves to "sign away" the rights to the mussel beds. As one of my informants put it:

> On the title deeds [to the laird's estate] it said that the Back Sands belonged to Ferryden fishermen as long as water runs and grass grows. He [the laird] also gave them the feu rights to Ferryden.[2] But there was jiggery-pokery with Johnson's over the area where the fishermen got their bait.

Malcolm Gray's account, which focuses on the economics and ecology of mussels, rather than the politics of fishermen and fishcurers, explains why mussels were such a critical resource for white fishing and why Johnston's would have been eager to control the supply:

> Until the middle of the century the needs of Montrose and its nearby villages had been met by natural growth on the local mussel beds where the fishermen leased beds for their supply. But the increase in the number of boats . . . threatened the exhaustion of natural supplies of bait . . . The South Esk with its wide tidal basin had at least two sectors suitable for the cultivation of mussels . . . and production was organised sufficiently to supply not only local needs but also to allow export to more needy sections of the coast such as the north-east. . . . The Dun beds were developed and carefully managed by the Montrose curing firm of Joseph Johnston, but even more interestingly the Rossie beds were managed on behalf of a fishermen's association. This contained almost all the haddock fishermen . . . of Ferryden and Usan and these met about two-thirds of their needs in this way; the remainder of their supply came from Johnston's . . . (Gray 1993: 247–8)

We also learn from Walker that the fishers of Arbroath, to the south and Gourdon, to the north, also relied upon Johnston's:

> Joseph Johnston and Sons ltd, Salmon fishermen, Montrose, organized the mussel trade in the Montrose basin in the 1850s . . . In addition to establishing a mussel fishery, J. Johnstons set up a delivery service to supply their customers with fresh mussels daily . . . (Hay and Walker 1985: 60)

However Johnston's obtained control of the mussel beds, no one disagreed on the outcome: the fisherfolk now had to pay Johnston's for bait. Thus they joined the ranks of other fishing villages where bait cost money. "My grandmother [in Burghead, to the north] was once in jail for stealing mussels from Lady McGregor. They all belonged to the laird," said Mrs Smith, an incomer widow of a Ferryden fisherman. By the late 1800s, then, Johnston's held not only the mussel grounds and local salmon fishing rights, but a virtual monopoly over the commercial fish trade, including both white fish and herring. Ferryden became, quite literally, a company town. One elderly man summed it all up: "the fish-curer is the enemy of the fisherman."

From the fishers' point of view, Johnston's was continually exploiting them. In 1857, the company persuaded the Ferryden fishermen to fish further out to sea, thus increasing the yield, but also the risk (Butchart 1968: 47). Soon they also engaged them directly to fish for both white fish and herring. The latter endeavor required larger boats and even longer stays at sea. In 1884: "Montrose was one of the chief places . . . which supplied the largest quantity of haddocks and cod and yielded the largest quantity of mussels" (Butchart 1968: 48).

For a time in the 1880s, the boom in herring meant relative prosperity for Ferryden. Fishermen were able to buy furniture and to bring back souvenirs of china and silver from distant ports, lending fisher houses a new air of gentility. Of this time, fisherfolk today boast that the water was so crowded "you could walk across the harbor on the backs of the boats."

But prosperity was a fragile and fleeting thing. The fishers nearly always owed money to Johnston's. The company's practice of extending credit subsidies led to it holding mortgages on the fishermen's houses. It also sold them boats which were to be paid for over time. With a few bad seasons during the depression of the 1890s, "the fishermen could not pay their debts. The boats were repossessed and a lot of ill-feeling was created and many people left the industry" (Butchart 1968: 51). One man confirmed this, telling me that his grandfather had been part-owner of a boat, but that "Johnston's didn't like to give up the largest share of a boat. Though boats were family run, they were mostly owned by Johnston's. Fishermen paid them back with interest. The fish went to Johnston's . . ."

Furthermore, villagers believed, Johnston's had undermined the Ferrydeners interests by buying large steam trawlers in an (ultimately unsuccessful) bid to compete with Aberdeen:

> The fishermen threw stones at them and refused to go on them because they said they would ruin the fishing. Johnston's had to hire men from Montrose . . . There used to be a portrait of one of the Johnston's family. They'd hung it in the Mason's Hall, but somebody took it down.

And around this time, villagers said, an effigy of the company chairman, Joseph Johnston, was hanged and burned in the village square.

By 1904, herring catches were already declining; only 50 to 60 men from Ferryden were now involved in the fishery. Numbers on the relief rolls began to rise. The First World War, of course, sank fishers' fortunes even lower as the seas became even more perilous and markets were cut off. In 1919, an attempt to sustain a new fishing company in Montrose lasted only two years:

> The company bought trawlers from the Admiralty and reconditioned them. But just after the war fish prices were low and the fleet was also laid up for more than a month due to the coal strike. There was also an increase in railway rates which put Scottish ports at a disadvantage compared to English ports. (Butchart 1968: 50)

Meanwhile, Johnston's was laying off fishermen and other workers. "Ma faither was a cooper at Johnston's. He had to make one barrel a week for nothin' to pay for the gas he had to use to see to work. There was no union." But after WWI, Johnston's stopped making herring barrels, so there was no more need for coopers. In 1936, Butchart (1968: 50) tells us, Johnston's stopped supporting white fishing as well.

Indeed, having blamed Johnston's for their continual impoverishment and indebtedness, Ferrydeners also blamed the firm for ending their role in the industry. Only the work of salmon fishing remained. However, according to my informants, Johnston's, having resented the villagers' defiant gestures, systematically refused to hire them. "My uncle tried to get a job there in 1918 but they told him they wouldn't hire anyone from the village."

By 1928, only 94 men and boys listed fishing as their occupation, and only 28 boats still lodged on Ferryden's shore. Unemployment soared, as did emigration. Unmarried women found work in the jute mills and the Chivers jam factor in town. Some boys and men became builders' laborers. But fishing, it appeared, was gone for good.

The Great Depression, of course, intensified these trends. Many Ferrydeners, seeking better opportunities, had left for the Clyde shipyards even before the First World War. Some of these returned in the 1920s to work in boat construction on nearby Rossie Island, but were soon forced to return west. Many kept on going, all the way to North America. "Until 1938, we were knocking from job to job." Mrs Johnson, born in Ferryden around 1910, recalled, "My father was a fisherman, but there was nothing for my brothers to do. Father decided to move the family to Clydebank to get opportunities for the boys in the trades."

Even before their economy soured, Ferrydeners were conscious of feeling trapped by circumstances, helpless in the face of overwhelming power. Like others who have seen themselves as dispossessed, Ferrydeners found solace in messianic religion. Encouraged by a series of roving evangelists, they turned to Jesus as a kindlier, if more distant, patron. They did not, however, turn to the Church of Scotland.

## Salvation and Dissent

During the early days of the village, Ferrydeners reportedly saw the Established Church as a forbidding place, with its pews filled with land-ward folk and the wealthy. They were so averse to attending there that, through the early nineteenth century, Ferryden was known as a "heathen" site. Its inhabitants were notorious for superstition and drink. Beginning in the 1820s, however, evangelical Presbyterian missionaries took an interest in saving these domestic pagans, the fisherfolk, along with those in isolated rural districts and the urban poor (Donaldson 1972: 98).

Ferryden's first religious emissary appeared in the 1820s. This was the Reverend Dr Brewster. According to the memoirs of a nineteenth century village schoolmaster, this intrepid evangelist met with significant resistance. Fisherfolk hid under carts, sheds, and upturned boats when word spread that he was on his way to collect a congregation. Women pleaded that they had to stay at home with the bairns, or insisted that "'I hae nae claes'" (Douglas 1866: 8). Gradually, however, Brewster prevailed.

He established a Fishermen's Society to encourage worship and insisted that all must be baptized, teaching the fisherfolk that the unbaptized were merely God's creatures, not God's children (Mitchell 1860: 43). On the Sabbath, all work, including fishing, washing, cooking, firelighting, mending – and nearly everything else – was prohibited. Only spiritual activities, such as Bible study and prayer, were allowed.

The minister was not simply a quixotic individual. Unbeknownst to them, Ferrydeners were being caught up in Kirk politics of a national scale. At that time, the Establishment was divided into two hostile camps: the dominant Moderates and the dissenting Evangelicals. The latter wanted to do away with state patronage and to eliminate the role of landowners in choosing ministers and paying their salaries. Moderates, including the aristocracy and rural gentry believed that the state should continue to support the Kirk and, in fact, to allow it autonomy and authority on a par with its own.

In 1843, in an act of tremendous consequence for the Highlands and for many Lowland parishes, as well, the Evangelicals seceded from the Establishment. The Great Disruption, as this was known, took "thirty-nine per cent of the ministers of the establishment, followed by about a third of the people" (Donaldson 1972: 98). They founded the Free Kirk and dedicated themselves to a program of exhaustive moral rigor.

The Great Disruption was far more than a factional dispute between rival theologians. It was a sweeping social movement that reached down into the lives of the working class and provided an outlet for the frustrations and angers of the disenfranchised. When Brewster led them out of the Established Kirk, Ferrydeners rightly construed this to be an act of open defiance against the holders of privilege, specifically the laird of Craig parish and the fish merchants of Montrose. Brewster's following grew.

During the next half century, the village became famous in eastern Scotland for intense devotion, in contrast to its pagan past (Mitchell 1896: 15). The evangelism that had brought them into the Free Kirk thus readied them for a wave of proselytizing that began to sweep them off their spiritual feet. Revivals – popular, public displays of new-found and reaffirmed commitment to Jesus – had been sweeping the Protestant English-speaking world from the 1820s onward (Carwardine 1979). These were often inspired by itinerant missionary preachers from Ulster, England, and the United States, but were frequently led by local men who had undergone sudden and dramatic conversion experiences.

The Free Kirk brought Ferrydeners into the religious arena; the revivals gave them a language and a forum for revitalization, as well as a voice for protest. Their messianic formulations allowed the fisherfolk to achieve some measure of psychological relief without directly venting their anger and thus risking reprisals from their social superiors.

After all, the fishcurers cared less about the fishers' spirituality than about their profitability. As long as economic relationships were not threatened and as long as public deference sufficed to maintain face, they could afford to regard the villagers' efforts with detachment or even approval. The Ferrydeners could thus achieve a kind of internally experienced revolution by joining the elect and spiritual reality could invert mundane hierarchy. In this sense, the religious movement in Ferryden was truly a "religion of the oppressed" (Lantenari 1963), as well as a "weapon of the weak" (Scott 1985).

William Mitchell, a shipowner, left a detailed account of events in Ferryden. According to him, Ferryden and Montrose each claimed to have held the first revival in the region:

> As in the great Reformation, it is doubtful whether Luther in Germany or Zwingli in Switzerland first saw the light and proclaimed the truth as it is in Jesus; as betwixt the fishing village of Ferryden and Montrose, few, if any, can accurately tell where the revival first began . . . the same causes that created an interest in the revival in Montrose, produced here [Ferryden] a kindred feeling, but much more intense. (Mitchell 1860: 7)

By the autumn of 1859, the fervor had reached a kind of critical mass hysteria:

> The burdened souls could not endure delay. People cried aloud for a meeting . . . The preacher was discoursing in most tender strains of the love of Jesus for fishermen, when a loud shriek for mercy broke the deathlike stillness . . . like an electric shock it affected all who had sympathy. The speaker's voice was drowned amid the general wail . . . one after another shrieked aloud to Jesus for mercy and falling prostrate, apparently dead, are carried out one by one to the vestry, till it is filled. (Mitchell 1860: 8)

Ecstatic experiences, exemplifying Lewis' (1971: 18) definition of possession as "the seizure of man by divinity," were frequent. Like the Anastenaria, the poor and stigmatized Greek firewalkers who seek physical and emotional healing through the power of the saints (Danforth 1989), fisherfolk sought relief from anxiety by allowing Jesus to possess them. During these episodes, the subjects could typically neither work nor eat. They spoke in tongues, had visions and became euphoric or hysterical. Typically, the possessed person felt him or herself to be a battleground for the forces of good and evil, God and the devil. The subject was passive but tormented, unable to make conscious decisions or control his or her behavior. The battle raged on until God triumphed and the frenzied soul knew that it was to be released from sin into salvation.

Mitchell's records revealed the intimate relationship between inner, emotional states and people's perception of their mundane, as well as spiritual status. In effect, each convert became transformed from a sinner who deserved the fisherfolk stigma – of being a marginal and unworthy person – to one who was lifted above the masses of the damned.

Evangelical Presbyterianism told Ferrydeners that the poor and oppressed fisherfolk could transcend their earthly subordination and triumph over worldly sinners who, they believed, were destined to occupy a lower, and somewhat warmer, realm. Thus, consider the biography of Christian Watt, the depressed fisherwoman I discussed in the previous chapter:

> When I grumbled about my dress at school, my mother said the fishers were the first chosen of Christ, so "Put on your creel in gratitude to his glory," she said. "Your fathers *are grossly superior to these tradespeople* who look down on you [italics mine]. They can navigate small boats by oar and sail to the Hebrides, Shetland, and Greenland, with nothing but the sextant set with the noonday sun, and the stars to guide them at night." (Fraser 1983: 17)

Moreover, the revivals served a performative function. Through public displays of possession, Ferrydeners could demonstrate their moral worth to those who had scorned them. For the first time in village history, outsiders praised them, giving them a glimpse of what it might be like to be considered "respectable." As I came to learn over years of talking with fisherfolk, respectability has been highly valued and long sought-after. Piety and zeal thus became prestige goods, costing nothing but emotional exhaustion.

The Temperance movement that accompanied the revivals did much to improve their reputations, as well. Long notorious for insobriety, the villagers became almost entirely teetotal. This marked a significant change in Ferryden's public image, for the stereotypical fishermen had been a reeling lout, his normally thick fisher dialect rendered unintelligible by drink. There was even a movement (ultimately unsuccessful) to rename the central village square as Teetotal Square. But for all this, the *communitas* engendered by enthusiasm suffered a blow, when, once again, the winds of national kirk politics came blowing through village and rent apart its precious spiritual unity.

## Wounds of Division

In 1900, The Free Kirk (outside the Highlands) united with the United Presbyterians, a group whose forebears had also seceded from the Established Kirk in the nineteenth century. The resulting United Free Kirk saw itself as remaining true to the principles of the Disruption and stayed outside the Establishment. In 1929, however, a nationwide movement to reunite the sundered Presbyterian factions embroiled Ferrydeners in a bitter contest.

Individual congregations throughout Scotland were asked to vote on whether to merge with the Established Church. In Ferryden, two votes were cast. My informants said that the first vote defeated the proposal, but the second reversed it. The stalwart United Frees refused to accept this and claimed that they were the only legitimate descendants of the "real" kirk of Ferryden. This left the village with two congregations and much resentment.

The reunion split friendships, sibling ties, and generations. People continued to argue over what had happened. Many claimed that the minister's wife and her brothers reminded him of the financial advantages of working for the Establishment. "They got him turned," my informants said. Another common accusation, voiced not only in Ferryden but in other fishing villages as well, charged that names of dead parishoners had been added to the winning side. Each of the current village ministers also mentioned this to me, though neither could commit himself as to its accuracy.

However, many members of the United Free Kirk were certain it was true. According to them, the decision could only be explained as the working of evil within the village. The minister was "turned," the congregation was not religious enough, and/or certain key elders were sick and unable to fight the proposal. One old lady vehemently insisted that had her father not died shortly before the vote, everything would have turned out differently.

Some people still found ways of fanning the flames. One elderly Established Kirk lady was well known for standing at her window, shaking out her rugs over members of the UF congregation as they walked to the evening service. Others still steadfastly avoided those who had been (or whose parents had been) on the opposing side. Members of each congregation generally declined to set foot within the purlieus of the other. When the two ministers organized a joint service one Sunday with the United Free minister presiding, a UF elder was heard to exclaim, "Fancy the minister of the Kirk setting under the minister of the 'separated brethren!" and, of course, refused to attend.

Thus United Free Kirk fisherfolk, devout abstainers and prayerful pietists, saw themselves as the only ones worthy of God's grace. Those who had "fallen away" and joined the Establishment had abandoned not only their Church, but their people. For their part, the Church of Scotland congregation, which now numbered quite a few incomers in its fold, saw the UFs as stubborn and divisive. Clearly, this event had shaken the foundations of their solidary edifice, partitioning it into two factions and undermining the identity of the whole.

The intense bitterness resulting from the reunion that split the village can be at least partly explained by the fact that Ferrydeners could no longer maintain a common front. The division between the congregations represented a "family feud," a breach that could be healed only by eliminating one side. No compromises, no negotiations, no peace offerings could obscure the wound of division itself. Ultimately, the mistrust engendered by this event was to undermine Ferrydeners' ability to speak with a collective voice about the oil base. But I am jumping ahead here.

## Social Class and Public Voice

Talking as I have been about unity and identity, an obvious question to raise at this point is how Ferrydeners have perceived themselves in terms of class: did they see themselves as sharing the same class interests? Talking about life within the village, they stressed the importance of kinship and mutual aid. They subscribed to Presbyterian beliefs that all those who are saved are equal in the sight of God. They cherished belonging to the fisherfolk, sharing a common past and a commitment to in-group equality. They often acknowledged their common circumstances by quoting a popular Scottish saying about equality, "We're a' Jock Tamson's bairns." Divisions of wealth were not the only way to rupture such equality. Indeed, anyone who put himself or herself forward in a public situation was likely to encounter some suspicion and be the object of gossip. Thus kirk elders, county councillors, and even the woman who organized OAP events all were targets of cutting remarks. As we shall soon see, this attitude was to inhibit their ability to respond to changes proposed for Ferryden.

They also held somewhat contradictory beliefs about Scottish society as a whole. At one point, they might appear to subscribe to what has been called the myth of Scottish democracy, or "the belief that Scotland is a more egalitarian society than England, and that social mobility is somewhat easier" (McCrone 1996: 113; see also MacLaren 1976).[3] This belief that a "lad o' pairts" (talents) can succeed if he only works hard enough is modeled on the image of the working-class youth schooled by dedicated teachers. Armed with piety and a fair amount of Greek and Latin, he (it is always a "he") goes out into the world to make good. The fisherfolk might cite examples of local lads who had done just that. But they were canny enough to realize that only a very few actually scaled the class ladder. Much more evident in their discourse, however, was the belief that the wealthy and the powerful almost always call the shots. They frequently spoke of "those in charge," a category that usually referred to people in Montrose or to rural landowners; it never included the villagers, themselves.

They would speak freely in these terms, but it was far more difficult to get them to speak about party politics. Many were immediately wary of such conversation. Some balked altogether when asked to reveal political preferences. As one anonymous informant said in a questionnaire I administered with almost total futility, "it is not etiquette to ask these questions." Apparently, by asking about voters' choices, I was violating the sanctity of the secret ballot. Someone remarked to me that it was actually easier to talk about sex.

Not everyone felt this way, thankfully. Joe and Elizabeth were a politically vocal, elderly couple and regular attenders of the Lunch Club. They taught me much about local political allegiances. Like many Ferrydeners, they were staunch supporters of the Scottish National Party's efforts towards independence. Indeed, their son was at that time beginning to build a political career within the SNP. In fact, the SNP was then widely popular with fishing communities who saw Scottish independence as way for their industry to get some freedom from British regulations and greater protection for their interests. Other parties, for a variety of reasons, were generally rejected.The Conservatives currently held the Parliamentary Seat from North Angus and the Mearns, where Ferryden was located. However, they were seen as party to all the social burdens villagers had had to bear over the years.

Nor did many endorse the Liberals, even though Ferryden had been a stronghold of Liberalism before the First War. According to Kellas and Fotheringham (n.d.: 146), "Scottish Liberalism was able to project itself at this time as a working-man's creed, and it linked up to Presbyterianism in preferring the ideals of libertarianism to ideals of class representation and collectivism". By the 1970s, however, many fisherfolk dismissed the Liberals as ineffectual.

The Labour Party, by far the most popular in Scotland overall, had some adherents among the fisherfolk, but was generally distrusted as the party of unions, cities, and Catholics. Indeed, as E. P. Thompson (1968) has famously impressed upon the readers of *The Making of the English Working Class*, class and class consciousness are not the same thing. Fishing communities, as marginalized enclaves, have had a complex and ambiguous relationship not only to bourgeois society, but also to the rest of what is objectified as the "working class." While fisherfolk clearly identified themselves as poor and downtrodden, they did not desire any alliance between themselves and other workers, whether of city, town, farm or mine. This attitude stood in sharp contrast to earlier days.

In the 1920s, Ferryden apparently underwent a temporary radicalization. It was known as a "red" village for supporting the Independent Labour Party, a socialist radical group that was part of a growing Labour coalition. The ILP was best known in the Clydeside area around Glasgow. Joe and Elizabeth said that the ILP had had "roomies" in the village "on the King's Roadie halfway up the brae on the left." Several factors might explain the ILP's popularity in Ferryden after the First World War. For a start, many villagers had begun working in the Clyde shipyards during the War, where they would have been exposed to the ILP during the heydey of Clydeside radical activity; they would have brought the message back on their many visits home (Lynch 1992).

Secondly, with fishing mostly gone, the villagers had nothing to lose in voicing political opinions. Inasmuch as they had lost an employer, they had also lost a local enemy. Third, in some ways, the ILP's fiery message echoed the evangelists' messianic appeal, promising a new world order. Knox (1990: 155) tells us that ILP leaders were also

> linked to the Free Church and the United Presbyterian. These churches, as a consequence of being locked out of the corridors of power, if not wealth, took a more critical attitude to the status quo and to the dominant institutions of Scottish society".

The ILP also advocated a national Prohibition act, which the Temperance-minded fisherss would have strongly endorsed (Smout 1986: 147). But the ILP was short-lived, reabsorbed into the Labour Party by the Second War (Kellas 1968). Its socialist radicalism was largely forgotten by the time that I arrived in the village.

Thus, it seems that Ferrydeners did not consistently identify themselves in class terms, nor did they consistently support Labour. And perhaps we should not be suprised. After all, as long as Ferryden's existence depended exclusively upon fishing, class-based action was not really an option. The overwhelming power of the fishcuring company and looming presence of Montrose made Ferrydeners feel extremely vulnerable. They had no allies. The effigy-burning incident mentioned earlier might be likened to a bread riot, a moment when anger and frustration became unbearable but which, having found an outlet, were quickly bottled up again.

But if a transcendent class consciousness could not flourish, place consciousness could. It was in Montrose, not in Ferryden, that the fish curers lived. It was that place that united Ferrydeners together in complementary opposition against outsiders. So it is to Montrose that we must now turn.

## In the Shadow of the Royal Burgh

To get from Ferryden to Montrose, one must cross the juncture of the river and the estuary. This is both a physical and symbolic divide. For Ferrydeners, the Basin represents a contested space and calls up memories of old injustices. Its tidal flux mirrors the fluidly ambiguous nature of village boundaries, sometimes clear, sometimes effaced. On the one hand, Ferryden appears to be an easily definable, encapsulated social entity. On the other hand, it looks like an outpost of the town. And indeed, Montrose has, over the years, imposed its power to draw the village ever more tightly into its orbit.

I choose this last word deliberately, for I find it useful to situate the relationship between village and town in terms derived from 1970s dependency theory: that is, of Montrose as a regional metropole and Ferryden as one of its satellites (Frank 1969). A satellite is to a metropole as a moon is to a planet. That is, the smaller body is caught by the larger's gravitational field. However, while unevenly sized astronomical bodies presumably coexist in a benign or neutral relationship, sociogeographical ones always entail power relationships. The satellite prospers only insofar as its activities benefit the metropole.

Any control over land base or resources that the satellite might claim remains contingent upon the needs and desires of its larger, more complexly organized and more affluent neighbor. The metropole therefore systematically "consumes" the satellite. For over 200 years Montrose has used Ferryden, dominating it both economically and politically. This history makes the conjunction of village and town an excellent vantage point from which to consider how place and power articulate and how place and identity intertwine.

A thousand years ago, Montrose was a small, fortified trading center built around a castle. In the thirteenth century, it received its Royal charter and became a Burgh (see Chapter 2). For the next several centuries, "Montrose was servicing a hinterland which marched to the south with that of Dundee and to the north with that of Aberdeen but which, inland and westward, had no competitor" (Lythe 1993: 91). But the merchants of Montrose looked seaward, as well. In the seventeenth and eighteenth centuries, local fortunes were built upon salmon, tobacco, slaves and smuggling (Fraser 1974).

The castle has long since crumbled away, but the town's strength as a market center has remained. Its position derives from its command of a dangerous but navigable harbor, as well as its accessibility by road and rail. The town's coat of arms, carved above the lintel of the Public Library, reads, "Mare Ditat . . . Rosa Decorat" ("The Sea Enriches, the Rose Adorns"). Sure enough, nearly every front garden today, no matter how small, contains a rose bed. The stiff, upright stems planted neatly in bare, brown earth culminate in petals of yellow, peach and red. They make a striking color contrast to the grey or dun-colored stone houses that stand, equally upright, behind them. When I first arrived there, during the height of the offshore oil boom, it seemed to me that an odor of bourgeois self-satisfaction filled the very air.

However, preceding years had not dealt kindly with the town. Despite the presence of two multinationally owned factories (Glaxo Pharmaceuticals and Cadbury-Typhoo), unemployment was high. By the end of the 1960s, harbor trade, the town's lifeline, had sunk to a new low. Thus when North Sea oil and gas came on the scene, the town's businessmen were more than eager to exploit new opportunities.

The Montrose Harbour Board of Trustees was critical in shaping the course of events. This exclusive and exclusionary, self-perpetuating body held unlimited authority over all harbor-related matters. Within its domain, it was virtually autonomous, answerable only to the Crown and to Parliament. Members of the Board were thus very powerful people, and fairly typical of Scottish entrepreneurs more generally in their involvement with local affairs (Slaven 1994: 163). Representatives of the town's major commercial enterprises, they were also active in local and district government, civic groups such as the Rotary and the Round Table, the Chamber of Commerce, various charitable institutions and the *Montrose Review*. They formed a clique, a core group of (virtually all) men linked by class, kinship, friendship, clientship and economic cooperation.

Clearly, to comprehend the sources of power over Ferryden, I would have to follow Laura Nader's advice (1972) and "study up". Thus I spent considerable time interviewing members of the Board, as well as other, closely linked individuals. The Harbour Master was one of these. He had played an instrumental role in luring the offshore industry to the area with promises of a cooperative business climate. I also spoke to local landowners, representatives of the Sea Oil Services Base and its client companies and local investors in the various businesses that had sprung up to service the new development. My goals were to learn the language and assumptions of entrepreneurship, especially with regards to Ferryden, to identify key players and, most fundamentally, to understand what the village had been up against.

In general, people were very free with information, including some about activities that skated rather close to the legal line, although it must be said that some of their generosity may have been predicated upon their apparent belief that I, a young, female, American graduate student, would not understand much of what they told me. Perhaps they were right. But I became privy to some extraordinarily candid musings on the joys of holding power. For example, one wealthy local farmer wished – with no trace of embarrassment or even tongue-in-cheek – that he could have been a plantation owner in the old American South because slaves, unlike modern Scottish farm workers, had to show "proper respect." Another landowner took a different, but complementary, view when he opined that the local countryside had remained "delightfully feudal" in its unspoiled character and in the deferential attitudes of its inhabitants.

But even my less brash informants did not hesitate to share details of their involvement in oil-related developments. It became clear that the single most important mechanism that kept the clique together was the sharing of information. When I asked how new entrepreneurial projects had gotten started, I would hear something like, "Well, I was having a drink at the Albert Hotel and James came over and we started talking. He suggested I might be able to get together with so-and-so, and get a new business going." Indeed, along with capital, information was the coin of their realm. News concerning potential buyers for land or property moved like lightning among them.

The timely communication of this information was facilitated by some common social characteristics. All of these men were local power brokers, though not all could, strictly speaking, claim membership in the upper class (as defined by the conventions of birth, education, and dialect, at any rate). They were also linked by ties of contract, kinship and clientship to more powerful individuals in other parts of Britain, including Edinburgh, Glasgow and southern England. Some also maintained social and economic contacts with members of the Angus aristocracy, such as the Earls of Southesk and of Dalhousie, each of whom had, as part of much more extensive estates, large holdings near Montrose. (A few even claimed genealogical connections to Royalty, though these ties went back many generations.)

In addition, most were well-connected to the Conservative Party. For example, the Tory Member of Parliament for North Angus and the Mearns, Alick Buchanan-Smith, owned farmland near Edinburgh and his wife came from an old Montrose family. Not all were ideologically driven, however. One of my more gregarious informants said, "I'll vote for Tory, for Labour, *or* even the bloody SNP, if they can get me what I want."

Moreover, each member already owned at least one substantial, well-established concern that did business regularly with national and multinational firms. Some traded in soft fruit, others in potatoes, still others in timber or salmon. Finally, they solidified their local presence by sitting on the boards of directors of local charitable and financial institutions.

So cohesive a group thus had no difficulty responding to an exciting new prospect that promised to lift the town out of its recession-based doldrums and bring new opportunities for profit-making. They knew that Aberdeen, then known as the "Houston of Scotland," could no longer contain the North Sea oil boom. The offshore supply industry had begun to reach outward to less crowded, less expensive, and, preferably, non-unionized east coast ports. Knowing this, they used their firm control over land, labor and local information to prevent established, Aberdeen-based Scottish offshore support companies from moving in to set up branch offices.

The Montrose group had its own plans. Several local farmers, builders' suppliers and fish merchants, all of them members of the Harbour Board, formed new companies to supply the offshore market with food, housing, laundry services, and local transport ("rope, soap and dope" in industry lingo). One local chemist (not a pharmacist) even set up his own business in oil field lubricants. Another boasted that he expected to set up his own merchant bank and, in a moment of masculine bravado, this same individual revealed that he and his friends liked to refer to themselves as the "Montrose Mafia" and had even written up a humorous document purporting to be a dossier in the files of "S.E.M.E.N. – the Society for the Extermination of Mafia Executives in Montrose." He reminded me of the small boys I had seen in Aberdeen, swaggering down the streets in the footsteps of a large-hatted Texan. Perhaps the urge to mimic American business stereotypes had simply proven irresistible.

In any case, the ambitions of the Montrose elite depended upon the success of a partnership formed between the Montrose Harbour Board and the Sea Oil Services Company (SOS), a subsidiary of the multinational corporation, Peninsular and Oriental Steam Navigation (P&O). The goal was to build an offshore rig and boat service base at Montrose. It was agreed that the Harbour Board would lease the site to SOS which agreed to relinquish its rights when it was ready to depart. (The Harbour Master told me he had dreams of turning the base into a major container port, but this never materialized.)

Since no suitable site near the existing commercial docks was available, they fixed upon the Inch Burn, the tidal stream that ran along Ferryden's north-facing shore, to which I have already referred. This choice was revealing, not just of the group's determination to make the project work, but of its frontier view of Ferryden, a Lockean view that village land was really an underutilized territory free for the taking. As we shall see shortly, this attitude can be seen as the obverse of the Ferrydeners' belief that they were being treated like a colony.

The Board then secured a government loan to dredge the harbor and use the excavated material to create 37 acres of landfill. However, in their haste to invest in offshore developments, the Harbour Board overlooked an obstacle which, for a time, appeared to threaten all its hopes of renewed maritime glory. As it turned out, their legal right to use the Inch Burn was not altogether clear. When the Trust was established in 1837, it

> was granted authority over the whole estuary including the tidal Basin, which was essential to its well-being, though no harbour works were to be built west of the bridges, and no authority was given over the south bank of the river [Ferryden], only within the water. (Adams n.d.: 42)

Construction projects in Britain require a formal planning permission process that allows – in theory, at least – for a period of time in which objectors may lodge complaints before work commences. At the District Office in Forfar, the former County seat of Angus, I found records that showed just how controversial the base had been from the outset. Among other things, there was a rather irritable correspondence between the County Planning Officer and the Harbour Board solicitor debated whether the Inch Burn lay within the Board's domain.

Many villagers had claimed that the Board had no authority to construct anything in Ferryden. In order to build quays along the edge of the base site, the board was therefore required to seek special permission from Parliament in the form of a "harbour revision order." Despite the Board's solicitor's intensive efforts, the order did not immediately appear.

Then an officer of a local company that claimed salmon fishing rights in the Inch Burn claimed that the disputed quays were already under construction and that they were interfering with his livelihood. The Board denied this, saying that the site merely contained the sheet pilings required to protect it from erosion. A public, Parliamentary inquiry in Aberdeen ensued and investigators found the Board guilty of proceeding in advance of permission and further rebuked it for offering "misleading statements." They ordered that all work stop until the revision order came through.

The base promoters were clearly nervous and began to pay attention to public relations. In order to "sell" the base project in Ferryden and forestall more objections, they launched a carefully coordinated campaign directed at both young and old. To the former, they promised jobs. To the latter, they emphasized the importance of "progress," of Ferryden's potential contribution to the regional and national economy. Those who would oppose such progress, they implied, were backward-looking and selfish. They wooed the old age pensioners with meals, gifts of glossy oil-field literature, and a bus trip to Aberdeen. Executives from firms like Hydrotech, Baker Oil Tools and Sea Oil Services also made a point of showing up for charity events such as the OAPs' annual sale of work.

P&O also did some huffing and puffing, threatening to pull out and go north to Peterhead if their schedule were not kept. But despite the mild scandal and the halt in construction, objections were "cleared" and work on the base was finished in time to satisfy their urgent demands. Montrose looked set to become "an east coast oil town" (Fraser 1974).

The base was operating by 1974. At any given time, 20 to 30 companies – many American-based – were in residence. At least 400 people worked there full time and more jobs were promised – particularly for Ferry-deners. Crucially, from the Montrose elite's point of view, business began to spill over beyond Base limits. More companies established construction and training centers elsewhere in town. At the commercial docks, trade increased. Bars, restaurant, retailers and hotels began to flourish as never before. The local press waxed ecstatic, touting Montrose's entry into the glamorous world of the offshore oil industry.

Through all of this, Ferrydeners were given virtually no voice. That does not mean, however, that they did not have plenty to say – to each other or to anyone else who would listen.

## Sold Down the River: The Sea Oil Services Base

If anyone had listened, they would have heard some Ferrydeners say that they had been "sold down the river." Actually, the river had been sold out from under them. The Inch Burn was quite literally transformed from water into land. In 1973, a Dutch-built cutter-dredger ship entered the harbor mouth and moved up the South Esk to deepen the navigable channel and then to haul the resulting landfill to the village foreshore. For months, work went on non-stop as the Inch Burn began to disappear. Villagers complained about the noise, the dirt, and the arc lights that shone into their windows at night.

These were temporary annoyances, however. The real issue for many villagers was the abrupt transformation of Ferryden from a quiet little community where the maritime memories could be relived with a glance and a gesture, to a dormitory suburb and "light industrial" site.

However, these views were not immediately available to me when I began my inquiries. The Montrosians I spoke to were unanimous in claiming that Ferrydeners overwhelmingly favored the project. Some had. William, a retired fisherman then in his late sixties or early seventies, was the village representative to the County Council and had allied himself firmly with the developers. Some said that he had sold or rented his old boat to the offshore industry. He insisted to me that the only opponents were "incomers, holiday-home owners . . . people with no real interest in the future of Ferryden." William considered himself the village spokes-man, so he was greatly insulted when I continued to ask other people what they thought. By the end of my fieldwork he would have nothing to do with me, and was reported to have stated publicly at a Community Council meeting that I was "a spy."

Other villagers spoke with enthusiasm of the new jobs for the younger folk, although they did acknowledge that there were only 20 of these jobs, and 14 were for cleaners. Others voiced some regrets but said they "would not stand in the way of progress." The powers that be had made their decisions and they were only little people in a little village. It was no good fighting the "higher-ups" in Montrose.

A small number of villagers were openly angry and had voiced their opposition from the start. They had tried to organize some collective action either to stop the base from being built or at least to weigh in on the details of its appearance. But in contrast to the 1920s, openly defiant behavior was no longer considered appropriate in Ferryden. "Fanatic" was the name given to one particularly vocal incomer, who had lived in the village for only a few years and who had engaged in a lengthy correspondence with planning officials and government representatives. Despite the rejection of organized opposition, however, some villagers expressed their sense of loss. I heard many of these at the OAPs' Lunch Club.

In a letter written to the County Planning Committee, one elderly woman who had returned to Ferryden after years of living and working elsewhere, voiced her dismay:

> I feel that I must protest at the sacrilege which has been and is still being perpetrated against our once lovely village of Ferryden . . . My husband and I had looked forward to the time when we could retire back to Ferryden and this we did eleven years ago. We were lucky enough to purchase a house directly facing the river . . . Today, our view has gone forever, the value of the house has slumped, for we are the nearest house to what was once the river and now we are faced with the prospect of looking into the back of an unbroken line of sheds . . . My husband is an invalid confined permanently to the house, and the only thing which gave him pleasure was watching the bird life in our burn and the boats on the river . . .

Many complained about the way in which information had been presented. During the four or five public meetings held at the village, Ferrydeners were shown slides of other onshore bases, models of the proposed work, and descriptions of the construction process. Many of the blueprints and models were highly technical – impressive, but not easily comprehended by the layman. The local newspaper claimed that all questions were answered and that no serious objections had been raised, but some of the villagers with whom I spoke recalled things differently. They said that a number of queries were ignored, or answered falsely, and that several very specific objections to a variety of planning details had, in fact, been voiced. These people said they felt "hoodwinked" and claimed that attempts to include the villagers in planning decisions were no more than a farce designed to satisfy government regulations.

The oil base stirred up feelings about autonomy and community boundaries, causing much talk and controversy, reawakening old disputes, and confirming the importance of fisher identity for a substantial section of the population. Few viewed the changes as merely topographical. Most understood that, at least on some level, the new industry threatened to put the final nail in the coffin of Ferryden's independence and sense of itself as a place of fishers. By annexing the village foreshore and eliminating the tidal burn, the base became a potent symbol of Ferryden's marginalization, not only from non-fisher society, but from the rest of the fisherfolk, as well.

Why, then, were protests not more vehement and better organized at the time of the original proposal? It is never possible to determine precisely why something did *not* happen. Nonetheless, several key factors were clearly at work in this case. First were the social divisions among the villagers: true Ferrydeners and Incomers; United Free and establishment congregations. In each case, animosities and mistrust constrained any possibility for collective effort. Second, was the sense of not being able to stand up to the "big folk" in Montrose, a legacy of dependency and powerlessness. In all cases, opposition only left you worse off than you had been before. Speaking out was futile and cast doubts upon your respectability. Third was the hegemonic ideology of progress so skillfully adopted by the oil base promoters. Always, the fisherfolk had craved approval from the outside and they could not abide being labeled "backwards" once again.

The sadness and bitterness it had all engendered were summed up to me twenty years later.

## The Last Ferryden Fisherman

In April of 1995, I sat in the living room of the last Ferryden fisherman, the man who literally embodied the end of an era. In a dry voice, almost without affect, Andrew recounted how, two years earlier, he had sold his boat, and in so doing, had closed the two-century-old chapter of Ferryden's commercial fishery. His career had spanned nearly 50 years. During that time, he had watched the fish stocks decline, and faced greater and greater demands for new technology, as well as ever-increasing competition.

Andrew began fishing at the age of 14, in 1947, joining the crew of his father's boat. In 1969 he built his last boat, the *Angus Rose*. In the 1970s, he moved from a house in an older section of the village into a new dwelling "up the brae," located in a modern and architecturally homogeneous housing estate. In material terms, he had done well – the signs of prosperity were evident in his well-built house and neat furnishings. But that day Andrew did not want to talk about his success or about his time at sea so much as his sense of where the village had gone and where Scottish fishing was going.

Our conversation was short and unsentimental: on my part a set of questions and gentle prodding; on his, a set of reminiscences tinged with bitterness. Andrew was not sorry to retire from the strain of hundred-hour work weeks at sea, but he regretted that no others would follow after him, and that the fishing village in which he grew up was no longer the same kind of place. He also knew where the blame for this should fall. A long series of rapacious entrepreneurs and incompetent bureaucrats had, in his view, managed to take a once-busy and productive place and transform it into a somnolent dormitory for "incomers." Andrew thought the local Council should have bought up and modernized vacant dwellings so that the Ferrydeners' children could live there, instead of leaving to find work and affordable housing elsewhere.

In fact, Andrew could think of few other people his age (61) from the old fishing community left in the village. Most of his peers and their children had left for distant places – England, North America, Africa and Australia – or for other parts of Scotland. The older folk whose memories had kept "the fishing village" alive were dying off. "We've just lost two," he said, implying a collective bereavement.

In short, the Ferryden Andrew knew had been done in by greed and indifference, by tricks and lies. Ferrydeners had no voice in the changes that beset them, and powerful people had made bad, self-interested decisions that left villagers in the lurch. The consequence has been, he said, that "Ferryden's biggest export is people."

## Conclusion

What, then, can we say about the ways in which identity articulates with place among those who "used to be fishers?" First, let us return to the old age pensioners. Just how did they re-imagine their community in the face of drastic change? They did this by telling stories about themselves, an activity that helps to constitute a continuing sense of importance and self-worth. The stories reflect upon both past and present and taken together, form a tightly woven narrative of injustices done to a subject people. Two themes emerged in their conversations. One was the idea of themselves as survivors, even heroes in a Christian sense of triumphing – if only morally – over evil doers. Discussions of the most recent injustice – the oil base – sometimes took on an eschatological quality, a final reckoning, as it were, for Ferryden.

In another vein, their rhetoric evoked striking parallels with the losses suffered by Native Americans. More than a hint of indigenizing inflected the way True Ferrydeners rendered the distinction between themselves and incomers. The former possessed the right to speak for the village; the latter did not. Of course, the further back one could go to establish such claims the better. Ferrydeners could not claim to be the first people in the wider area, but they could and did claim descent from the first residents of the village itself. *Pace* Hobsbawm and Ranger (1983), we might speak here of "the invention of autochthony".

As indigenous people the world over have found in contending with the various powers that oppress them, claims to land that rest upon history and "truth" draw upon different, generally incommensurate, kinds of evidence (see Bodley 1990; Clifford 1986). Indeed, the villagers' tales were more than suggestive of such land claims. They depicted powerful landowners and merchants as villains who would rape the village and its site for greed and profit. They, on the other hand, were the native fisher-folk, whose "ownership" of Ferryden was predicated not upon titles and state-sanctioned authority, but upon heritage and historical right.

The True Ferrydeners gave their account of village life and history a mythic quality: mythic in the sense that its shape and substance conveyed meaning and identity, not in the sense that it was false. As myths do, it established a charter for inclusion, a rationale, as it were, for the social dichotomy of insider and outsider. It also revealed the points at which fishers must negotiate tense and sometimes conflict-laden relationships between themselves and others. People did not always like each other or get along, but, with the exception of church politics, their differences were personal, rather than structural.

Sahlins' (1976) point about the locus of symbolic production might be applied here. Ferryden was a small, encapsulated, and face-to-face community enmeshed within a set of capitalist production relationships. In many ways it was in bourgeois society, but not of it. Certainly not "primitive," it nevertheless generated an internal value-system based in maintaining "the set of social (kinship) relations" (Sahlins 1976: 13). The relationship between the larger society and the small community, as between these two symbol-systems, was one of tension and contradiction.

Although the fisherfolk were forced to submit to the demands of the larger society in political and economic terms, and although they desired respect from the bourgeois society of, for example, the Montrose elite, they resisted complete submersion in its value system. The Free Kirk and the revivals made possible a wider appreciation of their virtues. These imbued their identity with a religious dimension that enabled it to became idealized as a defense against stigma.

The Ferrydeners' locally and occupationally based commitments to equality within and loyalty to the village can be explained in part as reactions to stigma, as establishing a framework in which notions of inferiority could be inverted. By generating pride in themselves and the rigors of their occupation, they could endure, withstand, and transcend the perceived inequities and iniquities visited upon them by the outside world. Only within a localist framework, where people had a sense of commitment to a particular place, could fishermen and women expect some recognition of their worth as persons and producers.

Even before the oil base, True Ferrydeners knew that the fishing was gone for good and that incomers were penetrating the village. They knew that their cherished community had not very long to live. Still, they could use the ties of kinship and memory to invoke its presence within a familiar setting. When the base was built, however, they began to lose even that ability and could no longer ignore the loom of a future in which the fishing village would play no part.

## Notes

1. The others were Usan, Gourdon and Johnshaven.
2. Feu-rights would mean that the fisherfolk had security in the village land, not just in their actual homes.
3. McCrone notes that in some respects, the myth is "not totally at odds with reality" (1996: 115). For example. Carter (1974: 274) tells us that a nineteenth-century farm servant in the northeast of Scotland could reasonably expect to move up the agrarian ladder as he matured, an opportunity "in strong contrast with arable areas of southern England, where most men in a cohort of young labourers entering agriculture could expect to be agricultural labourers at fifty".

# –5–

# Perpetual Crisis and the Making of the Fisherfolk

Well, what will we dae when the herrin's a' finished?
And what we will dae when the whitin's a' done?
And whaur will we gang wi' oor pursers and trawlers?
And how will we ever pay off the bank loan?

> (*Whaur Will We Gang?* As sung by Cilla Fisher,
> *Songs of the Fishing* 1983.)

Here come the Clearances my friend; somehow our history is coming to life
again . . . and up and down this coast, we're waiting for the wheel to turn.

> (Capercaillie)

When people talk about the state of the world's fisheries today, they
regularly invoke the idea of crisis. Images of sterile oceans compete with
those of burned-over rainforests in public imaginings of ecological
collapse wrought by giant multinational corporations. This sense of crisis
reflects a modern understanding of global unity and the notion of a
collective planetary future. However, it fails to engage with the experiences of those who must live with the daily and immediate consequences
of resource depletion and high-tech competition. Small-scale fishermen,
like miners and loggers, face immediate and dire problems as bureau-
cracies, politicians, and special interests of all kinds compete to dominate
the policy agenda. Fishers are also concerned with the long run, but they
must, nonetheless, pay their mortgages and send their children to university.
Their view of what constitutes the crisis, therefore, is likely to be significantly different from that of policy makers, much less of those who only
click their tongues over depressing headlines, or worry that their favorite
vacation beaches might be polluted.

Nor does this general view of global crisis consider how world-system
economics interact with cultural particularities in specific locales to
produce socio-ecological moments, except insofar as to bemoan a supposedly universal human propensity to mismanage the "commons" (Hardin

1968). Some have criticized this perspective concerning local ineptitude for its ignorance of the difference between capitalist and small-scale resource use (Cordell 1989; McCay 1989). They argue that indigenous management systems often work very well to preserve and distribute resources. Rather, it is the endless expansionism, competitiveness and ruthless insistence on efficiency of capitalist-driven extractive processes that more often result in the depletion, or even the exhaustion, of supposedly renewable resources.

This chapter and the one that follows home in on the local experience of crisis, exploring what the current socio-ecological moment means to people of Scottish fishing communities caught up in the processes of modern commodity production. What Habermas (1973: 1) points out in the context of advanced industrial capitalism has great force here, namely that "the crisis cannot be separated from the viewpoint of the one who is undergoing it". Fishers' interpretation of crisis is conditioned by a number of historical and social processes that no simple analysis of catch statistics or fisheries biology can reveal.

Specifically, we need to ask what is the meaning of crisis for those who have been chronically insecure. The idea of crisis normally implies a sudden shift, an imminent make-or-break moment threatening potential cataclysm, which cannot be avoided because, as Habermas (1973) also says, the means of resistance have themselves been undone. However, modern Scottish fishers see themselves both as persistent veterans of a more extended or chronic kind of crisis, and as active agents of history. In fact, the dread of disaster is never far from their minds. They express in a variety of ways a collective level of ontological anxiety that is rooted in the history and the discourse of their occupation. For centuries, each generation of Scottish fishers has, in its own way, seen its situation as critical. They speak frequently of how each cohort has learned from its elders never to take its livelihood for granted.

Yet, their confidence in themselves as fighters is never forgotten, as Cohen (1987) also notes for the fishermen of Whalsay. However, for the fishers of my acquaintance, taking "crisis in their collective stride," as Cohen puts it (1987: 150), seems to be an overstatement. Perhaps the Whalsay folk's further remove from mainland hierarchies and less experience with stigma as well as their scornful attitude towards "da Sooth" help to explain the difference. Cohen says that for them, the outside world (most directly, mainland Scotland)"was held at bay by a subtle inversion. The powerful centre was treated as inferior in terms of local values and as peripheral to local interests" (Cohen 1987: 27). Mainland Scottish fishers might also look down on the moral character of others but rarely had the luxury of regarding those others as peripheral.

Crisis may be fairly said to be a guiding theme of fisher life, and a theme that is invoked with increasing frequency. Scarce fish, heavy debts, and ever-sharper competition from foreign fleets have combined to make fishing an even more uncertain livelihood. In part, such uncertainty reflects the material and economic conditions under which fishing communities have always worked: the danger, unpredictability and usually precarious financial situation. In addition, this uncertainty also reflects the fisherfolk's consciousness of their social isolation and historically inferior status. Most believe that if they do not look out for themselves, no one else will. Or, as one fisherman said to me, "There have always been a lot of sharks in fishing." This wary consciousness permeates the ways they view the possibilities for both individual and social efficacy.

In this chapter, I will explore the current moment in the contemporary crisis, moving between written analyses of the fishing industry, modern observations of the fishing scene, and the ways fishing villagers themselves talk about it. Focusing on loss of life, livelihood and location in the world, I will investigate the question asked in the song with which I opened this chapter: "what shall we dae?"

## Crisis and the Fisherman's Work: Danger at Sea

My father came home,
His clothes sea-wet,
His breath cold.
He said a boat had gone.

George Bruce, fisherman-poet from Fraserburgh (b. 1909).

No one ever describes fishing as a secure way of life, either in terms of economic prospects or in terms of physical safety. As we saw in Chapter 3's discussion of women in the fishing villages, anxiety was a very real dimension of their existence. Each community has its own memories of disaster:

In the north east and north the fishermen's settlements clustered round the creeks and bays on that rock-bound coast. These natural harbours were quite inadequate to give protection in gales and there were disastrous losses in 1839, 1845 and 1848. In an official report in 1849 it was stated that along the miles of coasts of Caithness the fisheries were carried on by 1200–1500 open, undecked boats, manned by 6000–7000 fishermen and that there was no harbour that could be entered at all states of the tide or place of refuge in a gale. (Grant 1961: 264)

Isla St Clair, in her BBC program, *Tatties and Herring*, described the conditions at Wick harbor during the 1848 storm, blaming not only wind and waves, but human failure to provide proper lighting and moorings for the loss of many boats.

In fact, commercial fishing still has one of the world's highest mortality rates, despite radical changes in technology.

> There are 10–20 times more deaths [in fishing] than in other high-risk industries such as mining, construction or agriculture. In the last ten years 224 lives have been lost, typically around 24 each year . . . already in 2000, 13 deaths had occurred by mid April . . . (*Fish Industry Yearbook* 2001: 54)

According to the *Banffshire Advertiser* (4 August 1998) "In 1995/6, there were 77 fatal injuries per 100,000 fishermen. This is compared to 23.2 per 100,000 employees in the second placed mining and quarrying industries".

Like miners, fishermen may face death singly or in groups. But unlike miners, who never own the mines in which they work, those fishermen who do own their own boats live with the possibility of losing the very means of production. Livelihoods, as well as lives, are at risk. As McGoodwin (1990: 29) points out, "few land-based occupations present individuals with the risk of losing all of their productive capital – as well as their lives – every time they go to work". Anyone who has read Sebastian Junger's (1997) *The Perfect Storm*, about the doomed Gloucester swordboat, the "Andrea Gail," or who has seen the film made from it, will understand immediately what this means. To find similar stories, one has only to scan the pages of Scotland's premier fishing trade magazine, *Fishing Monthly*. A harrowing tale – with a happier outcome – was reported there in 1997:

> The fishing was good and the weather was fair to moderate . . . Spirits were high . . . when suddenly the sky blackened. The rain came down in sheets and the thunder roared as the lightning ran across the sky. Everybody was absolutely terrified as the massive lumps of water which were shown up by streaked lightening crashed down on the vessel's deck. It was though the very devil himself was present . . . The huge wave hit the vessel and lifted it clear out of the water, like someone shaking a wet rug on a rainy day. It all happened so quickly, human bodies and tangled fishing nets everywhere. When at last the vessel surfaced from its deluge of water and foam; five very crumpled and very scared men were clearly shown to be still on after deck; but where was the sixth man? (*Fishing Monthly*, 8 December 1997)

As it turned out, the sixth man had been washed overboard and was only rescued with great difficulty. The North Sea takes a steady toll, its rocks and storms snuffing out fishermen's lives with frightening regularity. Ferrydeners told me that fishermen did not learn to swim, for they believed that once the sea had gotten its hold, it would not let go again. Given the cold waters they sailed in this was not an entirely irrational belief. No matter how well built the ship, no matter how sophisticated the navigational instruments, the fragile shell housing men and gear remains at the mercy of the hidden undersea wreck, rocky shore, shifting sandbar, rogue wave or wild tempest.

My conversations with fishermen and their families often featured reminiscences about hair-raising danger. These were generally presented in tones that laced casual commentary with dramatic flourishes. In one conversation, an elderly man from the northern town of Buckie told me of a particularly bad day when he was shoveling coal during a trawling voyage:

> We was taken in an awful storm very near Cape Wrath. We didn't know what to do but run before the wind. It took two men to lift the hatch. The man I was lifting the hatch with looked at my face and said, "Jimmy, this is the last day you have to live." I was about twenty-three. If it hadn't a been for my good eyes, we would all have perished in the Pentland Firth. I happened to spot the light at Scrabster. I can see that man's eyes yet. We was the only boat shot our nets that night. The rest of the fleet kept in. The Pentland Firth is about the wildest place on the coast.

Some storms have been memorialized in poem, song and story as emblems of catastrophe and loss for fishing communities, or even, as in the case of the North Sea gale of 1881, for the entire coast. John Watt wrote *Windy Friday*, the saga of the storm that took 129 men from Eyemouth, on the southeast coast:

> Two score and five sailed out that day
> For the 'deep hole' they were bound.
> With all sails set from Eyemouth Bay
> None better could be found.
> And fourteen score o' fishers brave
> Sent out one heartfelt plea,
> That they'd be spared upon the wave
> To reap the white fish from the sea . . .
>
> From the Orkneys to the Channel Isles
> On that October day,
> The wind it blew two thousand miles

From Hoy to Newlyn Bay.
And seven score Mother's Sons and nine
They died off Eyemouth's shore.
These bonny boys who held the line
Would plough the seas no more.

The grinding turn o' the hearse wheel
In October Eighty One,
Made every man and woman kneel
In prayer for Eyemouth's Sons.
For this was the price they had to pay
The living and the dead,
And the price that Eyemouth paid that day
To earn her daily bread.

Such losses are hardly ancient history, as I was reminded by a retired skipper who now is active in fisheries politics.

There was a while when we were losing a lot of boats and crew in North Sea. This was in the 1970s. There was a lot of bad weather. Buckie lost two or three. That makes a big hole in a small community. Boats have got bigger, but that's not the whole answer. The "Acacia Wood" was lost recently and she was a top class boat from Lossie [Lossiemouth]. Boats would disappear and not be reported for a day or two. I spoke to the skipper of the 'Kestrel" who said he'd been speaking the night before to the "Nonesuch" and had a bad feeling he knew she wouldn't last the night.

And such devastating events still afflict coastal communities, some-times raising questions of responsibility and of blame. In 1997, the town of Peterhead saw four crewmembers die when the trawler, the *Sapphire* sank in three hundred feet of water some twelve miles from land. Only the skipper escaped. This tragedy was, sadly, common, but its aftermath revealed some changes in the way those bereaved are reacting to such losses. Once, it was widely accepted that drowned sailors were never seen again. However, the families of the *Sapphire*'s crew demanded that the government raise the boat and recover the remains. The families' actions, taken in part because of allegations of mishandling on the part of the skipper, did not sit well with everyone, particularly with the skipper's friends and kin. Within Peterhead, as well as within the fishing industry more widely, people debated the wisdom of such a demand. Many doubt-less feared the rifts to the community that might arise in the face of an investigation. Newspaper columnist Tom Morton commented:

> When I wrote last year expressing concern about what flew in the face of fishing community tradition, the reaction from throughout Scotland indicated that within maritime circles, if not political ones, attempting to raise the Sapphire was considered a mistake. (*Scotsman*, 24 March 1999)

The government was, in any case, reluctant to comply, doubtless confirming some fishers' beliefs that politicians were not their friends. On 4 August 1998, the *Banffshire Advertiser* quoted shipping minister Glenda Jackson as saying that

> The Government regard the sea as an honourable last resting place . . . We believe this is consistent with the traditions of seafaring which recognises the sea-bed as a grave. But we recognise that modern technology makes possible the recovery of relatively small vessels, although these operations will often be dangerous and costly.

Fishermen are aware that human error plays a strong role in their chances of returning from sea alive. In an article on industrial safety issues, *Fishing Monthly* (June 2000: 17) reported that "over a three year period in the early 1990s, an average of one fisherman was killed every eight days around the UK." Not all these were the result of bad weather.

> Almost 30 per cent of fishing vessel losses were the results of collisions or vessels going aground, and the majority of these accidents occurred in conditions of adequate visibility . . . Dr. Malcolm Findlay of the University of Plymouth Marine Studies . . . was reported in *Safety and Health Practitioner* magazine arguing passionately for a culture of safety to be introduced into the industry.

Many skippers would argue that they are highly safety conscious but also acknowledge that they do not always stick to the rules. I heard many tales of bravura and corner cutting that suggested a rather macho ethos of challenge and daring. One man spoke with pride about his days as a determinedly entrepreneurial fisherman, setting out in weather the other boats refused to face. With a strong sense of self-confidence and a willingness to take risks, he repeatedly won distinction for being Scotland's top-earning whitefish skipper.

*Fishing Monthly* frequently reports on safety issues such as the wearing of life jackets. Most fishermen have traditionally refused to wear these, arguing that they impede their ability to work comfortably and efficiently. Thus, if a man's foot is caught by a line and he is dragged overboard, he must depend on the quickness of his crewmates to observe his disappearance. The following article illustrates this quite starkly:

The crew of a 23 metre crabber were hauling in a fleet of pots during the late evening in heavy weather and snow storms . . . The vessel pitched heavily and the back rope, on to which the crab pots were secured came off the hauler. At the same time the pot which had just been placed on the table, was suddenly pulled back overboard before it could be released. As the pot went overboard it knocked one of the fishermen, who had been standing with his back to the hauling hatch, into the sea . . . [the skipper] swam 20 metres to the fisherman who was floating face down in the water . . . A rope was thrown to the skipper but he was unable to hold on to both the rope and the fisherman. Unfortunately, the fisherman was lost.

And if, as has often been reported, a man falls overboard when out alone (as is sometimes the case in lobstering), he has no chance at all.

An article in a northern weekly compared the risks of fishing to those of other dangerous industries, claiming that things are getting worse rather than better:

Fishing communities have always known the dangers the men who work in the industry face. Casualties have always been high. But now the industry has a worse safety record than any other sector of business. Over the past five years, the accident rate for all UK fishing vessels has increased significantly. And now the industry is No. 1 in the casualty stakes.

In 1995/96, there were 77 fatal injuries per 100,000 fishermen. This is compared to 23.2 per 100,000 employees in the second placed mining and quarrying industries. And though the number of vessels has been reduced significantly, there is no corresponding fall in the accident rate. (*Banffshire Advertiser*, 4 August 1998)

Articles from the same issue reported two local fatalities: a deckhand who died in a fall overboard and a crewman who drowned when his boat capsized.

If fishermen have symbolic practices designed to improve their chances of survival it is hardly surprising. Most accounts of fisher life from anywhere in the world emphasize the special belief systems and ritual practices of fishermen (Anson 1974 [1930], 1965, 1975 [1932]; Christensen 1977; Cook 1987; Gill 1993; Kalland 1995; Mullen 1978; Nadel 1986; Robbens 1989; Thompson et al. 1983). Graham Rich reports, for example, that Scottish fishing boats are deliberately kept plain because "the myth is that the sea can become envious of boats which are too beautiful. The sea will want to possess the boat for herself" (Finlay 1998: 86).

As I noted in Chapter 2, this focus on "superstition" has been frequently used to define fishermen as backward or primitive. However, it is common for those engaged in risky livelihoods such as farming, mining or fishing to employ mystical defenses. Doing so has nothing to do with an inherently pre-rational mentality. It has everything to do with a universal need to control the essential, but uncontrollable (Malinowski 1948).

The fishermen I met often mentioned the prevalence of what they themselves labeled superstitions, practices they believed were old fashioned but persistent. Among those that they mentioned, ritual avoidances predominated. We have already seen that women were bad luck for boats. Many also believed that ill-luck would follow the utterance of certain words on board, such as salmon, hare or pig. Some fishermen wouldn't even allow these words to be spoken in the home: "In oor hoose, ye coudna' say salmon. Ye had to say, 'the red fish.' A rabbit was a 'mappy,' and if ye met the minister, ye'd run and touch cauld [cold] iron." What struck me about these revelations was the mixture of embarrassment and pride in their voices. If such practices were seen as superstitious, they were also indices of the courage and luck necessary in the fishing profession.

Their perils involved more than the fear of drowning. As stigmatized people, fishermen have had to negotiate an often hostile social environment. They were also chronically beset by economic woes. Lummis claims that some East Anglian fishermen were more concerned with economic uncertainty than with the possibility of dying at sea, and that the numerous ritual practices they employed were strongly motivated by the volatility of their income (1983: 195). Well before the recent era of bank loans, computerized gear and restrictive fishing policies, a fisherman could drown in debt as well as in salt water. An older woman from Buckie recalled this along with the seriousness with which people took their obligations: "My father's boat was lost in 1929. There was no insurance, so we lost everything. My mother paid back every farthing the boat owned; the gear had been bought on tick [credit], along with the stores, the nets."

## Profit from Loss; Loss from Profit

Repeatedly, in conversations throughout the 1990s with men from Fife and from the Moray Firth, I heard that things are "out of control." The notion of "control" represents a tension, if not a contradiction, in their concepts of causation and outcome: on the one hand, the fishermen are, overall, a devout group, and believe that God, luck, and fate ultimately call the shots. On the other hand, raised in a Calvinist tradition that links individual merit to hard work, they are always striving to prove that they leave as little as possible to chance. By "control", then, they mean a sense that the parameters of difficulty are recognizable and that enemies are, at least, familiar, rather than that fishermen ever truly can manage all the conditions of their lives.

And these conditions have grown ever-more complex. Writing in the *Glasgow Herald*, Thomson and McIntosh speak of three nails in the coffin of the village fishery: the European Union, new technology, and capital intensification. Modern fishers, like modern farmers, are inextricably embedded in global capitalist relations and up-to-date technology. Just as the small farmer struggles – and often fails – to survive in an era when agribusiness runs the show, so, too, does the small fisherman encounter-face serious disadvantage in the face of bigger players (Fitchen 1991; Thompson, Wailey and Lummis 1983;). As McGoodwin (1990: 10) points out, "because small-scale fishing implies a small-scale capital commitment, it also usually implies small-scale power".

Indeed, given the advantages of size and new technology, it might fairly be said that investment capital has replaced labor as the fishermen's most indispensable resource. Actually, it is important to recognize that this trend is not so new: it can be seen as early as the 1880s, when, with the introduction of steam engines, trawling began to challenge line fishing as a commercial technique. Of course, these larger, more efficient boats threatened the livelihood of smaller operators. Fishermen were immediately concerned about the dangers of such competition, as well as of overfishing, but their protests went unheeded.

> The 1880s found the fishing industry in the grip of change and controversy as it had never been. Trawling, and the anti-trawling movement, were daily reaching new heights as the steam trawler began to make its presence felt. Aberdeen began expanding. Wick was visibly slipping from its position as premier herring port, and Peterhead, Fraserburgh, Buckie, Whitehills, Lerwick and Stornoway all grew rapidly . . . The 34 or so years between 1880 and 1914 were the most prosperous and eventful years the fishing had seen or ever will. Already fewer people were actually fishing but the catching power and size of the boats were increasing . . . All of this meant that the villages lost their most able fishermen to the nearest town with a safe harbour . . . the changes were ringing the death knell of such as Whaligoe, Clyth, Skateraw, Collieston, Pitulie, Portessie, Balintore and many others . . . (Sutherland n.d.: 70–3)

Today, without a state-of-the-art boat or combine harvester, neither fisherman nor farmer can compete in the modern market. But fewer and fewer people are needed to operate such sophisticated and expensive equipment, and fewer still can afford to purchase and maintain it. And so both farming and fishing households are disappearing or are being assimilated by larger enterprises. "Compared to farming as it is now conducted, fishing remains a labour-intensive industry – but only where boats continue to work" (Butcher 1987: 117). As a result, the community basis of fishing is also disappearing.

Another, corresponding change in the profile of Scotland's fishers is the growing class division between the successful and the not-so-successful. Two generations ago, most fisherpeople shared a substantially similar standard of living. Even the skippers – at least in the small-boat fishery – were not noticeably more affluent than those who worked for them. Skippers in this group, who were normally owners or part-owners of the boats, worked alongside their crew. In part, this was due to the Scottish share system, a practice of distributing income to all members of the crew after each trip. First, roughly one-half of the catch was set aside to meet boat expenses. Then, each member of the crew got an equal share of the catch (Baks and Postel-Coster 1977: 29).

Fishermen have taken pride in this arrangement, which they call the Scottish share-system, feeling that everyone puts forth his best in a truly collaborative effort that stands in sharp contrast to the practice of large factory trawlers, where skipper and crew are merely employees of distant, impersonal owners. But some of the new boats are introducing these more proletarian and alienating relations of production. Reports of firms like Asda signing fishermen up to exclusive contracts have hit the press as this book is being written. Such contracts are eerily reminiscent of the times when fishermen were bound to fish for a particular curer in order to work off their debt. "We were share fishermen. Now it's wages." Moreover, as the industry becomes more concentrated, it's wages only for some.

When I explain my research to people outside the fishing community as focusing upon the demise of the community-based fishery, they are often surprised. Many insist that "the fishermen are rich." They point to the elaborate and expensive ("Dallas") weddings reported from Peterhead and Fraserburgh – with stories of fishermen's daughters who travel to Italy to have their gowns fitted. They comment on the big houses of some fisher families. Everyone seems to know, or to know of, a fisherman with an enviably large income who drives fast cars, spends ostentatiously, and takes vacations in Portugal. Some also insist that the young fishermen are better off now. "There's mair fat on their backs," I heard one man say.

Fortunes are indeed being made. Reports of million-pound-plus boat investments are not uncommon. Since the late 1970s, those with sufficient capital and access to the industry have been doing very well, indeed. In particular, a few families from Peterhead and Fraserburgh own large purse-seiners that are reputed to be catching what some call "an obscene amount" of herring and mackerel. However, they are widely regarded and resented as exceptions. "They're the big fellows. An exclusive club; a closed shop." It is often remarked that a small number of families have bought up half of the available commercial licenses for the open-ocean pelagic species (fish that swim freely through the upper levels of the sea, such as herring and mackerel, as compared to the lower-dwelling, or ground fish). One fisherman commented, "there's enough fish for their need, but not for their greed. The purse net just catches everything." Writing in the *Glasgow Herald*, (*Glasgow Herald*, 17 December 1998; internet version from www.AlastairMcIntosh.com) McIntosh claims that

> some 3 dozen millionaires scoop-up Scotland's entire catch of herring and mackerel. Indeed, just 45 pelagic ships with 450 crew now monopolise an erstwhile community resource which, at the end of World War II, supported over 1000 boats, 10,000 crew and an even greater workforce on shore.

Thus we see how the rich get richer while the poor leave fishing: the number of people and places involved in the fishery has shrunk, leaving high profits for a few and decreasing opportunities for many, particularly the younger men. Those fishermen and families with sufficient capital, entrepreneurial skill, and a fair share of luck are doing extremely well and are steady consumers of high-end goods and services. As one Fife fisherman summed it up, "the boats are doing better in the last year or two, but there are fewer boats."

Overall, investment in new boats has fallen dramatically over most of the coast. One informant estimated that, in many places, the average boat is now at least twenty-five years old. An ageing fleet leaves the future gravely in doubt, as few young men can afford the extraordinary investment required to buy a new one.

It is clear that the fishermen are up against heavy odds. One obstacle is the sheer cost of entering the fishery. An article in *Fishing Monthly* (January 1998: 15) reports:

> A number of skippers in the Pittenweem-based Fife fishing industry are advising their sons not to go to sea but to obtain another trade . . . Apart from skippers telling their sons not to go to sea, another major barrier to entry to the fishing industry is the difficulty in obtaining licences. In some cases, licences can cost as much as, or even more than, the fishing vessels themselves, with the result that those without substantial financial resource cannot afford them while others who do buy have a heavy debt burden . . . There has been a one

third fall in employment since 1990 with a decline in the number of larger boats and an overall trend towards fewer and smaller boats.

On the other hand, a few fishing locations do appear to bear out the impression of industrial vitality. Aberdeen and Peterhead, on the northeast coast, have been top fishing ports in the United Kingdom for a number of years. They also cohabit with the North Sea oil industry, whose presence drives up both property values and harbor costs. Their western neighbor, Fraserburgh, is another striking example. The town suffered a "10 per cent fall in catching sector employment" between 1993 and 1997 (*Fishing Monthly* September 1999: 15). Nonetheless, Fraserburgh's multi-sectioned harbor area, known as "the Broch," hardly gives a hint that fishing is in trouble. The dockside is filled with vans and storage sheds. Forklifts shift rough wooden boxes lettered with the names of various processing companies. Boats – some of them immense trawlers – crowd the harbor.

Fraserburgh, in fact, regularly records large whitefish and herring landings. James Miller (1999: vii) writes of watching a catch being unloaded in 1995:

> the stream of herring seemed unending, as if one vessel had swept up in one excursion what several zulus and drifters [two older types of fishing boat] would have considered a week-long bonanza.

*Fishing Monthly* devotes considerable space to news of Fraserburgh's activities. It describes the town in vibrant terms, celebrating the latest harbor development project, such as the new refrigerated fish market built to EU regulations; the top European net maker who is relocating to the town (March, 1998: 17); or the deepening of the harbor channel to make it accessible at low tide (*Scottish Fishing Monthly*, January 1997: 10).

However, Fraserburgh's relative health is no guide to the overall state of the fishery and, indeed, it participates in a zero-sum game. Like Peterhead, the port has successfully captured a major share of a shrinking resource base and this has necessarily come at the expense of the small and mid-sized ports.

For most fishermen, affluence is elusive. Even those in work may be struggling, as a letter to *Fishing Monthly* from a Shetland fisherman points out:

> A young fisherman who is employed aboard what used to be a top-earner informed me that he is earning less than he would get on Jobseeker's Allowance . . . That is the truth from Shetland – hardly a picture of a thriving and prosperous industry. Since 1995 the Shetland fleet has been reduced by 21 working boats . . . (April 1999).

Where have the boats gone? Many perfectly good boats have been decommissioned (scrapped) in a concerted EU conservation effort to restrict access to fishing grounds. In 1995, a fisherman in Buckie told me that nine local boats had been decommissioned within the previous year alone. Fishermen watch all this with great dismay.

Those who remain in fishing often fight just to pay the bills. Many will soon be forced to leave for other kinds of work. Consequently, the industry is being beset not only by declines in stock, but also in loss of labor. *Fishing Monthly* (July 2001: 13) reported a serious crew shortage in Peterhead:

> A Peterhead-based fish selling agent has admitted that the white fish fleet is battling to plug the haemorrhaging of crewman to other industries in North-east Scotland . . . the problems currently blighting the white fish sector are forcing many young people to take up employment in the oil and construction industries where they can be guaranteed regular earnings . . . There is a lack of fish on the grounds and quotas are tight. There's no money in the industry . . . (even) the owners of many demersal vessels were seeking work with the oil industry as guard ships simply to ease the pressure on the fishing grounds.

A butcher in Anstruther left the fishing when he was in his forties. "I couldn't take it any more. Nine out of ten fishermen would take a job ashore if they could." "It's all changed now," said the wife of another retired fisherman. "My husband left the fishing a few years ago because it was such a hassle with quotas and all. We were losing money and not making it." Another said that her son had a boat. "But it's almost impossible to get into the fishing now, when boats cost over a million pounds." In a harborside pub in the Fife village of Pittenweem, I spoke with a young fisherman who was morosely waiting for incoming tide so that he could set sail with his crew. I asked him, given his gloomy comments about the state of Scotland's fishery, what young men entered the trade nowadays, rather than pursuing other careers. "The stupid ones," he said.

Such dour assessments are not hard to find. They convey recognition of the hard economics of modern fishing and the realization that these economics are unlikely to sustain an acceptable lifestyle for many. Few think matters will improve. A Buckie fisherman blamed the fishers' own shortsightedness: "Fishermen are mair greedy noo. In the past twenty to thirty years, they've nae been thinkin' aboot the future. Religion's been thrown overboard. Deep down, some of them are very stupid and think it'll come a'richt. But it *wilnae'* come a'richt. The boats are gettin' bigger," he said, "but the crews are gettin' smaller."

Evidence to support his view comes from the small village of Lossie-mouth, only miles to the west of prosperous Fraserburgh. Lossie is an example of the communities whose days of fishing are close to ending. Here a magazine photo caption tells us that: "The building of new flats on a site which was formerly home to fishing gear stores is a telling reminder that Lossiemouth's days as a fish landing port are almost over" (*Scottish Fishing Monthly*, November 1997: 11).

Lossiemouth is a typical example, but not the most extreme. In some places, the fishing, as we have seen in the case of Ferryden, has long been gone for good. Frequent warning calls for revitalization characterize references to those smaller ports that are still in the game. A headline such as "East Neuk fleet upgrade call" is followed by the claim that "The current economic conditions facing the village-based fishing industry simply do not permit investment to bring the fleet up to date . . . without modernisation, the industry will suffer a slow and inevitable run down" (*Scottish Fishing Monthly*, July 1995: 6).

To experience the scale and scope of this decline one has only to travel outward from Fraserburgh, which stands at the north easternmost point of the Scottish coast. Westward, the road spills out along the Moray Firth; southward, it coils around the headland called the "Knuckle of Buchan" along the North Sea. Most visitors know little about the more obscure ports that dot these coastlines. Many of the smaller settlements are barely visible from the road, as the A98 motorway dips inland periodically, sweeping one quickly (well, relatively quickly) along. To reach them a traveler must embark on narrower, more winding and often precipitous routes, some of which scarcely seem to admit the possibility of cars.

A list of these places cries the roll call of Scotland's maritime history. Their names ring out to those whose families have made their living anywhere along the coast. I like to repeat them, giving them (when I can) their proper local pronunciations. First, going west: Britsea (Broadsea), Sandhaven, Rosehearty, Pennan, Crivie (Crovie), Gamrie (Gardenstown), Macduff, Banff, Whitehills, Portsoy, Sinine (Sandend), Cullen, Port-knockie, Finnechty (Findochty), Portessie, Buckie, Buckpool, Portgordon, Lossiemouth, Hopeman, Burghead and Nairn. Of these, only Gamrie, Macduff and Buckie remain significantly active. Gamrie is a highly religious community whose family-based fishing fleet is still going strong (Knipe 1984), although they must now land their fish at Fraserburgh. Macduff's boatyards still get new orders to build and repair. Buckie, which now relies heavily upon shellfish, is still listed as one of Scotland's top 25 ports. But tiny Pennan is known today not for its fishing but for having provided the location of *Local Hero*, a film whose story flirts with the romantic idea of the quaint but impoverished fishing village lost in the slipstream of progress. Findochty and Cullen are heavily occupied by summer people. Portsoy (once also a source of the famed Portsoy marble) attracts tourists to its dramatic looking harbor and the crafts shop, but the water is generally empty of working boats.

The story repeats itself going south: Stonehaven, Bervie (Inverbervie), Gourdon, Johnshaven, Ferryden, Usan, Auchmithie, Arbroath, Crail, Cellardyke, Anster (Anstruther), Pittenweem, St Monans, Largo, Buckhaven, Granton, Newhaven, Fishherrow, Cockenzie, Port Seton, North Berwick, Dunbar, St Abbs, Eyemouth, Burnmouth, Ross. Of these, Pittenweem, in the East Neuk of Fife, and Eyemouth, near the Border, have new, up-to-date fish markets, but even these, like Arbroath, in southern Angus, fall into that ambiguous middle-range of ports whose future is unclear.

Some of the other villages on the list are now simply of historical, or even archaeological, interest from a fisheries point of view: Usan, for example, is simply a cluster of ruins on a narrow, rocky inlet; Ferryden ceased to be a working fishing port a generation ago; Auchmithie is best known for its role in *The Antiquary* (Scott 1907); and, as for Cellardyke, by Anstruther, where "every house was a fisherman's sixty years ago," its fleet is long gone. In sum, most of these villages are known today as places where "they used to be fishers."

Many articles in *Scottish Fishing Monthly* have emphasized the perilous position of the smaller ports. For example:

> Scotland's small fishing communities are in danger of being wiped out unless urgent action is taken to stem their decline. The situation is so serious that this month *Scottish Fishing Monthly* is calling on Scots Secretary Michael Forsyth and Fisheries Minister Raymond Robertson . . . to give our fishing villages valuable breathing space . . . At Pittenweem, for example, 2,672 tonnes of cod, haddock and whiting were landed in 1986. By 1994 this figure had slumped to only 783 tonnes, and the fall is continuing. In 1989 there were 318 regularly employed fishermen, but by 1994 this had fallen to 230. Billy Hughes of the local Fishermen's Mutual Association believes Pittenweem may no longer exist as a fishing community in 10 years time (*Scottish Fishing Monthly*, December 1996).

A school teacher from the local high school in the neighboring town of Anstruther, who is descended from a Pittenweem fishing family, says that "Pittenweem was once the center of the world." He has seen its decline reflected in the school curriculum. "Until 10 years ago, boys took a course in navigation [as part of their regular studies]. They stopped that when they could no longer get teachers."

But there is more to it than that. "The young lads want a better quality of life," says a middle-aged Fife fisherman. In Buckie, the North East Fishermen's Joint Group Training Association has been attempting to address this issue, working with an Aberdeen college to provide the sophisticated training for new recruits that would help ensure them relatively good paying jobs. In 1995, 65 young men were in training to get their deckhands' certificates. "So far we're managing to get all these boys berths, though it's getting harder," said an official of the Association. However, further south, in Eyemouth, a community development worker told me in 1999 that "seventy or eighty boys a year graduate from the High School and not one has gone into the fishing lately."

In large white type set against a black background, a headline in *Scottish Fishing Monthly* screams "Save our fishing villages!" The story inside warns of the "mortal threat to our villages" from the UK government's refusal to enact sufficiently protective policies:

> It is already too late for many villages, and most of those that do survive are a pale shadow of their former selves, with landings well down on the glory days of the past. It now looks as if the writing is on the wall for even these villages unless something is done to arrest the slide. (*Scottish Fishing* Monthly, July 1996: 6)

"Slide" is an apt word. It is very difficult to pinpoint the exact position either of the industry in general, or of many communities in particular. The process can be said to have begun at many points in time, and it is not finished yet. Some observers believe that the village-based fishery need not inevitably end, but merely awaits the appropriate adjustment.

However, just what must be done to save it remains in contention. The "industry" is neither harmoniously integrated nor self-regulating. And the fishermen's antagonists are numerous, distant and impersonal. Everywhere, now, the talk is of insufficient quotas, expensive licenses, bureaucratic regulations, poor fish prices, foreign competition, decommissioned boats and satellite surveillance. News accounts in local papers and industry magazines regularly employ a rhetoric of crisis, repeatedly employing such terms as crisis, catastrophe, and disaster. Calls for government assistance or policy changes have routinely sounded the death knell, not only of the small communities, but of whole fisheries sectors, even the entire industry.

For example, Aberdeen's daily newspaper, *The Press and Journal* (16 July 1975), ran an editorial saying that the United Kingdom Government's White Fish Authority was correct in speaking of "our fishermen being close to economic catastrophe". A few months later the *P&J* reported a "crisis facing the Scottish fishing industry . . ." and said that Tory Minister Iain Sproat "is convinced the industry is at death's door" (13 February 1976).

No longer do fishermen sing songs like this one from the Berwickshire coast:

> It's net after net is pulled from the sea
> With the hauling, the shaking, the one, two and three,
> And the herring that are climbing around your seaboots
> And slithering and sliding down into the shoots
>
> (Wood 1998: 55).

They are far more likely to sing – or listen to – songs like *The Final Trawl* by Cilla Fisher,

> For it's heave away for the final trawl,
> Singing haul away, my laddie-o
> It's an easy pull, for the catch is small,
> Singing haul away, my laddie-o
>
> (Cilla Fisher)

Or, the angrier verses of Matt Armour's *The Grey Flannel Line*, sung on his album, 'Memories and Rage':

> What bastard decided that I wilnae wark,
> Tae bring the fish in fae the sea?
> What bastard dressed up in a grey flannel suit
> Is making decisions for me? Dear God!

Armour, who hails from the Fife coast, says of this one: "Not all the vicissitudes inflicted on the fishing trade arose from our friends in Europe. Our own elected governments had to agree to them, and impose them with a rigour not seen in too many other community lands" (Armour 1998).

## Foreigners, Regulations, Bureaucrats and Protests

> Hesiod: an Epigram on the Common Fisheries Policy: All that we did not want to catch, we kept, and all that we wanted to take home we threw over the side (Finlay 1998).

Many fishermen seem to agree with dire predictions of the industry's demise, indeed, they have been voicing them for years. From their perspective they remain perpetually engaged with irrational, hostile and even malevolent external forces: many of them human. For at least the past 50 years, they believe things have grown worse as a shrinking resource base has pitted them ever more intensely against fishermen of different national fleets, from the Spanish to the Norwegians. The infamous Cod Wars of the 1950s through the 1970s between Great Britain and Iceland were one example.[1]

The mid-1970s produced another conspicuous crisis-point. In the 1960s and 1970s, Scottish fishing had enjoyed a brief boom period, when "the problems were those of adjusting to rapid success" (Cargill 1976: 2). In the mid-1970s, however, when OPEC tightened controls over oil production and a recession began to hit, fishermen had to face sudden rises in fuel and equipment costs for which they were ill prepared. Simultaneously, demand for fish dropped, lowering prices. And, with ever more efficient technologies, overfishing became a serious concern. By 1974, the boom had ended.

The increasing bureaucratization of fishing had produced a reaction among the fishermen, however. No longer were they content to let others manage their affairs. Many had been successful entrepreneurs and had gained considerable confidence in public arenas outside their own villages. Moreover, they were convinced that EEC policies regulating who could fish where, as well as compensation for skyrocketing fuel prices, were making everything worse. In March of 1975, fishermen from all around the coast (and in England, as well) decided on radical action. Lining up their boats one next to the other, they held a three-day blockade of all the major ports (Cargill 1976). The blockade ended after meetings between fishermen's groups and the government, with the fishermen feeling that some gains had been made. However, Cargill (1976: 52) concludes that many of these gains were illusory, but says optimistically that

> it is generally agreed that fishing gets a greater priority in negotiations and general debate than it did previous to the Blockade . . . Therefore it could be that the benefits of Blockade '75 which achieved so much in publicity and by public sympathy will be seen over the years to come.

Cargill's comment provides another example of the fishermen's need for public respect. From their perspective, when scientists and policy makers made decisions for the fishery without consulting fishermen, this was further confirmation of their marginal status in Scottish – and now, in European – society. By undertaking the blockade, fishermen were refusing any longer to have their views ignored. However, more recent reports about EC regulations and British government responses indicate that the battle had just begun.[2]

As resources shrank and competition increased, other countries began to enact protectionist coastal policies by asserting wider offshore territorial domains. These were accompanied by an ostensibly successful United Nations effort to reach mutually agreeable arrangements among states to allocate marine resources (including fish, seabed mineral deposits and offshore oil and gas) through the International Law of the Sea Conference. In practice, however, things have not worked out well. Accusations of cheating, lying and all forms of skulduggery abound.

It is, therefore, not surprising that Scottish fishermen charge what they perceive as the lawless fishermen of foreign fleets with creating many of their problems. They complain that the foreign fleets ignore regulations and catch – illegally – much smaller fish. "They're building their fleet up while we're runnin' doon. We're conservin' oor fish for they guys." The catching shortage has led to disputes of many kinds and on many levels, including quarrels between boats of different national registries and media campaigns against selected fleets. These quarrels have revealed and exacerbated existing tensions. The Danes are blamed for over-exploiting the stock of sandeels, a major food source for other species, particularly cod and haddock. But it is the Spanish who seem to arouse the greatest ire.

In 1995, Canada nearly set off a "fish war" with Spain when it detained a Spanish trawler beyond the 200 mile limit. The trawler, it claimed, was violating quota and size regulations while landing halibut from the Grand Banks. In a show of solidarity, ports all over Scotland flew the Canadian maple leaf flag, and Scottish fishermen spoke scathingly of the "greedy Spaniards" and alluded to the affray as a "moral battle." *Scottish Fishing Monthly* quickly blamed the Spanish for having "little regard for adhering to fishery rules and regulations" (May 1995: 4).

Anti-Spanish feeling clearly had not cooled much by the end of 1996, when the magazine blazoned "Spanish Shame" on its front page, in response to a report that the Spanish were openly flouting European Union minimum landing size rules. "The findings will come of little surprise to anyone in the UK and Irish industries where it is widely known that the Spanish fleet regularly lands undersized fish . . . with impunity" (*Fishing Monthly*, October 1996: 1). Some comments betray an envious tinge: "The Spanish fishing industry is huge and has a lot of political clout. They have taken full advantage of this to expand and modernize the fleet," said a man standing on the pier in Buckie. This comment reflects Scottish fishermen's convictions that they are marginalized not only within Europe, but by the British government.[3]

Unquestionably, many fishermen in Scotland today believe that they are being seriously disadvantaged by the current European Union's Common Fisheries Policy (the CFP, established in 1983), with its quota and management regimes, though it seems that most prefer to remain within the CFP and work for change. The CFP sets species quotas for each national fleet, allowing the Danish, the Spanish, the British and others their shares of cod, saithe, haddock and so on.

> The CFP uses the concept of quotas to share out the fish catch among the member states. This is done according to the principle of 'relative stability': the share-out is based on the track records of each country's fishing practices . . . The EC's own scientists and those in the International Council for the Exploration of the Sea give annual estimates of the size of the stock of the most important species of fish; these figures are used to determine the Total Allowable Catch (TAC) for each species . . . The TACs are then subjected to debate and negotiation, and are shared out, usually after much wrangling and horse-trading . . . (Miller 1999: 213).

Not surprisingly, no one is ever satisfied with the allocations or with the ways restrictions are imposed. "All Britain's rights were signed away to the EEC. Lots of us didn't realize the long-term implications" said one informant. Fish quota cuts proposed by the EC for the year 2000, for example, provoked howls of outrage.

> Employing 21,000 people in Scotland alone, fishing industry sources have warned that jobs are in jeopardy because of the TAC cuts . . . "A lot of fishermen are going to go to the wall. I can't think of any other industry that would be expected to make such a sacrifice without any kind of solution or form of compensation". (Dr Ian Duncan, secretary of the Scottish Fishermen's Federation, quoted in *Fishing Monthly*, January 2000: 1)

Along with the CFP, fishermen widely resent the scientists who provide the basis for management decisions. They claim, among other things, that scientists pay no attention to the vast store of knowledge the fishermen possess and that they derive their data from abstract models, rather than real experience. "There is a credibility gap," said one producers' organization leader (*SFM*, February 1996: 16). While no one has yet to burn a fisheries biologist or an EU official in effigy, as we saw the Ferrydeners do to a fishcurer, it is clear that scientists and bureaucrats have now become "the enemy of the fisherman."

Fishermen's policy concerns are articulated through a number of interest-based associations. One of the main ones is the Scottish Fishermen's Federation, founded in 1973, just two years after the introduction of the Common Fisheries Policy. Members gather regularly in often contentious regional meetings where personalities and politics come to the fore. Some fishermen worry about the extent to which the industry has become politicized, perhaps, as one skipper suggested, because all the foreign competition was causing the Scottish fleet to turn inward against itself. "A proud industry like the fishing industry cannot be run simply on sound bites and back biting" (Sutherland 1998: 18). In 1990, this infighting became apparent when a sizable group of Scottish and English fishermen formed a breakaway group called the Fishermen's Association Ltd (FAL). They launched a campaign called "Save Britain's Fish" (SBF) to lobby for Britain's withdrawal from the Common Fisheries Policy, which would have entailed withdrawing from the EU itself. Their rhetoric depicted British participation as evidence of blind obstinacy in the face of obvious solutions that lie in the power of the nation state.

> For British fishermen, the very existence of their industry and way of life demands that Parliament repudiates the foolish surrender of this vital national interest to a foreign power. No politician had the right to surrender these immensely valuable natural resources, which rightly belong to the British people, according to international law. (http: 222.savebritfish.org.uk/solfsh.htm)

SBF has proved to be a source of contention among Scottish fishermen, as tough times make for hard lines and strong politics. Some fishermen's groups have been staunchly supportive, others wary at best. "At first, people just laughed," said a prominent political figure in the fishing industry. However, SBF could not be ignored. In 1995, the Scottish White Fish Producers' Association publicly broke ranks with SBF, creating considerable bitterness among erstwhile friends.

In addition, many members of the Scottish Fishermen's Federation felt that those leading the anti-CFP campaign were fanatics who were damaging the communal spirit and sense of common cause that had always characterized the greater fishing community. As with the blockade, there was also, I suspect, a concern with how SBF was affecting the fishermen's public image. Given their history of stigma and marginalization, and in particular their reputation for excess religious zeal, many fishermen feel that their representatives need to appear modern, thoughtful and thoroughly rational. By contrast, one of SBF's chief activists is widely known for his intense, evangelical rhetoric. One of my informants said of him that he "starts with the book of Revelations. He sees a seven-headed monster from Rome destroying Europe."

Many, nonetheless, remained in sympathy with the organization's goals. "I don't like the EU. I would vote for coming out. Then we could control our own fishing. Brussels has taken too much power. Our fishing minister should represent us. They're probably right, *but*, if it's politically impossible, why waste time? We need to be released from the CFP without leaving Europe."

The British government is also high on the fishermen's list of trouble-makers. In their eyes, the government does not pay the fishing industry enough attention or respect. "Fishing is just a cottage industry as far as the government's concerned," said one. Echoing this sentiment, *Scottish Fishing Monthly* regularly criticizes government policy as ineffectual or worse. Warning that growing numbers of skippers are leaving the industry, Hamish Morrison, chief executive of the Scottish Fishermen's Federation was quoted as saying:

> I can't think of any other industry which is so important for employment and wealth generation to be treated this way. If a few jobs are lost in the textile industry, then the Government does all kinds of things to help out, but fishing, it appears, is treated differently. (*Fishing Monthly*, September 1999: 5)

Morrison's claim that fishing is disproportionately disadvantaged in government policy may be debateable, but it is highly consistent with the fishers' belief that non-fishers are fundamentally unsympathetic to their needs. The conviction that fishermen are "treated differently" echoes years of perceived low status.

Hopes that the newly established Scottish Parliament would change the fishermen's standing were dealt something of a blow when it immediately agreed to a new set of fishing boundaries with England in 1999. According to members of the Scottish fleet, the new configuration substantially reduced their control of coastal waters, "effectively ceding over 5000 square miles of traditional Scottish waters to the control of English authorities" (*Fishing Monthly*, August 1999: 2). They "called upon the [newly devolved Scottish] government to admit it has made a serious blunder" (*Fishing Monthly*, July 1999: 4). The Scottish Fishermen's Federation also claimed angrily that its members were excluded from discussions. It is hard to know whether this boundary revision has any practical significance, but its symbolic importance is undeniable. From the fishermen's point of view, it is yet one more indication that no one takes their views seriously.

With their long history of marginalization, fishermen believed that only drastic action would make officials listen to their grievances. Doubtless with pertinent memories of the 1976 blockade in their minds, Scottish fishermen waged yet another protest action in April of 2001:

> The imposition of cod closures in the North Sea led to the biggest fishermen's protest in years. This culminated in an armada of 167 fishing vessels steaming dramatically up the River Forth in protest at a lack of cash from the Scottish Executive to allow boats forcibly displaced from the cod fishery to stay in port with financial assistance, rather than being forced to plunder immature haddock stocks . . . The industry won plaudits [but no cash] for being conscious of the need to safeguard their future. (*Fishing Monthly*, January 2002: 7)

The EU, the British government, and now the Scottish parliament may be the most common targets for the fishermen's wrath, but they are not the only ones. We have already seen that fisheries' scientists with their unpopular, low estimates of sustainable harvests are widely derided. Even greater scorn is reserved for environmentalist groups that, the fishermen claim, are less concerned with human beings than with the fate of the grey seals that eat fish right out of the nets. To mention Greenpeace invites instant rage. "Everyone's in sympathy with whales but the seals – *shite*. We never saw seals in the Firth of Forth. Now seals are eatin' cod. I reckon seals are catching more fish than the fishermen," said a Fife fisherman. *Fishing Monthly* agrees. Policies protecting seals are "a symbol of everything the green movement represents, and, it would seem, takes precedence over everything else, including the interests and livelihoods of fishermen and their families" (*Scottish Fishing Monthly*, July 1995). Hence, when the Scottish Fishermen's Federation met with World Wildlife Scotland to discuss common interests, *Fishing Monthly* called the event "historic." Hamish Morrison, chief executive of SFF, saw the meeting as an opportunity to improve the stereotype of fishermen as wasteful predators: in effect, to reduce stigma.

> Mr. Morrison said that families in rural areas of Scotland often had no option other than fishing, and it was important that negative images of the industry must change. On this line of argument, Mr. Morrison cited the government's belief that all fishermen were guilty of black fish landings . . . It is the perception in this country that fishermen are victims. Victims of a perception of guilt. It could be concluded from this that the government believe that the fishing industry is full of dangerous criminals. (*Scottish Fishing*, April 2000: 4)

The distribution and consumption sectors of the fishing economy are also held to blame for changing the fisher way of life. Changes are even coming to the fish market. The old-style fish auction, where buyers congregate in the early morning to haggle over the fish boxes spread out over the quay, may be on its way out now that some ports in Europe are moving toward electronic marketing. This means that the large buyers, like supermarkets, can pick and choose from catches all over the country. As this happens in Scotland, the boxes of blue-veined shrimp, toothy, monster-headed monkfish, and silvery whitefish may no longer be spread out like a slippery cornucopia, to be picked over by discriminating buyers. As one man told me:

> People don't move around the market floor. They can buy from different ports at the same time. In fact, with the big boats and their satellite communications, sometimes the fish are sold before they even get to port. This will mean the end of the fish auction.

Supermarket firms like Tesco also contract with specific boats to fish only for them. By such means, they acquire consumable fish through a vertically integrated commodity system that reaches from the net to the display case. Many Scottish fishermen are very uneasy about this, seeing these super-owners as impersonal, absentee landlords with no loyalty to any particular producer or locality. They set quality standards and price structures and "cut off boats that don't deliver."

An Eyemouth man summed it all up by saying that

> the problems of fishing include legislation, quotas, and prices, and there's not enough new blood. The scale of commoditization has grown and the fishermen don't like it. Fish sold by the ton instead of by the box give processors, distributors, and retailers a bigger profit margin and fishermen lose control at an earlier stage.

The same fishermen who complain about inadequate consumption, management systems, and Green activists, however, also agonize over the ever-growing imbalance between pursuer and prey. As more than one fisherman said to me: "There are too many fishermen chasing too few fish." They see themselves as one of the last remaining hunters in a post-industrial world and worry about what happens to the hunter when his prey disappears. What will they become?

The above comments from Hamish Morrison about negative government perceptions notwithstanding, some fishermen have, in fact, become criminals. Fishermen know how serious the ecological situation is, but they openly acknowledge that no boat can survive without breaking the rules. Some become adept at evading surveillance from the Fishery Officers (a feat that is getting increasingly difficult) and landing "black-fish," that is fish that are undersized or caught over quota. Not all blackfish have been specifically targeted for catching, but are, in fact, fish that would otherwise have to be discarded.

As we have seen, EU fisheries management policy imposes species quotas on each boat. Every year, a boat may take a certain amount of any given species, depending upon its individual track record, based upon the amount caught the previous year. Once the limit is reached, a boat caught landing that species is subject to a heavy fine. While, in theory, this should reduce pressure on vulnerable fish stocks, fishermen say that there is no way of avoiding what they call a "bycatch," that is, unwanted numbers or species that get caught in the net. Once hauled up from the ocean, the fish are dead. If they cannot be landed legally within the quota, they must be dumped overboard or sold illegally, as "blackfish." The fisherman may run these into a non-registered port, sometimes selling them directly to restaurants. I was told in one village that blackfish were routinely landed there, "but we don't talk about it." So, as many fishermen see it, the choice boils down to one of irrational waste versus much-needed income, of complying with rules set by scientists and policy makers versus living as modern smugglers. Many fishermen now regard themselves as outlaws and indeed, technically, many are. They are firmly caught between the devil and the deep blue sea.

In an example of the fishers' need to defend their reputations, one skipper rationalized blackfish landings in the face of criticisms from the Scottish Fish Merchants Federation. The SFMF had labeled fishermen's catching practices as "reckless": "All I can say . . . is you cannot make wine out of water, you cannot make the available quota spin out all year. If no one was landing black fish then everyone would been finished about July" (*Scottish Fishing Monthly*, January 1996: 16).

Such stressful choices are enough to drive some men away from fishing altogether. One skipper told me without embarrassment that his son had been forced to give up the fishing because his nerves could not take the constant pressure of choosing between flouting the regulations and dumping perfectly edible fish. "He felt like an outlaw . . . He had a breakdown."

In 1995 I interviewed a retired skipper from the village of Portsoy, on the Moray Firth. Sitting in the lounge beneath an oil portrait of his boat, he mused about what he saw as an inevitable conflict between attempts to manage fisheries and the innately unruly character of fishermen.

I went fishing just after the war. I stopped fishing in '84 when I was fifty-four. My son is a chartered accountant in Saudi Arabia. He was never going to go to sea, so we sold the boat and cut my commercial ties to fishing.

I used to love being a fisherman. There was something different in every haul. It was like gambling. The white fish was exciting.

Fishermen are loners. All fishermen cheat. We could teach the Spanish how to cheat. If I went out to sea now, I would catch above my limit. Conservation and fishermen dinna mix. A fisherman is a hunter and he's got to catch fish to keep up his position and do his job. The better fisherman he is, the more against regulations he is, because regulations takes everybody down to the same level. There's no good and bad skippers after that. At the end of the day, fishing is cash. It's bred into us that we're hunters and the more fish we catch the better we're dong our job. We seem to be never satisfied, aye [always] looking for something.

It may well be that the fisher hunter of today also sees himself as prey, thus entitled to use any means possible to ensure his own survival.[4]

In sum, the problems besetting fishermen today proliferate at a rate and on a scale that overwhelm the locally based producer. The odds are so heavily against the newcomer and the smaller entrepreneur that it is not surprising that the younger generation is less and less likely to see fishing as a viable future. Few young men now find fishing an attractive career, perceiving it as difficult, dangerous, and always a risky proposition. So every slight to their integrity, every aspersion that calls up memories of stigma and the persistence of marginality, hurts them all the more.

## Misery Has Company: The North Atlantic Fisheries Crisis

Scottish fishers are not suffering alone, of course. An emerging global crisis in the fisheries, of which the North Atlantic is but one part, gives them plenty of company. In *Plundering the Seas*, Canadian biologist Richard Berrill reports that "the picture is grim everywhere you look" (1997: 2). Writing primarily, as he puts it, "from the point of view of the fish" (Berrill 1997: ix), he acknowledges the impossibility of preserving both fishing communities and communities of fish:

Fishing communities from Indonesia and China to West Africa, Western Europe and North America are dying as fish stocks collapse and as high-tech commercial boats make small-scale fishing operations unprofitable. Around the world, 200 million people depend on fishing to make a living, and for many that living is at risk. (Berrill 1997: 2–3)

Thus, like their counterparts elsewhere, Scottish fishers are caught in a cauldron of problems that has been bubbling up for some years. A quick survey from Norway to Newfoundland reveals anxiety over stocks in decline as well as about the often draconian management measures imposed to deal with them. This process has been intensively scrutinized by biologists, economists, journalists and anthropologists, and most agree that the outlook is bleak (Berrill 1997; Blades 1995; Chantraine 1993; McGoodwin 1990; Warner 1983). Berrill (1997: 2) says simply that "We are obviously close to, and probably exceeding, the maximum global catch that is possible to sustain."

Official reactions to the crisis in various countries have been slow, often bumbling, and always controversial. Controversy is inevitable, of course, because any long-term measures one takes to insure the fisheries' future by conserving fish stocks hurt the short-term interests of the fishermen themselves, who must "pay off the bank loan," as Cilla Fisher sings in the song which opened this chapter. In 1992, for example, the Canadian government imposed a moratorium on the Grand Banks cod fisheries; in consequence, life in many Newfoundland outports has subsided into a jobless misery made worse with the consequent closing of fish processing plants (Blades 1995; Davis ). In 1993, the once highly successful Faroese fishing industry suffered a precipitous collapse in the face of declining catches and international quota restrictions (James 1995). In October of 1994, the New England Fisheries Management Council recommended that Georges Bank, a major fishing ground for New England and Canadian fishermen, "be closed to fishing for flounder, cod, haddock and any other stocks deemed to be depleted" (*Hartford Courant*, 27 October 1994: A7). A typical headline for the American industry's *National Fisherman* now reads, "More Pain Ahead For New England: the Groundfish Crisis Continues, Putting Fishing Communities From Maine to Alaska on Alert." The article warns that cod and haddock stocks are recovering far too slowly, despite "painful sacrifice" and that "everyone knows what that means. More regulations. More pain. More boats going out of business" (*National Fisherman* 1997, 77: 30). None of this, of course, emerged overnight.

Since the 1950s, boats from all over the industrialized world have converged in the rich offshore grounds of the North Atlantic, leading to intense pressure on a number of species. By the 1970s, fishing technology had become so efficient and the rewards to fishermen so great that many stocks were in an acute state of depletion, exhausted by the efforts of what Warner (1983: viii) has called "the ultimate fishing machines", those immense factory trawlers that virtually vacuum the sea bottom and process or freeze the fish on the spot. Not only can they catch immense quantities of fish, but they can do so for weeks or months on end.

> On a clear day or night, some areas of the Grand Banks [off Newfoundland] are like crowded floating cities, with concentrations of coursing trawlers flying the flags of Britain, Canada, France, Germany, Poland, Portugal, Spain, the United States, the Soviet Union, and other nations. (Andersen and Wadel 1972: 3–4)

Other factors besides over-fishing have contributed to the problem. Pollution and habitat destruction, for example, have damaged salt marsh fish breeding grounds along many coasts (Carson 1962; Teal 1969). Changes in water temperature have also been implicated in some places. In the North Sea, industrial fishing (for non-human consumption) wipes out species, such as sand eels, which feed the fish stocks. Regardless of the cause, the consequence for fishing people worldwide remains the same: a competitive environment that makes village or locally based fishing communities very hard, if not impossible, to sustain.

## Vignettes of Loss: Nostalgia and Anger

If I had to choose one conversational theme that predominated over all else in my years of fieldwork, it would be that of regret for these communities and the way of life the fisherfolk remember. Here, I present here a series of vignettes that illustrate this regret. These are not to be dismissed as merely expressions of nostalgia. As people reconstruct and perhaps romanticize their own past, they create a reality that guides and motivates them in the present. Nor do they do this alone. The sharing of memories is a profoundly social experience, creating and reinforcing bonds between individuals and groups. It may also become the basis for communal action and politics (Connerton 1989). For them, the recounting of memory also became an implicit critique of progress, which they generally saw as something that "happens" to their villages. For example, as we have seen for Ferrydeners and their response to the offshore oil base, the past became an interpretive guide for present action or inaction. What Boyarin (1994) argues regarding how the politics of memory is employed to shape the nation-state can apply equally well at the local or community level. We shall see in the following chapter on heritage and tourism that fisherfolk employ memory as a way of making claims upon the present.

During many of my encounters with the fisherfolk, people explicitly pointed out their unhappiness with those aspects of modern times relating to the quality of community life. They lamented the loss of the fishing industry that had sustained it. Sometimes a sadness pervaded their voices as they compared present times with those of their youth. At other times, the tone was one of resounding pride at what once had been.

## David and Mary, in Nairn

One evening in the summer of 1993, I sat in the house of an elderly couple, watching their videotaped copy of an old film called *The Drifters*. This powerful documentary, made by film maker John Greirson in 1928, chronicles the offshore fishing industry in Britain. My hosts had dubbed in folk singer Cilla Fisher's voice singing *Whaur Will We Gang*? so that we listened to her lament for the modern fisherman's dilemma as we watched grainy, black and white, oilskin-clad fishermen wrestle with the sea from slippery, windswept decks. Heroic hunters, they relentlessly pursued their prey despite fierce winds, high seas and exhausting work.

As we sat comfortably ensconced in our armchairs, enjoying our tea and biscuits, a small group of friends and neighbors commented knowledgeably on the scenes unfolding before us, comparing older with modern techniques and recalling their own days at sea. They saw no incongruity in listening to a modern song play against the old film for they recognized versions of their own experiences in the old pictures. Yet they did wonder what, if anything, there was left "to dae" for an industry they saw as teetering on the brink of collapse.

The house where we gathered was in Nairn, a substantial seaside holiday destination and market town about twelve miles east of Inverness, on the large inlet of sea known as the Moray Firth. More specifically, we were in a harborside district of Nairn called the Fishertown, which Anson described in 1930 as "a little world all by itself" (Anson 1974 [1930]: 224). Although the Fishertown has no obvious boundaries demarcating it from the rest of Nairn, its streets seem to close in on themselves and to wind the walker into ever-narrowing spaces. I had first met David at the Fishertown Museum, a crowded, one-room affair that one can enter for a small fee. Except for myself, all those they had invited to watch the film came from a fisher family and remembered the days when the water was full of working boats, instead of the tidy yachts that occupy it now. That was during the days before Nairn's harbor was called (with a curl of the lip) a *marina*. "We're not over the moon about the change. It's a' yachties noo. It would be nicer if it were fishing boats," said one resident of the fishertown.

## Bob, in Buckie

In 1995, when Bob asked me if I wanted a ride in the fish van going down to Fraserburgh from Buckie, I accepted with alacrity. Not because I expected a particularly comfortable ride in the cramped vehicle, but because it was a chance to see a town I had heard much about. It was also an opportunity to travel down the Moray coast with a man who had spent all his life in the fishing industry and who had accumulated a vast store of local knowledge and information.

Bob had first "gone to the fishing" in 1937 in a steam drifter with his father. Back then, he mused, people's lives were happier. "There was not the covetousness. We bore things together. Ye were mair dependent on God. The fishing community was together. If there was a bereavement, everyone was all in sympathy. It's no that way now. Everyone's in competition wi' each ither. Ah'm speakin' truthfully."

Bob left the fishing in 1962 because he had joined the Close Brethren, a Christian sect found along the northeast coast of Scotland. "Ye had to be home every night for meetin'." Moreover, the Brethren had strict rules about who could associate with whom. Members could not take meals with non-members. "Ye couldn't have an unbeliever in the boat." Though Bob eventually left the Brethren, he still valued piety and spoke approvingly of the old days when no fisherman would even think of setting sail on a Sunday. "They lived God-fearing lives. But nooadays it's a' changed."

As we bumped our way around the bends and turns of the coastal road, I pestered him with questions: what was the name of that hill? How big was that village? When had the fishing died out in that community? Bob answered all my queries in great detail and with many anecdotes: all of the questions, that is, that had to do with places on the seaward side of the van. For the landward side, he had little to say, unless it was about prominent features of the landscape that provided sighting points for men at sea.

It was not that Bob was completely unaware or ignorant of non-maritime landscapes and lives. Nor was he, and nor is any fisherman, despite dense local ties, merely a "local," that purely imaginary creature who walks only village streets and dwells only in the cozy 'face-to-face' community of kin and lifelong neighbors. Bob was, after all, a citizen of modern Scotland – a taxpayer, a consumer, and a television viewer. As a fisherman, he had also participated in a highly sophisticated, internationally articulated industry. But it was the sea and the coast that drew his attention that day, as every day, for they provided him with the sense of expertise, or cultural mastery, that marked him as teacher and me as student. It was his seaside perspective that he was anxious to share with me and to elucidate, for this above all was his domain. Bob's descriptions and explanations of the fishing industry – its history, technology, and social value – were more than his gracious acquiescence to a question and answer dialogue initiated by an outsider. For him, they were claims to ownership of cultural capital (Bourdieu 1984), assertions of authority and attempts to ensure that at least the memory of fisher culture would be preserved, despite what he saw as the industry's decline.

Bob's talk took us down the coast and also back through time. He had a lot to say about harbors, markets and even whole villages that had changed or disappeared. The sight of a tumble-down house, a boat-yard, an old shed or even a stretch of empty sea set off a jumble of anecdotes, recollections, stories and observations about the days when fishing and its ancillary activities, including net-making and mending, coopering (barrel-making), and fish gutting, packing and selling, occupied nearly all the men and women of the villages that lined the Moray Firth:

> At one time there were 400 drifters at Buckie. At one time there were 126 at Portknockie. Buckie once had one-fifth of the whole British fishing fleet. They did gutting here. In 1912, the herrin' fishing was very prosperous. Fishermen invested their money in houses. In 1913 there was 1163 drifters in frae Yarmouth. Five thousand women gutters, mostly from Scotland. There was 1700 coopers. In the 1930s, there was a slump, and then the drifters were commandeered for the war. After the war, there was real prosperity until the 1980s. But purse-netters replaced drift nets. They were far too efficient. They say this is advancement, but modernization finished the fishing.

## David and Jim, from Anstruther

Later that same year, I was farther down the coast in an area known as the East Neuk of Fife. I stood in a Tayport scrapyard with David and Jim, two older members of the Anstruther fishing community. David had fished for longer than Jim, who had gone into fisheries management some years previously. Both had agreed to show me around some old, derelict boats that held special significance for them. As North Atlantic fishermen generally do, they spoke of the boats as female and as individuals, telling me, for example, that "She's had a checkered career." They described each boat in loving, intimate detail: her length, type, engine and gear, who had owned her, where she had sailed. One of them had belonged to Jim in the 1960s. Another, decommissioned (scrapped) in the government's effort to reduce fishing capacity, had never even spent much time at sea. "That was the crime of the century." They held the government responsible for its wasted life.

These were not inanimate objects that David and Jim discussed, but living, breathing organisms with personalities and quirks. Looking both thoughtful and rather depressed, the men mourned each loss as they conducted their tour of the yard. In a very real sense, the boats had marked the eras of their lives. Even an old wheelhouse, rusting in the sun, sparked reminiscences. I did my best to follow the abundance of detail with which they re-enlivened the wrecks, but of course I could not. You need a lifetime in the fishing to appreciate the subtle differences between the way that the bow rakes on one boat as compared to another. They had been trained to it. In their generation, every fisherman worthy of respect was expected to have an encyclopedic knowledge of fishing vessels. After all, a boat was, in a sense, an exoskeleton or a carapace, an extension of the fisherman's body that must be understood and maintained to perfection. It had to be "right."

David remembered his early days as a young deckhand and the informal, but continuous, training he had received. "The skipper would say, 'what boat d'ye think that is?' I'd answer and he'd say, 'Ye're wrang,' and I'd say, 'Ah'm no'.' He'd say, 'we'll wager fifty cigarettes, then. The binoculars were never out of my hands.' Each nuance of design spoke not only of different possibilities for speed, stability and efficiency, but of where the boat was built, and by whom. Boats were either ruthlessly criticized or lavishly admired. A fisherman could tell the differences between boats that would appear indistinguishable to a stranger. He knew that a builder would introduce minor variations into each craft as a kind of trademark. "There was no such thing as a standard drifter. They're aye different in some respect."

On this day, David and Jim alternated between expressing their aesthetic appreciation of fishing technology and their rueful conviction that only men from their own generation could truly understand. The social fabric that had made such knowledge possible was long gone, they thought. The overall quality of modern crews, as well as the ethics of skippers, had irrevocably changed. "Fishermen used to be so intelligent because there were so many people with brains who never had a chance at education. Now, what young man wants the life?" Not many, they believed. And those who did, moreover, generally lacked the patience and foresight required to do the job right.

## Jeannie, in Anstruther

In my landlady's sitting room, I met Jeannie, the daughter of generations of fishers from the Fife village of St Monans. As she spoke, she recalled the hardships and hard work her parents had endured.

Mum was a Dyker [from Cellardyke, next to Anstruther]. She was at Watson's oilskin factory. The war was hard. The government took the boats. There was bombs dropped at Pittenweem [the neighboring village]. After the war [when the fishing revived], they started the summer drave [herring fishing] off Peterhead. Mum mended all the nets. There was a lot of jellyfish died on the nets and they caused allergies. There was bad hay fever. Had to get the nets ready after the men returned from Peterhead, because then they went off to Whitby. I remember mending winter herring nets in the kitchen, Mum mending till the small hours of the morning.

It was out and in for the fishermen every day for the winter herring. We had to see them off, no matter what time of day. We could see all the lights out on the Forth on a clear winter night. There was at least a dozen boats. All my Dad lived for was a garret full of gear. It was a happy life when Dad came home frae Yarmouth. He brought presents, a bicycle, a doll, and a wee sewing machine. My dad was lost at sea coming around the Wash along the Norfolk coast. A fisherman's funeral was held on a Sunday. The men walked behind the coffin, and the women stayed in the house. When someone died, they stopped the clocks till after the funeral and drew the blinds.

These were hard days, but in the glow of recollection, Jeannie also saw them as "golden." She kept repeating that "those were happy times" when people took care of each other. In her conversation there were repeated hints that she had come to regard herself as an orphaned spinster, alone and with no longer any clear role to play in life:

People keep to themselves more now. There's a change in the wee communities. There are so many outsiders, ye don't know who people are. People used to drop in and relatives used to come on weekends. Now they watch television. I suppose that's progress. When my mither died three years ago [a centenarian], I went along to the fisheries museum. I was searching for something, I didn't know quite what, but I didn't find it.

## Alex and Peggy, in Buckie

Alex and Peggy were among the oldest folks I met in Buckie. Married for 49 years, he came from Buckie and she from the Black Isle, up north in Cromarty. They have a daughter in California. When I visited them, I found their small house filled with warmth and the smells of her baking. Her chief delight in those days, now that she was frail with arthritis, was to produce a profusion of fruit scones and ginger biscuits from her diminutive kitchen. When I interviewed them, Alex did most of the talking, comparing what life was like when he started fishing in 1931 with the way things are now:

When I grew up, no one locked their doors. When our mothers sold fish inland, the neighbors looked after you. Now there's vandalism. My wife's hands got glued together after they put glue all over the door. Houses get burgled. You're afraid on the weekends.

After we talked, Alex showed me around the Seatown, the area where most of the fishers used to live. The houses were all jumbled together, with no streets or squares rationalizing the neighborhood. "You just built where you felt like it."

## David, in Anstruther

In the spring of 1999 I heard yet more expressions of loss. My husband, Brad, and I were in Scotland for a brief visit and had gone sailing along the Fife coast with David, a recently retired and well-off skipper who now went to sea exclusively in his yacht. "Everywhere I look, I see ghosts," David said, as he gazed toward shore. "This boat has never seen a fishing net." His yacht, clearly a sign of affluence, is also, ironically, a symbol of loss, for yachts now outnumber fishing boats in many harbors. Looking from sea to shore, Brad and I saw only little harbors, quays, and sand, and the back gardens of comfortable, modern houses whose picture windows overlooked the shore. David, however, knew the history of it all. Every old building, every turn of the coast held memories: over here, his mother had worked in the oilskin factory; over there, an uncle had kept his storage shed and aunts had mended nets; further along, he and his cousins had played on the rocks and gotten into trouble. They had also learned to recognize their fathers' boats as they came in at last with the hold full of fish – or not, as the case might be.

David's vivid memories make him proud. "You know, the modern history of fishing is only 100 years, and I've been at sea for nearly half of it." For him, the chronicles of Scottish fishing are fraught with personal significance. He sees himself poised in an unfolding story of hope and loss, a story in which he recollects, for example, that " I knew the skipper who built the last sailing boat around these parts. That was Jim Tarvit's wife's grandfather. He built it in St Monans in 1904. Someone in 1904 thought they could sail the rest of their life. It's no that way now."

Because it is not that way now, David spends much time trying to save as many memories as possible, in particular by working to enhance the collection of the local fisheries museum, but he has not entirely given up on the future. Active in fisheries politics, particularly through the Scottish Whitefish Producers Organization, he takes a keen interest in debates over pertinent EU policies, about which he has very strong – mostly negative – opinions. But he does not place all the blame on outsiders. He also criticizes the younger generation for lacking the frugality he and his fellow fishermen practiced daily. "Every penny was a prisoner," he says of his long years of thrift.

> Fishermen pay their tax one year in arrears. Young boys get the same pay as older men on the Scottish share system. But the young ones couldn't spend it quick enough on cars and drink and one year later the tax man cometh. They'd spent everything they'd got.

He also talks with pride of how his careful ways have led to comfortable circumstances. A favorite story is of the time that he and his wife spent a weekend in a posh hotel, a place that would never have admitted fishers in years past. Sometimes, he also counterposes his own rags to riches story with a larger "riches to rags" theme of the Scottish fishery that has outspent and outfished its capacity.

David has been fortunate. He had a very successful career and his son now skillfully skippers his boat, which is fitted out with the latest electronic navigational equipment and fishing gear. When David was 62 and his son was 21, David took him aside and said, "Right. This is my last trip. Now you're the skipper. I was scared, but I didn't want him to keep looking to me for advice. He's doing well, though. He's got what it takes. He's a shrewd skipper, very meticulous."

Yet David is well aware that such continuity is exceptional and he is rather doubtful about the future, feeling guilty that when his son took it over, the boat was already 18 years old. He thinks it unlikely that his son's son will be a fisherman too.

## Conclusion: Back to the Future

It can be said that the fishermen I got to know well looked at their time at sea as fraught with crisis. Of course, they engage in an inherently dangerous and risky occupation that keeps the prospects of death or financial ruin at the forefront of their minds. Risk itself represents a continuity in their experience. Fishing has never been, and probably never will be, safe. Catches will always be somewhat unreliable, the weather always treacherous. Thus it is not surprising that most of the (many) folk songs sung by them and about them take up the themes of peril and ruin.

However, there is also the social crisis engendered by ecological, national and extra-national policies that today preoccupies them at least as much. The social crisis reminds them of both stigma and marginality. Stigma, because they believe that outsiders still regard them as having nothing useful to say; marginality, because it threatens the entire social fabric of their lives. It suggests that they may go from being on the margin to being pushed right over the edge.

Today, fishermen find themselves buffeted by complex agendas and market forces so large in scale, so distant and so unresponsive to local concerns as to represent a real discontinuity in their experience. Moreover, and perhaps most painfully as reflected in the vignettes I presented, for the first time in their history, many fishermen's work is detaching them from the communities where they live and generating class divisions among them. As we saw in the chapter on Ferryden, equality has long been ideal-ized within the fisher communities. Their nostalgic recollections provide them with a vantage point from which to critique the conditions in which they now find themselves.

While the Ferrydeners knew that they were likely to be the last full generation of fisherfolk within the village, the fishermen I got to know over the course of a decade of visits to the Fife and Moray coasts described themselves as the last of their breed, period. However, even as they positioned themselves as emblems of the past, their activism within fishermen's organizations showed that they are not ready to consign that past to oblivion.

## Notes

1. These came about when Iceland, a country heavily dependent upon fishing, extended its jurisdiction over coastal waters, first to 4 miles and finally to 200 miles offshore, preventing foreign fishermen from any access to the rich cod stocks that were flourishing there. British fishermen were among those most significantly hurt by this prohibition (Berrill 1997).
2. For a different perspective on the Blockade, see Cohen 1987: 292–321.
3. Warner (1977), writing on the New England fishery reports hearing similar statements from men who made foreign competition "the chief conversational topic of every trip".
4. Miely (1984) discusses the relationship between a Calvinist upbringing and the emphasis upon entrepreneurship in the Fife fishing village of Pittenweem, arguing that skippers' drive to succeed is strongly motiv-ated by the need for independence.

# –6–

# Fisherfolk under Glass? Memory and the Heritage Wars

"Our Future Lies in Our Past"

Motto of the Buckie District Fishing Heritage Society

## Introduction

The last chapter explored the meaning of crisis for people in Scottish fishing communities by presenting their views on the challenges of industrial decline and the erosion of community life. Here I continue to probe themes of loss and response but now I relate these more directly to a wider politics of identity, memory and representation. I follow Boyarin in arguing that we must bring both space and time into our discussion. Boyarin's (1994: 2) claim that nation states are constituted through a "temporal politics of memory" applies to other kinds of imagined communities as well. In addition to the Scottish nation and their own villages, my informants inhabit a wider community of fisherfolk. This community has now been permeated by the burgeoning "heritage industry" (Hewison 1987), in which fisherpeople's social recollections become a contested resource.

This chapter will look at the ongoing dialogue between "outsiders," in this case tourists, tourism developers, and museum professionals, and the fisherfolk who seek to control how they are being represented. We shall see that this dialogue in many ways recapitulates those that fishers have had with other kinds of outsiders for many years. Now, as ever, the arguments fishers make about their own importance and emplacement in the world are influenced not only by local conditions and local history, but by national and even international forces.

First, let me briefly recapitulate the circumstances that have led Scottish fishers to this moment of engagement. As the foregoing chapters have detailed, the fisherfolk are heirs to a long oral and textual legacy of insecurity, an insecurity that stemmed not only from economic disadvantage but from fishing's problematic status as a stigmatized occupation. Beginning with the First World War, the industry went through a number of critical turns, falling, rising and falling again but, as an employer of men and women, ever shrinking. Many of its smaller sites were stranded: like Ferryden, these became fishing villages without boats or fish.

Market collapses, expensive technology, and most recently, overfishing and desperately complex regulatory systems have made fishing an industry whose motto today might be "the survival of the fattest." Only those with solid capital to invest remain commercially viable. Like small-scale farmers and the family farm in many parts of the world, small-scale fishermen and their local places are struggling to survive in the face of large, well-organized competition. Many fear that their way of life and their identity as fishers are doomed and will be forgotten, that their villages, as meaningful places, will be absorbed into anonymity. Hence their memories are now taking on an almost painful significance.

The memories I refer to are both social and individual, although it is hard to tell the difference. At the point where individuals share their recollections with others, their memories become part of a collective discourse about the past, a discourse filled both with argument and agreement. However, the fabric of remembrance in common that Connerton (1989: 17) imputes to village life has been stretched, and even torn. As he also notes (Connerton 1989: 3):

> to the extent that their memories of a society's past diverge, to that extent its members can share neither experiences nor assumptions. The effect is seen perhaps most obviously when communication across generations is impeded by different sets of memories . . . the memories of one generation locked irretrievably, as it were, in the brains and bodies of that generation.

As we saw in Chapter 5, the older fishermen who provided so much of my information about both past and present face a yawning generational divide. When they talk about young people, their voices are either critical or resigned. They are keenly aware that few sons and grandsons will follow in their footsteps and that few daughters and granddaughters will have any knowledge of the work that women once performed. In effect, then, these fishermen are bereft of heirs. Who will inherit their legacy of skills and sea lore? This is a profound question for men whose memories are so deeply embodied that it is said of some that when they pace up and down, they always turn at the length of a boat.

It would seem that their only recourse is to transform social memory into historical reconstruction, to use Connerton's (1989: 14) contrast. In

other words, they feel compelled to concretize and embody their memories in texts, collections, performances and displays – many of these
housed in museums and heritage centers – so that their own descendants,
as well as outside visitors, will not forget them. This is their defense
against the probability that the past that they embody will become a
"foreign country" to the future that is nipping at their toes (Lowenthal
1985). It is also a way of bequeathing something of value to a future that
looks increasingly bleak. (See Lowenthal 1992 on "The Death of the
Future".)

As fishers involve themselves in the production of heritage they risk
ensconcing themselves in essentialized images of tradition and folk
culture. However, as we shall see, they are not imprisoned there. Nor are
they retreating into some mirror-image still life. As the previous chapter
made clear, many fishers are politically engaged in defending the fishing
industry at regional, national and European levels. However, just as we
cannot reduce fishers' willingness to participate in public displays as a
capitulation to others' desires, neither can we explain their efforts to
control these displays simply as some homogenizing notion of "resistance" (Brown 1996). A more useful way of viewing fisher heritage is as
a negotiation: with local and regional authorities, with visitors, with
promoters of Scottish heritage, and most generally, with modernity itself.

At first glance, fishers' interests in memorializing their way of life
might seem to dovetail perfectly with the rising national focus upon
heritage productions, as well as with Scotland's dependence upon tourism.
But, of course, the reality is more complex. The object of this chapter is
to examine such articulations and to consider their consequences. I will
therefore begin by examining Scotland's current heritage boom, one that
itself is part of both an international preoccupation with reclaiming,
preserving and reconstituting the past as well as a national quest for
defining identity.

## Heritage and National Identity

Around the world, heritage is on many peoples' minds.[1] Lowenthal (1994:
43) even goes so far as to call it "a realm of well-nigh universal concern".
Modernity's ruptures and connections – from diaspora to digital technology – now make heritage desirable, particularly when it seems that
local objects, meanings and expressions are about to disappear. Comfortingly, heritage depictions seem at first glance to be the quintessence of the
particular and the local, a statement of uniqueness. In this sense, heritage

selectively appropriates the past for the present, providing a legacy of tradition, invented or otherwise. Located in labeled buildings, famous ruins, landscapes ("natural" heritage), endangered languages, historical displays and reenactments (Handler 1985), heritage is especially conspicuous in museums devoted to local or national cultural expression.

Fisher museums and heritage centers reflect this preoccupation with the particular and local. The museums have been established by local people seeking to preserve their memories for their own communities, although many tourists also visit them. Heritage centers are didactic displays created explicitly to sell cultural authenticity and Scottish culture to an internationally circulating audience. Ironically, however, people, goods and ideas now move so far and so quickly that few experiences can be tied solely to a particular site or a particular cultural milieu. Appadurai (1996: 4) characterizes the "global ethnoscape" as constructed of "diasporic public spheres" which make an isomorphic equation of people to place impossible. Gewertz and Errington's (1999: 102–19) account of a law-and-order rally held in Wewak, Papua New Guinea, epitomizes just how globalized a local experience can be: Christianity, feminism, crime, class, Coca-Cola and indigenous values were all present in a public discussion about domestic violence. Thus the particular, the local and even the national are caught up in cultural imageries that transcend place (Wilk 1995).

It has been a century since the heyday of "salvage anthropology," when ethnographers were frantically recording fast-eroding cultures, and collecting as many of their objects as possible (see Stocking 1992). Yet, our preoccupation with saving objects and memories, often out of context, persists not only unabated, but among a much larger, non-professional category of people – that is, cultural tourists (Wood and Deppen 1994). Heritage tourism requires that tourists and heritage producers share what Wilk (1995: 111) calls a "structure of common difference". To consume heritage, tourists must be committed to certain ideas, among them that: a) the past is valuable and endangered; b) culture can be embodied, captured, commodified and put on display; c) the past can be authentically represented, thus eliding the fact that "the past, as it is materially embodied in museums and heritage sites, is inescapably a product of the present which organizes it" (Bennett 1995: 129); and d) everyone can participate in and compete for heritage and its economic benefits. Patrick Wright comments that "this quasi-archaeological sense of the past as recoverable, talismanic bits and pieces is linked with a supposition which lies at the heart of contemporary tourism, that the past is really there to be visited" Wright 1985).

Some see this as a dangerous trend. Robert Hewison (1987), for example, regards the many heritage centers and museums of folk life that have blossomed in Britain as indicative of economic and cultural decay, a commodified tradition substituting for the real, productive work that once underpinned social life. Rosie (1992: 170) dourly seconds this for Scotland and calls heritage museums "reminders of our failure to hang on to the markets we once dominated". "Historical Valium," parodies Andrew Mellor (1991: 93). Christopher Harvie (1992: 94) worries that not only work, but even ownership of heritage productions, will be further alienated from Scotland and that "present developments will turn us into a 'rest and recreation' area, a theme park on a huge scale owned by trusts in Switzerland and the Cayman Islands . . ." To see Scotland becoming a theme park means not only that the images of Scottish peoples, industries and ways of life produced and seen in museums and visitor centers are inauthentic and essentializing, but also that the Scottish people must increasingly accept and adopt these images as real or at least relevant. The "tourist gaze" might disrupt a local culture that some see as inherently fragile (Greenwood 1989; Urry 1990).

According to McCrone, Morris and Kiely (1995: 1), who write about the way Scotland itself has become a "brand," heritage is a

> thoroughly modern concept . . . It has come to refer to a panoply of material and symbolic inheritances, some hardly older than the possessor. We have constructed heritage because we have a cultural need to so in our modern age.

Lowenthal (1998: 1) locates heritage practices further back in European history but agrees with McCrone et al. that the current popularity and democratization of heritage is something new, a "self-conscious creed . . . whose praise suffuses public discourse".

The ideological aspects emerge sharply when heritage is employed in the service of national identity. Lowenthal identifies heritage as a " chief focus of patriotism" (1998: xiii). Charles Tilly (1994: 251) points out that dominant populations within the new ethnically diverse states of nineteenth century Europe began to establish the stuff of heritage in order to reinforce their cultural supremacy. Thus arose "official languages, monuments, museums, schools, histories, ceremonies, iconographies, currencies, postage stamps, and a wide variety of other cultural forms".

Nineteenth-century romantic nationalists were powerfully attracted to notions of national character, or essence, that reductively tied culture to the land. In northern Europe, particularly in Scandinavia and the Netherlands, the national soul was believed to reside in the countryside and in nature, newly threatened by industrialization.

Profiling an open-air folk museum in Arnhem, Netherlands, *Architectural Digest* magazine (1999: 92) notes that at the beginning of the twentieth century, when

> a wave of nostalgia swept over Europe . . . The founders of this museum believed that what made them Dutch – the folk culture of farmers and fishermen and artisans of the countryside – would not survive industrialization and had to be preserved in order to save some part of themselves as well . . .

Lofgren (1987: 59) in his analysis of how members of the Swedish middle class used rural society to define their own boundaries, concurs and elaborates:

> As peasant culture was threatened by industrial development, the interest in the natural, indigenous people increased. Scholars and folklore collectors saw themselves as a rescue team picking their way through a landscape of cultural ruins, where scraps and survivals of traditional life-styles could still be found. Through their enthusiastic work they helped to construct the myth of a traditional and national peasant culture . . . what was genuinely Swedish.

One of Sweden's earliest folk museums, built in 1891 at Skansen, included

> reassembled farm buildings, a manor house, craft industries, a log church, stocks, whipping posts [with] guides dressed in folk costume, with strolling musicians and folk dancers re-enacting traditional customs. (Bennett 1988: 70)

As we shall see later in this chapter, fisher museums and displays have also been appropriated as part of an attempt to construct a modern Scottish identity.

All such identity discourses are contestable and contested. In Quebec, Handler shows us that we cannot divorce the local uses of folkloristic images and pursuits from larger agendas of nationalism and economic development. Quebecois farmers have long been the focus of folklorists interested in rural custom as well as those engaged in defining Quebec's character and true patrimony in terms of rural life. In response, rural people have begun to collaborate in reproducing folk life for visitors. Many, Handler (1988: 80) says, are now even "marketing themselves as farmers". However, doing so requires them to profess a lack of modern attitudes as well as of modern material culture and thus confines them even as it gives them a new source of revenue. Handler (1988: 56) calls this process "cultural objectification". Ironically, of course, this also provides a means for rural Quebecois to participate in modernity – perhaps the only means possible, given their precarious economic position.

Like Quebec, Scotland is what McCrone (1992) calls a "stateless nation". This continues to outlast the re-establishment of the Scottish Parliament in 1999. It is also home to competing discourses of identity, none of which has established a clear hegemony. Devolution has meant that many decisions can now be made closer to home, but Scotland still is part of the United Kingdom, still sends representatives to London and still has a limited voice within Europe. Questions of heritage remain central to an ongoing debate over the core elements of what it means to be Scottish, as they do for the Quebecois, although the Scots have been debating this issue far longer. The problem of defining Scotland or Scottish identity is perhaps not quite so complex as determining "what is a Jew?" (a question I heard asked frequently in my own very secular upbringing) but it may come close, particularly as the Scots have their own diaspora and many apparently long to return, if only for a visit (Kirshenblatt-Gimblett 1998). (I met a number of these during my fieldwork. Many were searching for genealogical information and I came to think of them as "kinship tourists." I will return to these later on.)

Some writers argue that concerns with national identity grow as border contexts shift. Walsh (1992: 177), for example, points to a new threat from

> the increasingly important role played by multinational corporations and capital, the development of supra-national organizations such as the EC, as well as the strengthening of certain regional identities, or micro-national-isms . . . In Britain especially, the loss of Empire and the erosion of the power of the landed classes, certainly since World War II, should be seen as reasons for the emergence of a national heritage industry.

Indeed, McCrone argues that Scotland's "sense of difference and identity has grown rather than diminished" (McCrone 1992: 3) since its Parliamentary Union with England in 1707. This is hardly surprising, because the political merger was never fully accepted, the institutional merger was never complete, and the economic merger was very uneven in its effects. Moreover, English attempts in the eighteenth century to repress certain elements of Highland culture, notably in language and dress, have never been forgotten. Many who do not support the Scottish National Party's independence agenda nonetheless assert a strong feeling of Scottishness.

But on what is this "sense of difference" from things English based? It is one thing to articulate a set of shared grievances but quite another to make a positive statement about national identity.

Like Alice's dreamquest for the ever-receding egg on the shelf, such definition seems to elude capture. Despite McCrone et al.'s (1998: 632) assertion that Scottish identity is "largely uncontentious and unproblematic", explaining what that identity consists of is anything but simple. What kind of shared difference can transcend Scotland's myriad internal divisions? Tom Nairn (1997: 185), essayist and gadfly to all political parties, says that Scottish storytelling reflects "a form of cultural nihilism" that magnifies internal differences to the exclusion of national coherence, creating "mountain ranges of peculiarity".

It is thus difficult to know where to gain a foothold. Scotland's population is not homogeneous, popular representations of bonny Highlanders to the contrary. Even language unites Scotland only up to a point. Most Scots understand "BBC" English perfectly well, but few of them speak it and those who do are likely to be regarded as anglicized in other ways, as well as middle class. Fewer than one per cent of the population are native Gaelic speakers, but Scots English has many versions, as any inhabitant of Fife, or Aberdeenshire could – and would – tell you. This persists despite the efforts of generations of schoolteachers to instill "proper English" in the *bairns* (Kay 1993). The differences are so manifold that even transcribers for the new Scottish Parliament are having to consult dictionaries to make sure they get things right (Gilchrist 1999: 13).

Harvie (1977: 14) attempts to scale the ranges of peculiarity with a more culturally inflected approach. He says that there are two Scotlands: not, as one might expect, the Lowlands and the Highlands, but the "achieving society and the defensive community", bringing Scotland's bourgeois industrial advances together with its putative inferiority complex, sometimes called "the Scottish cringe." The latter can be seen in any number of self-deprecating references to Scotland as "parochial" (Craig 1996: 11).

Michael Russell (1998: xiv), Chief Executive of the Scottish National Party, says that Scots tell many stories about themselves, just as modern Scotland is a nation that is constantly rediscovering and reinventing itself. Some of these stories become fixed in the stories others tell, while others are less likely to be taken up. Take, for example, the despairing urban realism of novels such as those in Ian Rankin's detective stories. His protagonist, John Rebus, sees only the seamy side of Edinburgh. Irvine Welsh's anomic *Trainspotting* (Welsh 1993), looks at the world through the eyes of adolescent drug users, but only in literary circles do these prevail against the romantic likes of M.C. Beaton's portrayals of hapless Highlanders, now immortalized in a series by the BBC. Turning to film, *Local Hero*, with its setting in a quaint and quirky seaside village that manages to avoid the impact of North Sea oil, is arguably the best known portrayal of modern Scotland. Then, of course, there is *Braveheart*, popular both in Scotland and abroad, a deification of William Wallace that McArthur (1998) accuses of playing into a Celticized Scottish xenophobia.

Most answers to the identity question come back in some way to the idea of a shared history, but even here, interpretations clash. Some would argue that Scotland is an internal Celtic colony of the British Empire (Hechter 1975); or that it is the site of nationalist aspirations born out of uneven development and political frustration (Nairn 1977). Few will agree on a single answer. Certainly not the historians. As Brown, Finlay and Lynch (1998: 1) say about such a project, "it is necessary to confront a variety of Scotlands thrown up by the different ways in which images of Scotland and Scottishness have been created and recreated in the past."

In fact, it is not necessary to agree on the answer. The absence of unanimity does not belie the importance of the idea that Scotland exists. It is just that, like any heterogeneous society, "Scotland" includes too many subjectivities ever to be accounted for in any single descriptive scheme.

Nonetheless, the pursuit of Scottishness has occupied many people. Edwin Muir's travels through the country in the 1930s led him to describe Scotland as "a confusing conglomeration" (Muir 1935: 2). David Daiches (1975), Edinburgh University literature professor and the son of a rabbi, describes himself as caught up in the interplay of two identities. And well he might: J&B Scotch attempts to capitalize on Jewish Scottishness with an advertisement showing a kilted, bearded, yarmulke-wearing and bespectacled man blowing a shofar. It proclaims,

> Zayde wore kilts! Although Jews have a tradition of maintaining their cultural heritage, they also have the reputation of becoming an integral part of the community they live in. And Scotland is no exception . . . No matter where your friends or guests come from, serve them J&B to make them feel at home."

Angus Calder (1994: 52), cultural critic, suggests that

> A Scot is someone living in the area which comes under Scots law, so long as that person also supports Scottish athletes against those of other countries or identifies strongly with some other aspect of Scottish culture – our folk-music, say.

This leaves Scottishness wide open. By that definition, I am a Scot when in Scotland, after all.

Given such debates, how do purveyors of Scottish heritage decide which face of Scotland to project? The answer to this lies in what sells. Nairn (1977) reviles "that vast monster of Tartan kitsch" that stands for Scotland in all too many venues. Perhaps the best known example of this is that dreadful musical, *Brigadoon*, which elevates Highland life to a dream-like Utopia. By the time its American hero returns to that magical, once-in-a-century Highland village to rejoin his true love, the audience is greatly relieved, having wondered why it took him so long to recognize the obvious advantages of life among the jolly, embracing, tartan-wearing denizens of the glen. Not surprisingly, *Brigadoon* was not even filmed in Scotland, Hollywood "having found nowhere in Scotland that looked like Scotland" (Bruce 1996: 39). This is a problem that won't go away: much of *Braveheart* was filmed in Ireland.

Scottish tourism at all socioeconomic levels is best known for such Highland-inspired imagery, accompanied by some highly inventive heritage promotions aimed largely at North Americans (Ray 2001). Tartanry sells well. Anyone who passes through a Scottish airport or who ventures into one of Edinburgh's Princes Street shops can hardly fail to miss the plethora of plaids, as well as the ubiquity of clan references. For the many North Americans who wish to claim actual Scottish descent, a bevy of willing genealogists is ready to help them discover a Highland connection. Some of this Highlands obsession can be laid at the door of Sir Walter Scott and other early nineteenth century romantics (Bruce 1996: 9; Cannizzo 1999; MacDonald 1997; McCrone et al. 1995; Nadel-Klein 1997; Trevor-Roper 1983; Withers 1992). Even before Scott, however, the Highlands, with its wild scenery and Gaelic-speaking people, had become a destination for travelers in search of an exotic "other" within Britain (Chapman 1992; MacDonald 1997; Urry 1990, 1995).

Such images both transcend and are refracted by class. Visions of the country as a vast, untenanted "huntin', shootin', fishin'" estate dominate the elite market, though, as Wightman tells us, such estates are a relatively recent phenomenon (1997: 171). Upmarket hotels and resorts drape tartan fabric everywhere and keep their male employees kilted. *Vogue* magazine recently touted a stay at Cawdor Castle as an education for those still unsure of what Scotland is really all about (August 2001: 142). Exclusive, private resorts, such as Ackergill Tower in Caithness, or Skibo Castle in Sutherland (once owned by Andrew Carnegie), offer – along with haggis, bagpipes and deferential servants – such exquisite amenities as falconry demonstrations or archery lessons – that is, for those able to afford the facility's astonishing membership fees. In the case of Skibo, one can also hire the castle for a wedding, as Madonna recently showed the world.

The heritage on offer here is little more than a set of tartan-draped props arrayed upon a costly stage set. It is doubtful that most of its consumers care all that much about it as long as the golf, the salmon fishing and the food are first rate. The inequities and brutalities of Scotland's history, of course, receive no mention at all. Skibo sits almost under the shadow of a statue of the Duke of Sutherland, infamous for his role in the Clearances. "Cleared estates have come to represent landscape in Scotland just as soldiers in kilts inform our image of what it is to be a Scot," say McCrone et al. (1995: 6), though few tourists have any clue about what the Clearances were, or that the land was once more densely populated (McCarthy 1998).[2]

Alluring as these upscale venues may be, their consumers belong to a select group and visit a small number of places. The money they spend is concentrated. Marketers must construct attractive niches to draw the widest possible variety of visitors to the widest possible variety of sites. In effect, they must both exploit and combat the emphasis upon the Highlands. One strategy has been to emphasize Scotland's strong international connections. Edinburgh's new Museum of Scotland proclaims that its mission is to represent Scotland to the world. Its exhibits highlight foreign – particularly transatlantic – connections established through trade and technology. These explicitly appeal to members of the aforementioned Scottish diaspora: those North American, Canadian, Australian, and South African expatriates and their descendants. Many celebrate their Scottish roots while at home through Highland festivals complete with bagpipes, haggis, and caber-tossing (Ray 2001). At Spanish Bay golf resort, in California, bagpipes wail every night at dusk, presumably to delude the upscale patrons into thinking that, by playing golf, they are somehow "at home" in Scotland. The Scottish Tourist Board (STB), created in 1969, is not shy about exploiting this sense of community, however imagined it might be.

The trick is not only to lure these people to Scotland for their holidays, but to disperse them around the country. While tartanry brings visitors to Edinburgh as well as to battlefields and castles in the Highlands, vast sections of the country are left alone until they can transform their failing industries into attractive tourist locations. The STB is one of the key players here. Its official mission is to "promote Scotland at home and abroad as a tourism destination . . . [and to] develop tourism outwith the main tourism areas" (Scottish Tourist Board 1998).

Examining some STB literature, McCrone, Morris and Kiely (1995: 85) cite a consultant's report that requires heritage sites to have "core elements which are *intrinsic to* Scotland in some significant way".

Properties preserved by the National Trust for Scotland must also exemplify this. The Trust's magazine, *Heritage Scotland* (1990), announces that "the purpose of the Trust is to serve the nation as a cabinet into which it can put some of its valuable things where they will be perfectly safe for all time and where they can be seen and enjoyed by everybody". Highland battlefields, stately homes, archaeological sites – preferably Pictish – and rural environments all come under the Trust's domain. However, other Lowland venues must be more creative. Small wonder that there has been an ever-growing array of museums. In fact, museums and heritage centers are one of the few growth industries left in recession-battered Scotland. Since the early 1980s, the number of museums in Britain has more than doubled, and "the Scottish Museums Council gives Scotland more museums per head than any other part of the United Kingdom" (Rosie 1992: 159).

Now that I have established the broad context of Scotland's interest in promoting heritage, it is time to take a closer, ethnographically informed look at the ways fisher heritage articulates with this endeavor. This also returns us to the people I have come to know over the past two decades, the people whose lives are now being woven into the heritage fabric.

## Heritage Trails

Tourism is now one of Scotland's largest industries in terms of employment. A 1997 pamphlet from the Scottish Tourist Board tells us that "Over 13 million tourists took overnight trips and spent nearly £2.7 billion, supporting around 8% of all employment." Visits to castles, monuments and churches emerge as the favorite activity for overseas visitors (83 per cent), while museums, galleries and heritage centres draw 58 per cent. Heritage is clearly a lynch-pin for the tourist economy. Of course, the vagaries of Scottish weather tend to encourage indoor events for all but the most hardy souls.

Tourists can now seek heritage by following a designated trail, an itinerary designed by the Scottish Tourist Board to "sell places" (Kearns and Philo 1993). As targets of what Gold and Gold call "formal place promotion" (1995: 22), tourists must be convinced of the value of a cultural "experience" (Rojek and Urry 1997). Travelers' imaginations are lured down particular paths and pasts to the "stories" of whisky, weaving, mining or fishing. These are presented as examples of Scottish industry and culture. A Trail encodes as many meanings and purposes as the varied agendas of those who travel or reside along it(Rojek and Urry 1997). These include casual Scottish, English, or overseas tourists who just want something different from the mainstream tourist experience, as well as returning members of the diaspora looking to discover and reclaim family heritage.

The Fishing Heritage Trail extends from the Shetlands to the Borders. Its 10 regional sub-sections encompass 43 communities designated as "major attractions." These range from the very large, like the port of Aberdeen, to the very small, like the bird-watching mecca of the St Cyrus cliffs. Despite this and other differences among them, however, Trail advertisements impose a narrative uniformity on Trail sites. These reinforce the perception that most Scottish fishing villages are fundamentally the same. Thus the local becomes subsumed as a demonstration of the general, as Urry has said. Crail village, in the East Neuk of Fife, for example, becomes a sign of "the Scottish fishing industry" (Urry 1995: 133). On the other hand, some distinctions must be played up to avoid the "if you've seen one fishing village, you've seen them all" dilemma of marketing locality.

Therefore, tourist literature also highlights a particular feature for each site – marked sights, in MacCannell's (1989) usage. These include a seventh-century missionary's cave in Pittenweem, for example, a notable church, or even, as in the case of Eyemouth, the horrendous disaster of the 1889 storm that I referred to in the previous chapter. To lure visitors along the path, promotional brochures and advertisements emphasize the authentic, the secret, the mysterious and the hidden, as well as the idea of age-old continuity. Consider two examples from different brochures:

> When you take Scotland's Fishing Heritage Trail, you're setting off on a journey into the past. Men have fished from this rugged coastline since the end of the Ice Age; today fishing remains man's last great hunting activity. It still offers the thrill of the chase, the fascination of the sea and sailing – and it has brought about a particular way of life, with its own customs, speech, dress, festivals and superstitions.
>
> North East Scotland's Coastal Trail offers a maritime adventure, a journey of nearly 200 miles . . . By way of lonely sandy shores, cliffs and shingle tidelines, past hidden fishing villages tucked in coves and bays . . .

Such language rightly arouses suspicions of manipulation and exoticism. The second advertisement, in particular, has one wondering whether some of these fishing villages, like Brigadoon, might even be enchanted. This idea can be successfully purveyed in part because many coastal locations appear to be isolated, like the villages of so-called primitives, in a "land that time forgot" sort of way. Of course, as MacCannell (1992:

285) points out, this is an impossible position to sustain, given the inter-connectedness of all sites in the postmodern world, as well as the mundane structures of the modern fishing industry. However, mythmaking under-lies all tourist sites, which are distinguished as such by their "natural, historical or cultural extraordinariness" (Rojek 1997: 52).

Promotional statements also refer to the enduring, essential values of fishing people as well as to their colorful beliefs and customs:

> Scotland's fishing industry has undergone dramatic changes in the course of its history: it has experienced heady booms and gloomy slumps. It has become even more complex in its technology, ever more demanding in its calls on capital and in its need to respond to market forces, to catching quotas, and to changing types of fishery. But the basic skills of the industry – the resilience, seamanship and judgement of the individual fisherman – remain the constant factor . . . This is part of a broader truth about fishing communities . . . The sense of continuity is strong and the past lessons learnt are handed down from father to son, mother to daughter. This, as much as any of the features you may visit on the trail, is the true wealth of Scotland's Fishing Heritage.

The "broader truth" alluded to here says that fishing villagers can tran-scend hardship and adapt to anything life can throw at them. Economically and socially marginalized sites are sanitized for tourist consumption. Ironically, these may be the ones that are most picturesque. Their very failure to be competitive has protected their architecture, roads, quaint houses and stone-built harbors from destruction in the name of progress. This enables heritage displays to direct tourists' eyes towards those emblems of the past that fit the model of "industrial heritage."

> In focusing on industrial heritage, it was decided at the outset to concentrate on industrial sites and buildings which are no longer in production . . . work-places (i.e. industries in production which are open to the public) were excluded . . . ("Industrial Heritage and Tourism in Scotland: a Review" 1996: 6)

Many active fishing communities thus find themselves in an awkward, painful but sometimes even humorous position, when they are represented both as obsolete and as enduring. Rosie sees this problem exemplified by the case of the North Carr Lightship, once moored as a floating museum in Anstruther Harbor, where "the past has banished the present" (Rosie 1992: 158):

> The plight of the North Carr seems to encapsulate the conundrum presented by Museumry and what has come to called the heritage industry. Important

artefacts should be, perhaps must be, preserved for posterity. But the loss of use and purpose can be painful to see. And the process can render them as irrelevant as the North Carr's blind and empty light tower. And the waxwork "crew" will never replace the squads of ex-trawler hands and Caithness fishermen who used to man the ship.

Overall, the Trail projects a halcyon vision of fisher life. For good or ill, the history of stigma and poverty has been erased. Danger is admitted because there is no getting around it. Besides, it adds to the romance. So visitors can experience a vicarious nostalgia and even a sense of awe, untroubled by politicized flashbacks to destitution, ostracism, or anger. Ignorance, as they say, is bliss, or in this case, romance. The Trail reveals no ruptures, no disturbances. And tourists seldom ask about what is not there.

*Wives of the Fishermen*, Angela Huth's novel about fishermen's wives in the East Neuk of Fife, depicts such visitors and their illusions rather bitingly, in tones that echo film maker Dennis O'Rourke's representation in *Cannibal Tours* (1987). This documentary offers a scathing indictment of how tourists construct their own version of reality in Papua New Guinea, unaware of local people's needs, problems, or, most especially, of their views about the tourists themselves. Like O'Rourke, Huth sees tourists as unthinking consumers:

Abroath Street, once only known for the poverty within its thick-stoned houses, was by now a generally smarter place . . . roofs were patched, window frames gloss-painted, the wood of old front doors turned yellow and red and blue. Strangers with cameras, in clothes to match the front doors, were often to be found wandering down the street these days – their eyes more dulled than amazed by the sight of what one of them explained to Myrtle was surely "living history". (Huth 1998: 32)

Not all fishing communities suffer from such indignities, though this absence may be a burden as well as a blessing. Like Ferryden, with its offshore oil base, places now too far removed from the picturesque because of modern developments have been excised from the Trail. Because they are largely spared the tourist gaze, they lack the economic advantages that visitors may bring, as well as the public recognition that comes with being a heritage site. They are twice cut off – first from their fishing past and now from their heritage future.

Of course, putting such displays together takes considerable planning and coordination, not all of which can be laid at the door of the Scottish Tourist Board. The list of parties involved includes public agencies, private firms and individual entrepreneurs. Politicians also become involved in the act, from local councillors to Members of Parliament, Members of the European Parliament, and, since 1999, Members of the Scottish Parliament. In my more recent fieldwork visits, I worked closely with members of fishing communities who participated in heritage production, examining how their views articulated with those of museum professionals. To begin exploring these articulations,, I will now go to the East Neuk of Fife, where tourists, museum curators, heritage seekers and fisherfolk interact on a daily basis.

## A Stop Along the Trail: The East Neuk of Fife

People like to sit in Anstruther and believe they're in a fishing village. (A fisher informant)

The 15-mile stretch of coast along the Firth of Forth known as the East Neuk of Fife is widely regarded as one of Scotland's more picturesque spots and "is Scotland's only designated Maritime Heritage Area" (East Neuk: Building a Maritime Adventure). Visitors are welcomed by a road sign, courtesy of East Neuk Company Limited, bearing a picture of the iconic fisher lass, whom we met in Chapter 3, with her striped petticoat, knotted head scarf and creel. A stop into any newsagent's shop in one of the East Neuk's villages and towns – Largo, Elie, St Monans, Pittenweem, Anstruther, Cellardyke and Crail – reveals numerous flyers, also decorated with the fisher lass logo, that similarly encourage visitors to view the area in static, ahistorical terms, as a living "time-capsule":

Each village retains its own individual characteristics virtually immune from the passage of time. Small, white-washed buildings with red pantile roofs crowd into small winding streets. The streets lead to secluded little harbors containing a profusion of ropes, nets, creels, and boxes: testimony to the existence of today's small East Neuk "fleet". It is little wonder that these towns are among the most photographed areas of Scotland.

Alongside these flyers are the ubiquitous little pamphlets about local history and folklore. "What to see in St Monans: a guided walk" is such a one. With scant references to modern times, its effect is to convince the reader that the twentieth century has been largely irrelevant to this part of the East Neuk (Martin 1991).

The people of Fife are used to the visitors who have appeared along the coast with greater regularity than the herring for well over a hundred years.

After all, Thomas Cook, father of mass tourism, introduced his first excursion tours to Scotland in 1846. Other entrepreneurs were quick to follow suit. Durie and Ingram (1994) tell us that George Washington Wilson, a professional photographer of the late nineteenth century, set out to sell pictures to "the growing tourist market in Scotland". While the increasingly popular sport of links golf in nearby St Andrews was one of Wilson's chief subjects, he also did many studies of fishing, including boats in the harbor and fishwives on the quay.

But, as a tourism worker from the Borders fishertown of Eyemouth (site of yet another fisher museum) said to me, "the bucket-and-spade" days of beach-lolling are gone. Visitors now want a more varied itinerary. In 1989, the tourist industry launched the "East Neuk of Fife Maritime Project," described as

> a partnership composed of seven national, local authority and voluntary sector bodies . . . the Scottish Development Agency, North East Fife District Council, Fife Regional Council, St Andrews and North east Fife Tourist Board, the Scottish Tourist Board, the Scottish Fisheries Museums Trust and the East Neuk Merchants and Traders Association.

The partnership, managed by East Neuk Ltd, was explicit about exploiting heritage as a substitute for the once-thriving fishing industry:

> As the area possesses a distinct identity deriving from its former dependence upon fishing activities, the tourist marketing concept utilises this "maritime heritage" in order to promote the area as a specific "product" within the increasingly segmented Scottish and UK holiday markets.

The prospect of being turned into a holiday "product" does not sit well with every resident of the East Neuk. Some, indeed, are greatly annoyed. Take those in Pittenweem, for example. Pittenweem's narrow roads and wynds curve down from the top of a steep hill to meet the harbor. This is protected from storms by a wall of concrete and stone and is bounded by the fish market, various shops and offices, and a cluster of scrubbed white cottages. Described as "The pretty village where fishing is still the main way of life" (Fife 93), Pittenweem, like several other villages in Fife's East Neuk, has so much heritage value that the National Trust for Scotland has restored a number of its historic houses. Strangers cluster on the quay to photograph or sketch the brightly painted fishing boats. A summer colony of people from other parts of Scotland and England occupies many of the old houses.

Even academics have been seduced by Pittenweem. An archeological survey of Pittenweem, written in 1981 and sponsored by the University of Glasgow, is prefaced in florid, even gushing prose:

> There is something touching in the sight of such old towns as Pittenweem, Anstruther or Crail left as they were two hundred years ago, as if the spirit of progress had overlooked them – not unlike old maiden ladies shut up in their garrets, unwilling to forget the days of their early beauty, although the bloom has faded long ago – still able to boast of their royal degree, and ever thinking to themselves what might have been were it not for their more fortunate rivals Dundee and Glasgow, and even Kirkcaldy, luring the young men away. (Simson and Stevenson 1981)

For all its prettiness, however, Pittenweem has another, more mundane face. Its port sustains what is left of the Fife fishing fleet. Its new fish market is built to European Community standards of hygiene; directly across the road sits the office of the Fisherman's Mutual Association. The harbor wall where tourists wander is also the work site for fishermen unloading boats and making repairs. In other words, the green and orange tangles of net and rope that are scattered about are not stage effects. However, tourist literature does not reveal that Pittenweem is struggling, along with the rest of Scotland's smaller fishing communities, to maintain a foothold in the fishing industry.

Nor will the visitor hear about the conflicts that inhere in relying upon the picturesque. A harbor-front shop-owner told me, with great scorn in his voice, about a proposal to re-cobble the now smoothly-paved harbor area in order to make the place look more old fashioned and quaint. Slippery and uneven, cobblestones are not an ideal work surface. The fishermen who mend their nets there and climb in and out of boats each day were outraged. "Pittenweem is a working port; we don't want it turned into a marina," one said. The cobble proposal reveals that power issues surround heritage representations. As Urry (1995: 27) says, heritage claims are "socially organised memories that are invoked as authoritative sources of being able to speak a place".

I heard fishers voice similar sentiments voiced at Anstruther:

> Anster has changed for the worst. For example, if a Pittenweem boat has a torn net, there's very few places in Anster you could haul it in and mend it. This *promenade* here [said with derision] . . . we used to mend our nets, had room to spread them out. Not now. You try to do repairs here – it's all for pleasure boats. They're trying to transform a beautiful working village into a tourist trap.

Fisherfolk under Glass

The Anstruther and the Pittenweem fishermen are finding that their authority is slipping away as others attempt to "speak" their place. The owner of a shoreside pub acknowledged that tourism boosted his business, particularly when times were slow for the fishermen. He also owned that tourists provide some entertainment value for local people: "Fishermen like to have tourists come into the bar so they can tell them yarns." Both Brody (1975) and Puijk (1989), writing about rural Ireland and northern Norway, respectively, have also noted that for some people in particularly remote regions, a seasonal influx of strangers is, on balance, a welcome diversion.

On the other hand, he said, "we don't want to be like Anstruther" (where tourists are truly thick on the ground, only a mile away). In other words, in limited numbers tourists were acceptable, but no one wanted them to dominate village life. Nor was the distinction between "kinship tourists" or expatriates seeking their roots, and other, less focused strangers, a factor in their local attitudes. As Pedregal (1996: 59) notes for a southern Spanish community, "as the number of tourists progressively increases, tourists cease to be individuals and become stereotypes".

Anstruther in summer is indeed a busy place. Pedestrians overflow the sidewalks. Mothers with babies in prams and elderly ladies in pastel raincoats doing their shopping must compete for space with visitors who peer into shop windows and snap photographs. Teenage girls with plucked eyebrows and jet black hair totter along on gigantic platform heels. Brash-voiced boys slouch along behind them, navigating the shoals of sticky-faced children bearing ice cream cones and sweets. All are blown together by the sharp winds off the Forth. It is a relief finally to push through the Fisheries Museum's polished wooden door and enter its shadowy, quiet world.

## Power and the Museum World in Anstruther

Every fisherman is a wee bit prood o' the museum (A member of the Museum Boat Club)

The Scottish Fisheries Museum is one of Anstruther's chief attractions. Established in 1967, it claims to represent the entire Scottish fishing industry from all around the coast. It is a complex place that embodies all the dilemmas of heritage. Part "cabinet of curiosity," with archaeological relics and miscellaneous objects relating to seafaring; part art exhibit with portraits of fishermen and women wrought in oils and watercolors; part archive, with an enormous collection of photographs, tapes and documents; part demonstration of industrial progress, with its linear succession of exhibits routing the visitor from past to present; part instantiation of local identity; and part heritage discourse: the museum is all this and more. (See Walsh 1992.)

When I first visited it in the early 1970s, it was merely a couple of rooms with a jumble of local artifacts, little funding, and less renown. Today, the museum has joined the list of National Heritage Sites, competes successfully for money from the EU and the Scottish Museums Council and has expanded into several adjacent structures. It is almost fully wheelchair accessible and has received public honors, including "a Civic Trust Award, an Architectural Heritage Year Award and, in 1976, the Museum of the Year Award for Scotland" (Hume and Storer 1997: 109). The Scottish Tourist Board now places the Museum among the top 20 industrial heritage sites in terms of visitor numbers. In the early 1990s, these averaged around 30,000 per year and come from all over the world, including Japan.

After paying a small admission fee, the visitor is guided from the shop to an inner courtyard where a few upturned boats amid piles of nets lie about on the cobblestones. Then one makes a choice: in through the main door or up a side stair to a special exhibit on domestic life known as the Fisherman's Cottage. If one chooses the former, the route is straight-forward, leading from prehistory and marine biology through the various technological eras: sail, steam and diesel power. Along the way are displays on whaling, fish processing and navigation, among others.

Climbing the stair to the cottage, one finds a room filled with "good" furniture and fancy ornaments, including a locally made grandfather clock, a Japanese lacquered box, and a harmonium that was built in Canada. Some rather scruffy-looking mannequins represent a small nuclear family. A box bed sits against one wall. The whole exhibit is staid and idealized, conveying fishers in their "Sunday best," and affluent fishers, at that. In this sense, it contrasts strikingly with a domestic exhibit in the fisher museum at Arbroath, up the coast. There, a harried woman is attempting to cook a meal while a baby cries and a cat, perpetually suspended in the act of filching a fish, meows plaintively (sound effects courtesy of a repeating tape).

I visited the cottage one day with David, whom we met in the previous chapter. It was a fine summer day and he entered wearing a polo shirt and sunglasses. These seemed out of place in the chilly half-light of the cottage, but as he spoke, he made the place his own. The space had, in fact, once belonged to him. He had used it to store gear and as a work area for the two women he employed to mend nets. Even a basket that stood outside the door had once been his. As we surveyed the room's contents, he reminisced about domestic details. He told me, for example, that the biscuits on the table were ships' biscuits called "hardies" because they would last for weeks. He also recalled the fisherwomen's passion for cleanliness and how each would scrub her section of the pavement all along the village of Cellardyke, where "all the Anster fishermen lived." "The worst thing that could happen to you in Cellardyke was to be 'spoken aboot.' If you didn't keep clean you would be 'spoken aboot.'" He recalled his mother boiling clothes and then pounding them in an old, modified herring barrel. Many objects provoked him to say, "that could have come out of my granny's hoose . . . I remember my mother's mother before she died – she lived in Cellardyke – we're only 50 years removed from being pretty primitive."

David had done such an effective job of making me see the museum though his eyes, that I found myself upset when others failed to appreciate it. Thus it was that, while browsing in the Anstruther "fisherman's cottage" one day, I experienced one of those moments when the ethnographer realizes how close she has come to her informant's point of view. I was showing some American visitors around the exhibit and I asked them if they had seen any of the other fishery museums. They had not. When I told them that this was the biggest one, a woman said with satisfaction, "Well, that's nice, we've hit the biggest then," and hurried away down the stair. It was not, perhaps, as egregious a remark as the famous, "if this is Tuesday, it must be Belgium," the kind of comment often associated with American travelers. Nonetheless, I was glad none of my fisher friends, and particularly David, were around to hear this casual dismissal of their efforts.

Such "ugly Americans" stand in sharp contrast to those who consider themselves part of the Scottish fisherfolk diaspora. These are the kinship tourists to whom I referred earlier. Looking for heritage of a different sort, they search for recognizable faces among the museum's many photographs; some even comb patiently through the archives for details about their ancestors and how they lived.[3] These seekers tend to tour the coast. I once overheard a visitor to the tiny fisher museum in Nairn say to his child, "Look at that photo. There's granny, baiting the lines." A museum volunteer commented on them as "exiles," saying, "This gives them a sense of stability in their lives to know their family history." In Anstruther, I encountered a number of similar visitors, including two from New Hampshire who were looking for the man's grandfather. "We think he came from Pittenweem . . . he was a fisherman and probably left around 1850 . . ."

But it must not be forgotten that tourists are not the only visitors to the museum. It is also a collecting point for a more local, if dispersed, imagined community and a place in which to imagine that community reconstituted. Those claiming fisher identity or direct descent from those who did, often visit the museum and make vehement, critical comments about the selection and accuracy of exhibits. The criticisms stop, however, when they reach the museum's Memorial Room, where plaques to those fishermen drowned at sea cover the walls. The room was built initially at the suggestion of a fishermen's association and anyone with ties to the fishing community may put up a plaque to honor a lost kinsman. Casual visitors are excluded, so mourners and rememberers can sit there in silence.

Many leave flowers, particularly on the anniversaries of boat losses. "It's when there's no body recovered, no burial, this serves as a grave," said one museum worker. A look at the visitors' book for 1992–3 showed that relatives had come from as far away as Australia and Zimbabwe, but by far the greatest number were from the Scottish coast. Many left little messages: "God Bless Donald," "In memory of a beloved father," "Joe, I remember you," "Grandad lost at sea, skipper Caledonia." This is, in many ways, a sacred space and, as we shall see a bit further on, occasional attempts by museum staff to manage it generate considerable hostility.

The museum also works with a boats club. This group of men takes responsibility for collecting and maintaining old fishing boats and its members often do not agree with Museum policies about preservation. Their prize possession is the "Reaper," a 74-foot-long wooden sailing boat that dates from about 1900. She is used as a kind of floating emissary for the Anstruther museum. A few club members regularly take her up and down the coast for special events and on educational missions. "We have to be careful what waters we take her into – she's a sweet old lady," said one crew member, who also complained that the Museum would not let the club fit her out with the appropriate artifacts:

> There's an Aladdin's *Cave* up there, lassie. There's half a gartlin' [great line]. I dinna ken why they won't let us have some o' them things for the *Reaper*. A boat like this would always have had a brass barometer and a weather cock on the wall. They've got them up there and they won't let us have them. Mebbe it's because the stuff's on loan but we could sign a note and return them after the trip.

These men wanted more accuracy from the museum, but others didn't want the museum at all. Not all fishermen were pleased to see their way of life put under glass. Different attitudes tended to reflect different generations. As one man from Pittenweem said to me, "working fishermen are not so happy to think of their industry as something that belongs in a museum." Another concurred: "fishermen don't want to think of themselves as part of a dying industry." A young boy standing near him said simply,"it's crap."

However, a number of the East Neuk's older fishermen have been heavily involved with the museum, so much so that I once heard them referred to (snidely) as "heritage aristocrats." For them, the best definition of heritage might be the sympathetic one (in contrast to the critical ones I mentioned earlier) that Ray (2001: 7) offers in her discussion of North American devotees of Scottish culture: "something of a rhapsody on history [whose value] . . . lies in its perennial flexibility and the strength of emotions it evokes". These fishermen devote a great deal of time and thought to the museum. While they are not always rhapsodic about the results, they have powerful feelings about their efforts, as well as about the kinds of truth they believe the museum should show the world.

In this, the oldest and largest of Scotland's museums devoted exclusively to fishing, we find a rich venue within which to examine the contested meanings and uses of fisher heritage. These range from the national to the local, the native to the "professional." As one former curator said to me, "a museum is a strange thing to have representing a living community. You're fragmenting someone's life, splitting things up and putting them in glass cases." Yet local people wanted their pasts so preserved, at least in the beginning.

One of the founders told me that a local builder had first broached the idea for a museum in 1962. His family had all been fishing folk, and he had watched unhappily as a lot of valuable material was thrown away when the old men were dying off. He and his friends began a collection and called for donations. These practically flew in, as people scoured attics and storerooms. Every object came with a personal story about a local family. All, moreover, were entailed, as donors expected their gifts to be put on display (and would complain loudly if they sat in storage).

As I toured the museum with various fishermen or huddled with them over tea in the chilly museum cafe, I learned a great deal about the many ways in which objects reveal social relationships and about the politics of exhibition. It immediately became apparent that the fishermen do not trust professional curators. In particular, they do not and cannot subscribe to what Gathercole (1991: 75) calls "curatorial knowledge:"

> Curatorial knowledge, however, is much more than knowledge about artefacts;
> it is . . . part of a museum culture, within which curators define, maintain, and

extend their roles . . . The measure of curatorial productivity, therefore, is one of ideas, expressed as texts of one form or another. Thus we find another paradox. Artefacts are, in the contexts of their parent cultures, indigenous instruments of production . . . Once they are transferred to museums, however, they become some of the instruments of production which curators use to demonstrate their professional roles and to delineate their productive relations . . .

So any artifact on display is a potential site for disagreement (O'Hanlon 1993: 90). For example, several informants took great care to tell me that the Fisherman's Cottage should properly have been called "the Fisherman's Hoose [House]." Farm workers had cottages, they said. Fishermen had hooses. In another instance, one man pointed derisively to a replica of a Scottish dugout boat, circa AD 500, saying, "What has that to do with Scottish fisheries? It's just a lump of wood and a waste of money."

Such comments naturally aroused my curiosity about the social dynamics of exhibit making and so I set out to interview not only fishermen, but museum staff and curators. Over the years, the museum has had a succession of curators whose goals for the museum typically derived not from local experience and sentiment, but from a delocalized, professional culture with *a priori* ideas about what to do with objects. It was the Edinburgh-based Scottish Museums Council (based in Edinburgh) that suggested the need for a professional curator and general manager. The tenures of these curators have typically been short. The first one stayed for 12 years; the next lasted six months. Subsequent curators have had varied tenures but all have been plagued by local politics, disputes and competing agendas.

Baxandall (1991: 36) notes that museum exhibits are always complex and dynamic productions involving a three-way conversation:

Rather than one static entity representing another, I would prefer, as more productive, a notion of exhibition as a field in which at least three distinct terms are independently in play – makers of objects, exhibitors of made objects, and viewers of exhibited made objects.

This helps to explain much of the dynamics of exhibition politics in Anstruther. There, the political engagements of exhibition are further complicated by the fact that many people occupy more than one position in this field. Disentangling the perspectives of makers, exhibitors and viewers is enormously difficult. Hooper-Greenhill (1992: 7) says that "power within museums and galleries is skewed towards the collecting subject who makes decisions in relation to space, time and visibility; in other words as to what may be viewed, how it should be seen, and when this is possible." In the Anstruther museum, the role of "collecting subject" has never resided in only one individual. Donors have continually warred with curators over the right to make decisions. Their passion for their own versions of appropriate use, accuracy and truth lead them inevitably into conflict with those whose background is strictly in the academic or museum setting.

The curator must answer to a Board of Trustees that includes local fishermen, businessmen, solicitors, bankers and one university academic. Fishermen still dominate the curatorial committee. One former curator explained some of the challenges he had faced in the 1980s:

> I found that just being local, even though not from the fishing industry, was an advantage. But I was not local enough, because I came from another part of Fife. For the people of the East Neuk, Pittenweem is the center of the universe . . . The fishermen were very proud of their heritage and wary of outsiders. We had a student from Queen's University working with us who was told a lot of lies. People didn't want to reveal details about their families and didn't want their lives misrepresented. They even told one researcher in St. Monans that a boat was to be covered in the best Fife butter prior to her launch, for superstitious reasons! A lot of these people are frightened of academics. They also want only the positive side of things to be represented.

My informant also found himself becoming caught up in the changing climate of museum development, as heritage began to be perceived as a profitable, as well as a national, enterprise:

> In the Fife Region, the Scottish Museums Council are all getting into museum politics. Working at the museum became a seven day a week job. For a couple of years, I was going to meetings twice a week. The politics got intense as the Scottish Development Agency and the Scottish Museums Council worried about duplicating resources along the east coast . . . But more than this, there was the frustration of not being able to get on with the job. Paper work and meetings took the place of working on exhibits . . .

Early in this curator's tenure, in the early 1980s, pressures to reconfigure the museums's identity to reflect that "intrinsically Scottish" quality that McCrone et al. (1995) have remarked upon, began to plague him. The museum then retained a distinctively East Neuk stamp, despite the presence of exhibits from elsewhere. Was it to remain a truly local enterprise, or should it broaden its remit to include all of Scotland?

From the beginning, the museum had been called the Scottish Fisheries Museum, and it was felt that we needed to reach out. We went out with the fishermen on boats, up to the Shetlands and all around the coast. In the 1970s there had been a big change in technology and people were throwing things away.

A subsequent curator, whom I will call William, came to Anstruther from England and had a particularly difficult time. He deplored how his instructions and demands were flouted. "This is an area of advanced parochialism, where people delight in nit-picking and in seeing things go wrong. This is true elsewhere, but it seems to be fairly marked here." He attributed the criticisms he received to his status as an Englishman and an outsider. He also understood that local people and curators have very different agendas. However, his understanding did not translate into sympathy for the fisherfolk or an interest in compromise:

> This town is still a close-knit community and it's hard to penetrate socially. In fact, I find it easier to collect things from the west coast than locally. The locals got all upset when I changed the steam gallery [devoted to the days when steam succeeded sail]. I rearranged the layout so that the models could be seen from all sides, to make it more three-dimensional. The collection itself was substantially unchanged. Yet some locals think the gallery has been ruined because the change came from an outsider . . .

With William, the ongoing war between fishermen and curators seemed to intensify. Doubtless, his belief that the fishermen's memories were often faulty and rambling did not help. But then, his views were not unique. A non-fisherman resident of the town explained fisher resistance to curators in terms of ignorance and stubbornness:

> There are tremendous local resources, but local people don't understand some aspects of the museum ethic, especially issues of restoration, research and authenticity. If you've been a fisherman for fifty years, you believe you are an expert. But we've found that their memories are not always reliable and stories will get mixed up. They don't believe that upstart academics could possibly know better . . . Restoration is another issue. Locals want things smartened up, fixed and painted, but sometimes that means a loss of material . . . We have a lot of handymen who are invaluable – old retired fishermen who get paid a pittance and turn around and spend the money on things for the museum like paint. The problem, though, is that they make decisions for themselves. For example, they'll decide the curator is wrong about where to put an object and they might move it. Once they took a very old object collected from up north and decided to paint it.

The question of restoration is always contentious. For example, in O'Hanlon's discussion of a Highland Papua New Guinean exhibit at London's Museum of Mankind he mentions the debate over whether to clean a Wahgi shield:

> The question raised the issue of what it is that an artefact is valued as embodying. Is it the shield as a perfect example of its type, a kind of snapshot in time, taken grime-free at the outset of its career? Or do we seek, rather, to preserve the evidence of the shield's biography through time, even when (as with the grime) the evidence also begins to obscure something of the artefacts' original purpose? (O'Hanlon 1999: 80)

In the case of the Anstruther artifacts, the fishermen's desire to clean and paint was not necessarily to render them pristine. Rather it was to show a different aspect of their biography: objects in use were frequently cleaned and renewed; only discarded objects would have been left dirty. As we have seen, in reference to the pride fisherwomen took in scrubbing their doorsteps, it is part of the fisherfolk's "presentation of self" (Goffman 1963) to display clean objects. In their minds, to display a dirty one would embody the wrong value.

Various curators spoke of the need to preserve objects, maintaining the physical integrity by locking things away, if necessary. However, what museum professionals saw as a commitment to conserve rare objects and delicate materials was widely interpreted by the fisherfolk as sacrificing living history for sterile academic purposes. Some of the fisherfolk believed that the museum was in danger of being taken over by "those toffee-nosed buggers" and "lady do-gooders," as some referred to a few people from nearby St Andrews. They believed that such a take-over would seriously distort and dilute the meaning of fishing for those who visit the museum.

Fishermen employed various subversive tactics to undermine this process. One day, as a fisherman member of the board was trying to explain to me the difference between winter and summer herring nets, he said, "Go and pick them up, so you can feel the difference. They say you're not supposed to, but you just go and pick them up." I did, of course. Not only did I want to feel the nets; it would have been a serious breach of trust to indicate allegiance to what were, for him, a foreign set of standards. Moreover, in telling me to pick up the nets, he was asserting his role as *de facto* curator.

One of the few women active in the museum's creation also voiced her concerns over the influence of professional staff. An octogenarian in failing health, Mary had previously given museum tours, including one for the Queen Mother. In recognition for her work, "I had to go to Buckingham Palace and get an MBE. I'll give that to the fisher museum." She was proud of the award, but even prouder of her fishing lineage:

> My grandfather was drowned when my father was 12, in one of the first steam drifters. He went to do a week of fishing in February, for white fishing. There was a bad storm and she never came back. It was the fourteenth of February in 1900. But their sons went to the fishing. My father left school after his father drowned. But he was an intelligent man and he took his skipper's ticket when he was old enough. He could help me with my maths because he knew navigation.

She was still deeply committed to writing and preserving fisher lore, but deplored recent changes in the museum. "When it opened, the museum was mainly about people. Now it's about things. We looked for stories about people. It was not so much a museum as a demonstration of history. Now it's not a place for homey talk. It has changed its ethos." As for the current curator, who was then on his way out, "I'll be glad when he's away. He lost things. He didn't think things were important that were very important. He didn't know anything or anyone among the fisherfolk."

One local man was especially notorious for opposing the curators. "Robert" was descended from a fisher family, but never went to sea himself. Despite a career spent in teaching mathematics, he had amassed an astonishing array of facts about fishermen and fishing boats. When I went to see him, he sat me down in an armchair and first established his fisher lineage. "My mother was from Boddam, near Peterhead; my mother's father went to the whaling. My father had three sailing yawls and two motor yawls in my time." Then he told me about all the things that were wrong with the museum, blaming the growing influence of academics from St Andrews for the many mistakes he saw there.

From his perspective, museum politics had seriously degraded the quality of exhibits. He spoke of those who had "staged a coup and got fisherfolk knocked off the committee." Local fishermen had been alienated from the museum by outsiders, "university and business people who like to be important. I've noticed there's an element in the town which values incomers more than local folk." According to him, local experts have been ignored. "There are six kinds of fishing and I've never met anyone who's worked on more than four of them. So you have to *listen* to people. These folks don't listen."

Peter was most aggrieved over an exhibit depicting a late nineteenth-century fish-curer's premises. In the antechamber of a large room sits a mannequin hunched over a typewriter. The mannequin represents a fish merchant, an employer, as we have seen, of considerable local power. One day, Peter identified the mannequin's waistcoat as having once belonged to a local man's great grandfather, who had been a fisherman. When he saw the man on the street, he roared, "why William, d'ye ken, yon mannie in the museum is wearing your *great grandfather's waistcoat* with a *collar and a tie!*" Peter was outraged at the idea that a fisherman's clothes now adorned a fish merchant. No man who wore a fisherman's waistcoat would ever have been found working at a desk or with a typewriter. The mistake was also critical because, as we have seen, during the period depicted, fishermen and fish merchants stood in tense, antagonistic relations to each other. To conjoin them symbolically, albeit unwittingly, in an exhibit violated a significant structural opposition within the fishing community. The resulting marriage of the unmarriageable was, in effect, a monster.

But the monstrosity was only evident or relevant to those in the know. When I questioned the present curator about the decision to use the waistcoat, he said that no one had thought that it mattered very much what the mannequin wore. To him, the exhibit was accurate in all the ways that counted. A non-fisher board member said that the intent had been to display the fish-curer's documents and that the clothes were "just things that the museum had handy." But to local fisherfolk, this was a breach of major proportions. The story circulated widely throughout the town. For us, it provides a telling example of Kishemblatt-Gimblett's (1998: 149) point that "a hallmark of heritage is the problematic relationship of its objects to the instruments of their display".

I listened to many conversations about the museum collection and its personal meaning to the people who devoted so many hours to its making. As might be predicted from what we learned in the previous chapter, many of their stories were about boats: when and how they were built, and most particularly, how accurately they have been depicted either in books or in models. Even objects outside the Museum came in for such scrutiny. An antiques dealer in Pittenweem told me that he had displayed a group of model boats and found that "all the old fishermen came in to have a look. One of them said, 'You'll have to tell the man that built this boat that he's gotten the stay in the wrong place.'"

One member of the museum staff said that the fishermen were so concerned with accuracy because

You're dealing with men mostly above the age of fifty. When they were young, you were belted in school if you got things only 90 per cent right. They had to be 100 per cent right. They feel you have to tell people the accurate story – a stranger can't be satisfied with only half a story. This should accord with what a museum does, but it doesn't.

More importantly, however, was that almost all of the boats seemed to have a personal connection to a kinsman. In other words, as when fishermen talked about actual boats, they were relaying family history. "My grandfather/uncle, cousin/nephew/brother sailed aboard her/ken't the man who built her/lived across the road from her skipper/was her first skipper."

Not all conflicts concerned displays: the museum itself could be a contested space. Thus, Mary recounted how she had met a friend coming out of the museum one day. Jessie, then about 70 years of age, had lost her son some 20 years previously when his boat had foundered. Not only had she had put up a plaque in the Memorial Room that read, "In memory of David Meldrum Hughes Aged 19 of Pittenweem. Lost on 2nd February, 1966 from the boat 'Honestas' LH 370," but she also visited the memorial every two weeks, setting flowers in a vase near the wall. When Elizabeth met her, however, she was in tears. Some woman in the museum had told her she had no right to sit there and she had fled. Mary said, "your folk have been fisherfolk in Anstruther for 300 years. You have every right to be in there." As she told me the story, her voice rose with indignation over the affront. "That woman was an *incomer*."

This incident reveals more than the persistence of the distinction between incomers and fisherfolk. It speaks to the fact that heritage cannot be contained within museum walls, confined to a designated space and subject to hierarchical decision making about what does and does not matter. We can follow this argument by moving out of the museum into some more private spaces, where fisherfolk collect and produce texts and displays of their own.

## Heritage Domesticated: the Importance of Being Erudite

Not only the fishermen but also their houses speak volumes about heritage. Every living room, or lounge, is filled with memorabilia of the sea: paintings (at least one of the fisherman's boat), photographs (ditto) and model boats. Every time I visited a fisher couple at home, I asked for a guided tour of the art and artifacts. These were always happily granted and accompanied by a long stream of reminiscences.

In addition to the artwork, many of the older fishermen have also amassed a large store of books and notes relating to the fishery. Their personal libraries often included weighty industrial texts as well as the bound volumes of reminiscences, verse, and local histories. These have titles like *Fishing in Old East Lothian* (Gibson 1994); *Broughty Ferry in the Days of Sail* (McMillan nd); *The Berwickshire Coast* (Wood 1998); *Aul Torry: O' Fish and Fowk* (Atherton 1992); *Fishing the North East* (Taylor n.d.); *Steam Fishermen in Old Photographs* (Elliott 1979); or *One Foot in the Sea* (Smith 1991). Over the years, I have benefitted from the generous loan of many such publications. In fact, I have seldom had to ask for them. My informants would unearth them from their shelves and press them upon me, eager to display the prodigious chronicling capacities of indigenous fisher writers. Thus, when David presented me with a copy of Peter Buchan's collected poems and stories, he told me "you'll learn everything you need to know about the fishing if you read that book. I take it to sea with me."

In laying claim to specific authors and texts, the fishers also ratified their own status as fisher experts who could transmute and incorporate the works of others into not only *local* knowledge, but *reserved* knowledge, that is, kept only for themselves and for those with whom they chose to share it. Such acts of sharing or withholding further enhance the value of insiderness by reminding the outsider (whether curator or anthropologist) that fishers still controlled access to their pasts. They, the fisherfolk, were the patrons and dispensers of understanding. Outsiders were dependents, knowledge-clients who may not receive all that they ask for or comprehend it when they do.

This also had the effect of inverting power relationships based upon formal education, a significant class marker in British society. Such inversions provoked reactions, however. An academic, non-fisher informant asserted a counter-claim to authority when he derided the "flurry of pamphlets being produced all around the coast; many are very badly done and privately published. This is just using heritage for status reasons. It's a waste of time and energy."

Whether or not the volumes of local history were completely accurate, fisher poetry was vivid and evocative. It was also voluminous. I refer here not to the astonishing quantity of poetry that has been written *about* the fisherfolk (by writers such as Alistair MacLean, Robert Louis Stevenson, Robert Southey, Iain Crichton Smith, and Rudyard Kipling), but to the poems written *by* the fisherfolk. Many fisherfolk are very fond of poetry, writing it, reading it, and reciting it. Most of it is meant to be spoken aloud. Often sentimental, it tends to be highly concrete, with compelling renderings of boat and home and harborside. However, it is rarely personal or introspective. Most poems mark places and recognizable experiences. Although the writers would no doubt appreciate a wider audience, they do not need it to justify their efforts. They write to each other, to celebrate a way of life.

"'Poetry Peter' Smith: The Fisherman Poet of Cellardyke", born in 1874, wrote poems "in the main for recital at church and other social gatherings" (Watson 1992: 89). According to Watson, who edited a volume of his work, Smith also wrote in order to preserve local dialect.

> Yet tho' we sing the same auld tunes,
> Ilk [each] country's words ha'e different soonds.
> In Aberdeen we've quines [women] and loons [men],
>   And foo [how] and fat [what].
> In Fife's red tiled, auld farrant [old-fashioned] toons,
>   It's hoo and what.
>
> (Watson 1992: 112).

Nellie Watson, born in Cellardyke in 1895, wrote of old days but also commented on the present. In 1949, she reminisced about the winter herring, which were already in decline:

> Thae days saw hunder-barrel shots
> That a' were brocht frae oot the Firth
> And sune the herbour was astir
> Wi boats a' scamlin' for a berth . . .
> The Hame Toon was sae busy then
> And HERRING often filled oor dish,
> But noo there is this awfy change –
>   what's happened tae that HUMBLE FISH! (n.d.: 1–2)

Peter Buchan (1917–91), the widely read Peterhead fisherman whose work my friend David admires, also wrote for a fisher audience. The jacket biography of his *Collected Poems and Short Stories* describes him as "the voice of Scotland's northeast fishing communities" noting that he wished to present fishers in a kindlier light than the one often used to illuminate them. "He started to write short stories to portray the 'middle ground' in fisher life which had formerly been portrayed at the two extremes of either drunkenness or religious fanaticism . . ." (Buchan 1992).

In a story that begins like a homily to fisher pride, he goes on lovingly to mock the fishers' competitive obsession with cleanliness,

Visitors to the Moray Firth coast are usually favourably impressed with the spick-and-span appearance of the houses of the fisher folk.

The immaculate paintwork on both wood and stone is positive proof that a great deal of work and not a little money have been lavished on these dwellings, which altho they are not of granite, are nevertheless soundly constructed to endure the rigours of the north-east climate.

This is not the arrogant pride of bigsiness or conceit but a softer, milder pride in such things as heritage and birthplace . . .

Seldom will you see a BCK [Buckie] boat in an orra [shabby] state. Nae fears! The BCK lads, are, on the whole, 'verra parteeclar' with their craft . . . (Buchan 1992: 205)

In Buckie, where we are about to go, Isobel Harrison reigns as local poet. She is fully bilingual but she writes exclusively in the Doric, or northern dialect of Broad Scots. Her poems, published in a volume called *En Kin Ee Mine Es?* (*And Can You Remember This?*) with the support of Moray District Council, concern the homely details of life in the Buckie of the 1930s, when she was a girl. Poverty, sharing, humor and thrift inform her verses and above all, the warm recollection of an enveloping community:

> Fin I wis a wee quinie, it aye seem't tae me,
> My Dad wis hardly iver hame, aye awa tae sea,
> My Mam wis aye in the hoose, fin we come in fae play,
> And nivir seemit tae chainge, bit wis wyvin ivery day! . . .

> The Worrel wis a wee sma placie, safe an affey secure,
> Bounded be a way oh care, an an innocence sae pure,
> The days afore the war, we maybe wirna gran,
> Bit Lord we hid athin that wis necessary tae man!! (Harrison 1992: 21).

Harrison, who traveled a great deal throughout her life, has now returned to her birthplace in Buckpool, where the fisher community was once concentrated. I met her there, at Bob and Nessie's house across the road from where I was staying, "the most traditional part of town," she told me. Our conversation was an intense lesson in heritage, although she never referred to her memories in that way. Her talk, emphasizing the independence and resourcefulness of the fishers she had known, was replete with references to particular characters, jokes, and games. Much of her lore, she said, came from her grandmother, a formidable character, it seems:

I had the great benefit of sleeping next to her from the age of twelve until she died. I got all her stories. When my grandfather was thirty-four, he was carted home in a net-cart and the doctor came and diagnosed TB. Grannie set him up in a loft near the window and fed him a tonic with eggs in it and he lived to be seventy-four.

Grannie became known as a healer, treating sore throats with iodine and making beef tea and saving the fisherfolk from having to pay the doctor's fees. And when her labors failed, she also *strauchtened* (laid out) the dead.

In the indigenous voices of Smith, Buchan and Harrison, we hear strong notes of nostalgia. However, it would be a mistake to think that they point monotonally backwards. Like my older informants in Anstruther and Ferryden, they are also speaking about age, loss and modern times by saying, in effect, "We're still here. Let us tell you how we lived." My capacity for listening to them generated some comment. It even led one of my informants to announce, "I ken what anthropology is: it's the study of auld men!" Like the elderly Jews of Myerhoff's (1978) Aliyah Center, they embraced this conversation to maintain vitality and to leave a legacy, not just to inherit one. And thus they teach us what heritage is really about: it is not just about what has been handed down from the past, but about how to live in the present, as well as about what to leave for the future (Huby 1992). As I said at the start of this chapter, the motto of the Buckie Heritage Society, to which both Peter Buchan and Isobel Harrison have belonged, reads, "our future lies in our past."

## Buckie

Travelling north from Fife to the Moray Firth coastline, we could visit other fisher museums.[4] But it is in Buckie that the competing orientations of heritage – towards locals or towards tourists – emerge even more starkly than in Anstruther. Here the locally established Heritage Society faces a competitor in the large, expensive and purpose-built heritage center called the Buckie Drifter Project, whose motto reads, "Catch the Spirit of the North East." The Heritage Society is a truly indigenous, grassroots affair reliant upon donations and small entrance fees; the Drifter is a sleek product of the tourist industry that cost about one million pounds to construct.

Unlike Pittenweem and Anstruther, Buckie (population 8,800) has not been a major tourist destination. In fact, so parlous has its status been in the tourist industry that in 1995, despite the opening of the Drifter Project, Buckie's local tourist office was threatened with closure. This aroused much ire:

> The decision can only mean astonishment in the Buckie and Cullen areas as to its absurdity. Within the last year . . . the new Buckie Drifter, has been opened to act as a tourist flagship and provide a platform for developing a

tourism base in the Buckie coastal area . . . (*Banffshire Advertiser*, 14 March 1995: 1)

However, the town is neither beautiful nor picturesque. Its commercial center contains a number of rather seedy shops, chain stores, and desultory cafes. Its sidewalks are often empty. It is hardly a tourist's idea of the perfect vacation spot.

But Buckie proper is not all there is. When people speak of the town, they refer to a thickly settled coastal strip that extends eastward from Buckpool to Portessie, once separate fishing settlements. The shoreline is rocky, with no sand beach to draw the summertime crowds. At the heart of these settlements today is Buckie harbor, which hosts an active, though troubled, fishing fleet. Many of the boats are small and well worn. Lately, shellfish, primarily prawns and nephrops, or Norway lobster, have been the mainstay for the large, enclosed fish market. There one finds a bustle of activity, with workers, mostly retired fishermen, helping to weigh and grade fish. Picking up large, iron hooks, they drag fish boxes to the waiting vans, then drive the vans, or fish lorries, to other ports. When the auction is over, they repair to the fisherman's cafe across the road to light cigarettes, drink tea and coffee and to talk about how bad times are getting. They appreciate the Heritage Society but have many qualms about the Drifter, which they see as having been imposed upon the town.

These fishermen like the Buckie Heritage Society's "Heritage Cottage" much better. It sits just behind the town library in a graceful little square. Founded in 1986 by a group of local fisherpeople who, like the folks in Anstruther, were worried about preserving the artifacts of days gone by, the Society claims to be "more than a museum, much more! . . . where people fae a' the airts [places] can meet." The Society is an all-volunteer organization whose main collection consists of an astonishing number of old photographs, as well as a set of video and audio tapes of people's reminiscences. The artifacts are crowded and jumbled. Much remains in storage. Unlike the Drifter Project, which focuses exclusively on the days of steam drifting (roughly from the 1880s to the First World War), the Heritage Society welcomes all material relating to Buckie's fishing history. As a result, there is far more material than can be displayed. The *Banffshire Advertiser* (7 March 1995: 1), in an article headlined "Cramped!" quoted Society Chairman Peter Bruce as saying that "There's enough material in our possession to fill a building twice this size." That was probably an understatement.

True to its claim, the cottage is a convivial place. It is open about 20 hours a week, staffed by volunteers (most of them in their seventies or beyond) who drink tea, sort through the massive collection of photographs and happily chat about the old days of fishing with any visitor who happens by. In the summer of 1994, they received some 900 people. Some of these visitors are the kinship tourists whom we first met in Anstruther. However, the Heritage Society, while locally respected, was not doing much for Buckie's lagging tourist industry.

For some years, efforts to increase Buckie's share of the tourist market had languished. With the growing popularity of heritage, Banff District Council decided in the early 1990s to launch a second heritage site, this one lavishly funded and architecturally *avant garde*. By 1993, a professional manager had been hired. Work went quickly and the Buckie Drifter Project opened in 1994. The power struggle over domain began immediately. On a visit to the Heritage Society in '93, shortly before the Drifter Project was built, I sat chatting with a few members when the new manager of the Drifter Project came by to collect information. Her manner was brisk and the presence of an anthropologist hardly put her off her stride. When I asked her about plans for the new museum, the old men quickly said, "oh, that'll be for the tourists." She immediately responded, "no, no, it's for local folks too." The old men remained unconvinced. "That's right," they said, "it'll be for the tourists." After she had gone, they pointed out that she was an incomer.

Like the people of the East Neuk, the old men of Buckie were not opposed to tourism *per se*. Yet, they would have agreed with the woman from the small fisher museum in Nairn, further west, who said, "We're not particularly interested in tourism, we're interested in preserving the community." These men thought, in fact, that tourism would probably do some good for the local economy, but they also saw it as essentially irrelevant for their purpose, which was to keep and make available the memories of Buckie's fishing past for those who really cared about it. Moreover, further conversations also revealed some concern that the Drifter would attempt to acquire the Society's collection of photographs, tapes and artifacts. The old men adamantly insisted that these would stay where they were. Others were not so sure. Still, everyone was clearly anxious that ultimately, the Drifter would efface the Heritage Society and eclipse its efforts.

Rivalry with the Drifter began to mount. The Society's newsletter, *Heritage News* (1993: 3) reported concern that an artifact promised to the Society "would end up in the Drifter." On the following page, it tried to reassure its readers:

> Our work and display will be totally different to the Drifter, yet complementary to it. We will continue in Heritage Cottage, to do what we do best, to do what

our members expect; namely to provide a down-to-earth, no frills, home for the photos and exhibits which have been entrusted to our care and a 'hamely' welcome to all our visitors from home and abroad.. (1993: 4)

Some claimed that the Drifter's designers had ignored local expertise and created a superficial display. In 1993, Bob's words strikingly echoed those of Mary, my Anstruther informant, who lamented the growing impersonality of her museum's ambience:

The new heritage opening up may help or it may not. I would have put the Buckie Drifter Project nearer the town, so you could see the sea and have easy access to the town. I don't approve of the site, but they got it cheap from Grampian [Regional Council]. They'll take over the Heritage Society. The new curator is an outsider and can't tell the story the way the local folk can. The fishing communities along the coast, from Peterhead to Lossiemouth, they work together. If I ran the museum, I'd have them tell people stories.

However, the worst insult was the first manager's failure to invite members of the Buckie Heritage Society to the gala opening ceremony. This was a *faux pas* of epic proportions. Word of it sped down the coast so that I heard of it not only in Buckie but in Anstruther as well. A number of fishermen now refused to set foot inside the Drifter and only one or two agreed to work with the Drifter as local experts.

The next Drifter manager, who started work in 1995, had local ties and a better understanding of how to engage with the community. The *Banffshire Advertiser* reported that she

would like to see the quayside alongside the Drifter come alive, with real people taking part in the recreation of history. Anyone who could spare some time to demonstrate net-making, gutting or any of the other quayside jobs which were part and parcel of harbour life during the time of the steam drifters, is asked to get in touch with her.

She went on to call for people to feel a sense of ownership. She also attempted to separate the roles of the two institutions:

I want the people of Buckie and the surrounding area to see it as their heritage centre . . . *It's not a museum, it's a visitor attraction* [italics mine] . . . and to increase its appeal we need the help of local people who are in the know about the periods we are recalling . . . Anyone who could spare some time to demonstrate net-making, gutting or any of the other quayside jobs which were part and parcel of harbour life during the time of the steam drifters, is asked to get in touch with her. (*Banffshire Advertiser*, 14 March 1995: 1)

Under her aegis, the Drifter was promoted as part of "the Buckie Experience," which includes the working harbor itself, the fish market, and the Royal National Lifeboat station. "Experience" is an increasingly popular concept in heritage productions and it figures strongly in the Drifter's approach. Kirshenblatt-Gimblett (1998: 138) notes that "the term indexes an engagement of the senses, emotions, and imagination" that signals a "self-conscious shift in orientation away from the museum's artifacts and toward its visitors". And indeed, with an early twentieth-century polling station where one can cast a ballot for or against becoming teetotal, and the Drifter deck where one can walk on board and even stand in the wheelhouse, experience is on offer. In contrast to the Anstruther Museum, visitors are even encouraged to touch things, such as the cloth-made "herring" inside an old cooper's barrel, or the bedclothes of an old box bed. Preservation is not the watchword here. The Drifter is intended to make a profit.

In one pamphlet, the visitor is explicitly invited to "experience the past" through "a journey back in time." This journey is marked by performances available through modern technology in the form of an audiocassette.

> Go on board a Buckie Steam Drifter, find out how many fish it took to fill a barrel and listen to the Buckie loons [men] and quines [women] as they talk in their distinctive dialect. Join in the activities by mending nets and packing fish and become part of the Buckie Drifter Experience.

In some ways, the Heritage Society and the Drifter have much in common. As I said earlier, a heritage center, as opposed to a museum, is more specifically intended to provide a didactic, but enjoyable experience. In a heritage center, a greater part of the display is constructed using replicas or simulacra and brings visitors into close contact with the exhibits. By contrast, in a museum, curators anguish over accuracy, authenticity and preservation, within the terms of the museum profession. Neither the Buckie Drifter nor the Heritage Society is a museum and this accounts for part of the competition between them. The simulacra of the Drifter are pitted against the artifacts and conversation of the Society. And it remains unclear which side will win out.

In some places, it seems, the line between museums and heritage centers is being blurred. In an address to a museums conference in Glasgow, Patrick Boylan commented on the irony of changes besetting the museum community as heritage centers arise to challenge their domain:

> . . . real museums seem desperate to deny their own status and market themselves instead as 'heritage centres' or 'experiences'. Well, I have news for you,

the Disney Corporation has now put the grand-daddy of all 'centres', the Epcot Center, on to an independent non-profit basis, declared it to be a museum after all, and applied to the American Association of Museums for Accredited Museum status. (*Museums Journal* 1990: 29)

He further remarks that proponents of the "new museology" in Europe

argue that the true limits of the museum should not be the boundary walls of the museum building and its grounds: they should be the whole of a defined geographical territory, which might be a small village at one extreme, or a whole country in the case of a true national museum. They further argue that the subject matter of the 'new" museum's operations should not just be the collections within the museum building, but the total patrimony, natural and human (including the individual and collective memory) of that defined territory . . . (Boylan 1990: 32)

To my ear, the idea of a "total patrimony" sounds a lot like "heritage."

## Conclusion

Both Buckie and Anstruther celebrate fisher heritage, but they do so in very different ways. Anstruther's museum concentrates on the past but also brings things up to date. It celebrates inventiveness and progress. In that way, it models the heritage industry's desired spirit of intrinsic Scottishness, to which I referred earlier. Despite a lingering East Neuk emphasis, it is a national museum in more than one sense. Its exhibits evoke different parts of the coast; but more importantly, its focus on changing technology recapitulates Scottish pride in industry and invention, the "achieving society" of which Harvie (1977) spoke, whose products are featured prominently in Edinburgh's Museum of Scotland. It links Anstruther to a wider world in which Scots have traveled and made their mark.

In Buckie, which still has a working port, both the Society and the Drifter focus exclusively upon the past. Their displays call up local history and local memories without saying much about external linkages. Buckie's heritage productions closely resemble those of other small, local fisher museums, but the heritage stakes in Buckie still matter a great deal to those whose lives have been given over to the sea. Everywhere that people deplore the present (and that would seem to be pretty much anywhere), they invoke some other time as an idealized contrast (Lowenthal 1985; Wright 1985). Indeed, as the previous chapter showed, modern fishing communities find themselves at a juncture where the latter has largely failed them. Hence, to recapitulate, the motto of the Buckie Fishing Heritage Society: "Our future lies in our past."

Will Scotland's fishing communities have any choice about how to manage themselves as sites of industrial heritage? Some signs suggest that they will. The idea – however facetiously expressed – that Scotland and its localities could be transformed into a series of museums and thereby lose all cultural integrity rests, I believe, on two mistaken ideas. The first is that such a transformation could truly fast-freeze communities: that time and social dynamics would essentially stop in the interests of preservation. To the contrary, it seems to me that the debates over heritage in Scotland's fishing villages affirm that fishing people still have something to say.

The second idea is that museums themselves are truly "about objects, and not about people," as my informant lamented. But her very lament, and the controversy that surrounds every move museum people make, assert that the objects in the fishing museums may sometimes be seen as hostages in a battle for control over the definition of heritage. In that sense, they are entirely about people and their ongoing social relations.

As we saw in Chapter 5, a fisheries crisis extends across the North Atlantic. Not surprisingly, heritage centers are following in its wake. Canadian government subsidies have encouraged the development of outport tourism in Newfoundland, for example, but these have not successfully replaced either the economic or the social benefits of an active fishery. Davis notes that some residents say bitterly that they now live on "a reservation" (Davis, personal communication).

Filmmaker Richard Wheeler's (1994) documentary about the town of Lunenberg, Nova Scotia, visits a fisheries museum, commenting that "fisheries museums are beginning to replace the fisheries". In the US, we find that Gloucester, Massachusetts, has for many years marketed itself as a tourist attraction. There, visitors can follow a red-lined sidewalk trail down to the historic parts of the harbor. Soon, many say, the red trail will be all that is left of the fishery.

This does not mean, however, that all heritage sites can be read in the same way. Analyses of tourism in Europe to date have often followed a paradigm of pessimism, exemplified by Davydd Greenwood (1989), who argues that cultural tourism almost invariably purges local practice of authenticity and cultural initiative except as dictated by the profit motive.

Hewison (1987) and Harvie (1992) both apparently presume that heritage centers and community museums are institutions imposed by a hungry and expansive tourist industry and thus have little organic connection to their host sites. But as we have seen, many museums are indigenously sponsored by local people seeking to ensure their mark on Scotland's future. Caring for history is not a pastime reserved solely for Scotland's elites.

That people pay admission to fisher heritage museums may validate the fishers' belief in their own self-worth. So the answer to the question of "who benefits?" may not entirely exclude the locals after all. In that sense, Greenwood's assumption that tourism renders authenticity impossible may be shown to rest on a static and exclusivist view of meaning. To the contrary, heritage sites encode multiple, contested, and mutually constituted meanings, linking local people to national and diasporic communities as well as locally instantiated, transnationally based economic processes. Scottish heritage is not a coherent identity or ideology, but rather an ongoing discourse that is rife with ambivalence and disagreement, or as Rapport (1993) would put it, with "conversations" that take place in a variety of significant contexts.

Fisherfolk deploy heritage as a way of surviving in a manner they deem authentic. If, as McCrone et al. (1995: 25) suggest, Scottish heritage is "doubly peripheral" to core English heritage by being defined as outside the center both geographically and culturally, then the heritage of Scottish fisherfolk must be seen as peripherality squared, because fisherfolk themselves occupy a doubly marginalized space: socially and geographically separated from middle-class Scottish society. If they possess heritage, it may be both blessing and a peril. Blessing, because they actively enjoy it; peril, because they cannot control or contain it.

"Who owns the past?" then, is a question that too often translates reductively into issues of economic and political power, into contests over the meaning of places and debates over the value of preservation. As Herzfeld (1991) argues in his analysis of time, place, and power in Crete, such contests and debates draw upon larger issues of identity, issues that raise questions about national and cultural boundaries. Unlike the Rethemniots, however, Scots fisherpeople are ambivalent about their heritage being pressed into national service. They do not (yet) feel forced to edit themselves for external consumption, but they are aware that they must be vigilant if they are to participate in the conversation.

## Notes

1. Indeed, heritage productions that depict national and local culture histories abound. We find analyses of them, for example, in Crete

(Herzfeld 1991), England (Hewison 1987; Lowenthal 1998; Taylor 1994; West 1988), France (Hoyau 1988), Guyana (Price and Price 1995), Hawaii (Boniface and Fowler 1993), India (Appadurai and Breckenridge 1992) Quebec (Handler 1988), and the United States (Dorst 1987; Gable and Handler 1996; Kirschenblatt-Gimblett 1998; Ruffins 1992), to name but a few.

2. Lorne Rubenstein's (2001) new book is notable for its exceptional attention to the bloodier side of bonnie Scotland.

3. Some of these are, no doubt, avid participants in the Scottish heritage phenomenon that Ray (2001) details for the United States. See also Lowenthal (1998) on "Being Innate."

4. Fisher museums proliferated during the 1980s and 1990s. Sites include Aberdeen, Anstruther, Arbroath, Buckie, Eyemouth, Lossiemouth, Nairn, Peterhead, Oban (on the west coast) and Wick.

# Afterword: Scotland in the General and the Particular

And so we come to the end of our voyage along the Scottish coast. We have stopped at more than one destination, for my ethnographic quest could not be located in a single place. To understand the play of forces affecting Scottish fisherfolk, I had to leave my first site, Ferryden, and look elsewhere. Once, "the field" was an idea that ethnographers could take for granted; today, it has become far less easy to define (Gupta and Ferguson 1997). For the anthropologist, as for the fisherfolk, a place can no longer be taken for granted as a fixed social or "ethnographic locale" (Rodman 1992: 640).

Old certainties about the integrity of field sites and their value as microcosmic representations of a larger reality have given way to a revived concern about social fluidity and the commensurability of our comparisons (see Kapferer 1990). As we have seen, the tourist industry's happy depictions of ancient fixities notwithstanding, modern Scottish society is typified not by sites fixed in tradition but by mobility and change. The days of many communities based upon single occupations, such as weaving and mining, as well as fishing, are past, along with the activities that gave rise to them. Workers in such places have been made redundant and have joined the larger Scottish labor force, shifting to a variety of jobs as demanded by fluctuations in a capitalist labor market, or subsisting on the dole.

So many grandchildren of fishers are now indistinguishable from anyone else in the population. Former miners now drive taxis. Many of the places where they live are no longer filled with others who have shared the same industrial experience. They have fallen victim to what John Foster (1992: 215) calls a "culture of migration". Now virtually everyone has relatives abroad, from Ohio to Sydney. Indeed, one of the first questions a Ferrydener asked me upon hearing that I lived in New York City was "My cousin Joe lives in Brooklyn. Perhaps you've met him?"

But some fishing communities remain and still express the very essence of places where locality, in Appadurai's (1995: 205) terms, is a "general property of social life". They are face-to face – even, one might say, "in your face". They contrast starkly with Auge's (1995: 78) notion of the "non-place," where people live in the electronically coded, increasingly evanescent interactions of a "world thus surrendered to solitary individuality, to the fleeting, the temporary and ephemeral". As astute readers of global trends, fishers worry that this fate might also befall them. They have no wish to inhabit any version of what Kunstler (1993) calls *The Geography of Nowhere*, referring to that vast, dis-cathected and anonymous wasteland called suburbia.

Hence they cling tightly to fisher identity and try to preserve what is left of the fishing industry, despite the stigma, marginality and stereotype that have marked their lives. As we have seen, community identity is precious to them, in part because it has been the one thing they could count upon, apart from the insecurity of life and livelihood.

Writer Christopher Rush grew up in St Monans among fishers who cherished their way of life. In *The Scotsman*, he writes about his uncle's decision to retire from fishing because of too many regulations and too much bureaucracy. It sums up quite neatly how identity is now on the line and how bitter its loss can taste:

> My uncle, who once stepped out of his front door and was fishing in the Firth minutes later, has lived to see most of the fishing culture that was his livelihood fossilised overnight in the Anstruther Fisheries Museum . . . Each time a fisherman goes out he risks his life. But to do so for a way of life that was virtually a religion, which was saturated in and strengthened by formal piety, and in a spirit that was a cocktail of faith and fortune – that seemed somehow acceptable. The gladiator was on his own with God. Who'd be a fisherman nowadays?" (*The Scotsman*, 1997)

The question of the future remains a difficult one. Today's globalizing economy has made such sites as fishing villages appear to be curious relics: ironically enough, that also makes them ideal sites for heritage centers and museums that reassert the importance of locality. One result is that their economic problems are not taken seriously. They are simply expected to market themselves as simulacra of their own ancestors.

In the context of current discussions in anthropology of place as a cultural construct, the localism of fishing villages might be considered almost "overdetermined," in that such communities form virtual Rubik's cubes of significance. Every path, route, intersection and work space interlocks with every other, housing memories of birth, death, love, hope and insult. Within their boundaries, intimacy is inescapable, though it may generate discord as much as harmony. Perhaps, then, fisherfolk should be candidates for inclusion in the next issue of *Cultural Survival*'s volume on *The State of the Peoples*, a survey of groups whose physical or cultural persistence is in doubt. After all, the Highland Celts are already included there.

However, the term, "cultural survival" carries a double entendre. As I pointed out in the first chapter, its older, currently less reputable usage takes us back to Tylor's notion of survivals and the idea of folk holdovers atavistically lurking within the body of the West. As we have seen, modern tourism plays upon this meaning, conflating the folk with the primitive and exoticizing the marginal. From this perspective, as we have seen, fisher localism is a sign of quaintness (read parochialism). This, of course, rules out the idea that fishing communities live in the present.

Such a de-politicized view provokes us to think about the other meaning of cultural survival, the explicitly advocative one adopted by the above-mentioned compendium. This view asserts the rights of indigenous or otherwise disempowered and encapsulated groups to have a place where they can live upon their own terms. Such rhetoric is not foreign to the fisherfolk. Indeed, it circulates quite widely. As Jedrej and Nuttall explain in their book, *White Settlers* (1997), the growing presence of English incomers in the depopulated areas of Scotland has provoked many people to liken the Scots themselves to internally colonized, indigenous populations in North America. When the True Ferrydeners lament their loss of community, they blame incomers for taking space that fisherfolk should occupy. For them, as for the rest of the fisherfolk, locality is "a structure of feeling" (Williams 1976) and they feel it very deeply.

Nothing is simple about the experience of people who gaze at a past they see devalued and who imagine a future in which they have no role. It is hardly surprising that many glance back often to recall a time and place full of warmth and sharing. They do this despite their equally vivid memories of hardship and insecurity. This complicates their vision of the present. Few fishing communities enjoy consensus on how to manage current uncertainties.

In this, of course, fishers are hardly alone. One has only to look at Scottish writer William McIlvanney's 1985 novel, *The Big Man*, to realize that fishers are not alone in such feelings. His protagonist, a village man, not a crofter, is lured by city slickers to a life of risk and danger. Ultimately, his longing for community and local identity draws him back home, even though home (in Ayrshire) is not quite what it used to be. Still, it owns him, claims him and will not let him go:

His former sense of his past seemed to him now about as incredible, as untrustworthy as it had to Betty. He found himself questioning the shared identity he had found there. But even as he questioned it, he was confronted daily with the stubbornness of place, the hauntingness of its familiar associations. (McIlvanney 1985: 83)

This 'stubbornness of place' is what this book is all about.

Elsewhere I have called for anthropologists to represent Scotland as "a set of articulating arguments" (Nadel-Klein 1997: 89). By arguments I mean the terms people use to explain who they are and to lay claim to distinct identities *within* Scotland. These claims, whether of locality, ethnicity, occupation, religion or class, all say something about the range of possible ways to be Scottish. They exist in dialogue with each other. When David says, "I'm from Fife," he is saying that his family came from there, that he learned his trade there and that the Fife coast is home to him. When he says, "I'm a fisherman," he is also saying that he is not a farmer or an accountant. He is claiming an inheritance, a legacy of pride and skill as well as of stigma and marginality. His legacy binds him to others who make the same assertion.

Thus I do not deny Cohen's argument that social identity, national or otherwise, is mediated through the person and thus retains properties of uniqueness (Cohen 1996; 1999). However, I emphasize the bonds that make identity a collective as well as an individual experience. Only by searching for the mutual entailments of claims or arguments can we gain a deeper understanding of how the particular and the general are related. How Scotland's fishing communities survive depends in part upon what their inhabitants want but also upon others' visions for them. To learn about fishers tells us much about power, hierarchy and boundary-making in Scottish society.

Moreover, the concerns that I have raised in this book go beyond Scottish borders. Anthropological debates about Europe today acknowledge the centrality of history while they address all kinds of fractures, disputes, assertions and claims. In the age of European "union," we find that questions of "identities in Europe" and European "identity" are conjoined twins, and not just at the national level (Bellier and Wilson 2000; Boissevain 1994; Goddard et al. 1994; MacDonald 1993).

Locality remains significant throughout Europe, contradicting occidentalist assumptions that Europeans and other "Westerners" are freely moving individuals who inhabit only a wider, cosmopolitan culture (Carrier 1992; Nadel-Klein 1995). However, it is certainly the case that localized or at least *located* certainties face new challenges. Place, space and territory no longer lock us in – if, indeed, they ever did. Nor do they enable us to make clear, unambiguous claims of status and identity.

Without them, however, we are disembodied, unmade, and impotent. People are still widely inclined to identify themselves or others with specific areas, whether cities, towns or villages. As creatures and creators of a spatially ordered world, we continually construct our lives in terms of origin and destination, home and away, places where we belong and places where we are not welcome, zones of comfort, and zones of danger.

Some might say that setting Scottish fishing communities in a context of cultural survival lacks credibility. After all, they are not Filipino hill tribesmen or Amazonian head hunters. Their physical survival is not on the line, nor are they objects of state-sponsored genocide. Nor, perhaps, is their way of life so obviously a distinct "culture." In other words, they have been exoticized, but not enough! Furthermore, their dependence upon endangered marine resources loses them allies, such as those in the environmentalist movement, who might otherwise be sympathetic to the plight of the under dog.

It is much less contentious to submerge the issue within the process of heritage making. From this perspective, one can see how the heritage industry manages to link local people's desires to maintain their way of life with the more widely-encompassing impulses of nationalism. Local identity is "reimagined" (Macdonald 1997a) as part of the larger project of presenting a Scottish identity to the world. Thus, when fishers assert ownership of their cultural legacy, the heritage industry enfolds it into Scotland's patrimony. Stereotypes become sanitized and celebrated; marginality becomes a resource, and stigma is generally overlooked.

Some see in this process a traducing of authenticity that renders cultural survival moot. Others see it as a practical way of solving economic problems. In either case, we are well beyond the purely theoretical here. As academics, we can suspend our textual battles; we can quite literally put them aside with the papers on our desks as we go out into our gardens. I do not share these bleak, condemnatory, and ultimately homogenizing views of heritage. As I have shown here, fishers are not merely passive figures in static tableaux. They are creative, assertive actors in a swiftly moving play, attempting to write their own scripts for the future. As Macdonald (1997b) has revealed about the intensely tourist-visited Isle of Skye, local people may be very sophisticated in their engagements with modernity. For the fishers whom I have come to know over the past quarter-century, the act of telling their heritage cannot be put aside. It is part and parcel of the fabric of everyday existence. The act of telling – whether through song, poem, autobiography, ethnography, museum or heritage display – is an argument for their worth and their right to place.

So having told the story of Scotland's fisherfolk, I hope I have answered the question of why should anyone should care about these few thousand people in their small communities. My own journey toward the answer began in the 1970s, in Ferryden, where a local drama pitting small against large and poor against wealthy had unfolded shortly before my arrival. I pursued the story back in time and outward beyond the village: beyond the east coast and beyond Scotland. To discover the sources of Ferryden's predicament meant linking the village to the nation, to Europe and to the North Atlantic.

I have learned much along the way. I have learned that every bit of food we eat has a story behind it. I have learned that connecting the local to the global, a trendy phrase today, is a political commitment, not just an exercise in theory building. For as soon as we turn that phrase around, and connect the global to the local, we realize that all of our actions, as citizens, have consequences far beyond what we can see. And I have learned, most of all, about enduring marginality and facing loss. Marginality is the perpetual frame that surrounds the fisherfolk. Even the wealthiest and most successful fisherman (and there are a few) knows that his livelihood is precarious and that public policies rarely reflect his interests or even take him very seriously.

Many readers of this book may ask what they have in common with Scottish fisherfolk. I would answer that most of us experience some degree of marginality in our lives and all of us experience loss. Even if we live relatively secure, middle-class lives, we are marginalized by the sheer scale of our globalized existence. Daily news accounts of war, famine and oppression leave us feeling intensely powerless, in part because we have been taught to care about the problems of so many people we will never meet.

Ironically, perhaps, we care more about them than about those closer to home. It is a common feeling, I think, that those "like us" somehow have greater control over their lives. However, the processes forcing fishermen from their livelihoods at sea are not separate from, or in their origins all that different from, those forces that drive millions of peasants and tribespeople off the land in remoter settings. But remoteness and numbers should not matter. If we can only care about the big tragedies then we truly lose sight of what humanism means. We should care about the fisherfolk because their story is fundamentally one that entails us all. What I hope I have done in this book is to use anthropology and history to bring the fisherfolk into our view and within the reach of our empathy.

For too long, Scotland's fisherfolk have been ignored as part of Scotland's modern story. They are even virtually absent from Edinburgh's

Museum of Scotland. As I write these last pages, I find myself wondering what my fisherfolk readers will make of my project. I hope that they can take some pride in it, knowing how crucial they have been to its fulfilment. I hope also that they will see it as an attempt, which it is, to send their voices more widely around the world, to those in land-locked professions as well as to fishers on other coasts.

# Bibliography

Adams, D. (n.d.),. *Usan or Fishtown of Ullishaven*, Brechin: Chanonry Press.

—— (1991), *Johnshaven and Miltonhaven, a Social and Economic History*, Brechin: Chanonry Press.

—— (1993), 'The Harbour: Its Early History', in G. Jackson and S. Lythe (eds), *The Port of Montrose,* Wainscott, NY: The Georgica Press.

Aitken, H. (1973), *A Forgotten Heritage: Original Folk Tales of Lowland Scotland*, Totowa, NJ: Rowman & Littlefield.

Allison, C., Jacobs, S. and Porter, M. (1989), *Winds of Change: Women in Northwest Commercial Fishing,* Seattle: University of Washington Press.

Andersen, R. and Wadel, C. (eds), (1972), *North Atlantic Fishermen: Anthropological Essays on Modern Fishing*, Newfoundland Social and Economic Papers No. 5, St John's, Newfoundland: ISER.

Anderson, B. (1983), *Imagined Communities*: *Reflections on the Origin and Spread of Nationalism,* New York: Verso.

Anderson, B.G. (1990), *First Fieldwork*: *the Misadventures of an Anthropologist*, Prospect Heights, Illinois: Waveland.

Angus District Council (1977), *Montrose Local Plan: Report of Survey*. Forfar.

Anson, P. (1974 [1930]), *Fishing Boats and Fisher Folk on the East Coast of Scotland*, London: J.M. Dent & Sons.

—— (1947), 'Sea Fisheries', in Meikle, H. (ed.), *Scotland: A Description of Scotland and Scottish Life*, London, Thomas Nelson & Sons.

—— (1965), *Fisher Folk-Lore,* London: The Faith Press.

—— (1969), *Life on Low Shore*, Banff: The Banffshire Journal.

—— (1975) [1932] *Fishermen and Fishing Ways*, East Ardsley: EP Publishing Limited.

Appadurai, A. (1995), 'The Production of Locality' in R. Fardon (ed.), *Counterworks: Managing the Diversity of Knowledge*, London: Routledge.

—— (1996), *Modernity at Large: Cultural Dimensions of Globalization*, Minneapolis: University of Minnesota Press.

Appadurai, A. and Breckenridge, C. (1992), 'Museums are good to Think: Heritage on View in India', in Karp, I., Kreamer, C. and Lavine, S. (eds), *Museums and Communities: The Politics of Public Culture*, Washington, DC: Smithsonian.

Ardener, S. (1993), 'Ground Rules and Social Maps for Women: an Introduction', in S. Ardener (ed.), *Women and Space: Ground Rules and Social Maps*, Oxford: Berg.

Arensberg, C. (1959), *The Irish Countryman*, Gloucester MA: Peter Smith.

—— (1961), 'Community as Object and as Sample', *American Anthropologist* LXIII (1): 241–64.

Arensberg, C. and Kimball, S. (1968), *Family and Community in Ireland*, Cambridge, MA: Harvard University Press.

Armstrong, K. (1976), *The Participation of Scottish Women in Village Politics*, Unpublished Ph.D. thesis. University of Pittsburgh.

—— (1977), 'Women, Tourism, Politics', *Anthropological Quarterly* XLX: 135–45.

—— (1978), 'Rural Scottish Women: Politics without Power', *Ethnos* 43: 51–72.

Asad, T (ed.) (1973), *Anthropology and the Colonial Encounter*. London: Ithaca Press.

Association of Scottish District Fishery Boards (1977), *Salmon Fisheries of Scotland*, Farnham: Fishing News Books.

Atherton, D. (1992), *Aul Torry: O' Fish and Fowk*, City of Aberdeen.

Auge, M. (1995), *Non-Places,* London: Verso.

Bachofen, J. (1861), *Das Mutterecht*, Basel: Benno Schwabe.

Baks, C. and Postel-Coster, E. (1977), 'Fishing Communities on the Scottish East Coast: Tradition in a Modern Setting', in M. E Smith (ed.), *Those Who Live from the Sea: a Study in Maritime Anthropology*, St Paul: West.

Bamberger, J (1974), 'The Myth of Matriarchy: Why Men Rule in Primitive Society', in M. Rosaldo and L. Lamphere (eds), *Women, Culture and Society*, Stanford: Stanford University Press.

Barclay, W. (1922), *Banffshire*, Cambridge: Cambridge University Press.

Barth, F. (1969), *Ethnic Groups and Boundaries*, London.

Baxandall, M. (1991), 'Exhibiting Intention: some Preconditions of the Visual Display of Culturally Purposeful Objects', in I. Karp and S. Lavine (eds), *Exhibiting Culture*, Washington DC: Smithsonian.

Beaton, M. (1985), *Death of a Gossip*, New York: Ballantine.

Bell, C. and Newby, H. (1976), 'Husbands and Wives: the Dynamics of the Differential Dialectic', in N. A. Barker and S. Allen (eds), *Dependency and Exploitation in Work and Marriage*, London: Longman.

Bellier, I. and Wilson, T. (eds) (2000), *An Anthropology of the European Union: Building, Imagining and Experiencing the New Europe*, Oxford: Berg.

Bennett, T. (1988) 'Museums and "the People"', in R. Lumley (ed.), *The Museum Time Machine*, London: Routledge.

—— (1995), *The Birth of the Museum*, London: Routledge.

Berreman, G. (1972), 'Race, Caste, and Other Invidious Distinctions in Social Stratification', in *Race*. Special Issue: Race and Social Stratification 13: 4.

Berrill, M. (1997), *The Plundered Seas*, Vancouver: Greystone.

Bertram, J.G. (1869), *The Harvest of the Sea*, London.

—— (1883), *The Unappreciated Fisher Folk: Their Round of Life and Labour,* London: William Clowes & Sons.

Blades, K. (1995), *Net Destruction: The Death of Atlantic Canada's Fishery*, Halifax NS: Nimbus.

Blair, A. (1987), *Croft and Creel: a Century of Coastal Memories,* London: Shepheard-Walwyn.

Bloch, M. and Bloch, J. (1980), 'Women and the Dialectics of Nature in Eighteenth-Century French Thought', in MacCormack, C. and Strathern, M. (eds), *Nature, Culture and Gender*, Cambridge: Cambridge University Press.

Bochel, M. (1979), *'Dear Gremista': The Story of Nairn Fisher Girls at the Gutting,* Nairn: Nairn Fishertown Museum.

—— (1982), 'The Fisher Lassies', in B. Kay (ed.), *Odyssey: Voices from Scotland's Recent Past,* Edinburgh: Polygon.

Bodley, J. (1990), *Victims of Progress*, Mountain View CA: Mayfield.

Boissevain, J. (1994), 'Toward an Anthropology of European Communities?' pp. 41–56 in Goddard, et al. (eds), *The Anthropology of Europe: Identities and Boundaries in Conflict*, Oxford: Berg.

Boniface, P. and Fowler, P. (1993), *Heritage and Tourism in 'the Global village',* London: Routledge.

Boserup, E. (1970), *Women's Role in Economic Development,* London: Allen & Unwin.

Bowick, J., Lee, J. (eds), (1880), *Montrose Past and Present*, Montrose: David Davidson.

Boyarin, J. (ed.) (1994), *Remapping Memory: the Politics of TimeSpace*. Minneapolis: University of Minnesota Press.

Boyes, G., (1993), *The Imagined Village: Culture, Ideology and the English Folk Revival*, Manchester: Manchester University Press.

Boylan, P. (1990) 'Museums and Cultural Identity', *Museums Journal*, October 29–33.

Brandt, V. (1971), *A Korean Village: Between Farm and Sea,* East Asian Series No. 65. Cambridge MA: Harvard University Press.

Breitenbach, E., Brown, A. and Myers, F. (1998). 'Understanding Women in Scotland' *Feminist Review* 58: 44–65.

Britan, G. (1974), 'Modernization' on the North Atlantic Coast: The Transformation of a Traditional Newfoundland Fishing Village' pp. 65–82 in Andersen, R. (ed.), *North Atlantic Maritime Cultures,* St John's: ISER.

Brody, H. (1975), *Inishkillane,* New York: Schocken.

Broun, D., Finlay, R. and M. Lynch, M. (eds), 1998, *Image and Identity: The Making and Re-making of Scotland Through the Ages,* Edinburgh: John Donald.

Brown, G. M, (1995), *Beside the Ocean of Time,* London: Flamingo (HarperCollins).

Brown, J. (1983–4) 'Land Beyond Brigadoon', in *Sight and Sound* 53: 40–6.

Brown, M. (1996), 'On Resisting Resistance', *American Anthropologist,* 98(4): 729–35

Bruce, D. (1996), *Scotland the Movie,* Edinburgh: Polygon.

Bruce, N. (1934), *Twilight of Scotland,* Glasgow: John Smith & Son.

Bryson, B. (1995), *Notes from a Small Island,* London: Black Swan.

Buchan, D. (1984), *Scottish Tradition,* London: Routledge & Kegan Paul.

Buchan, J. (1936), *The Free Fishers,* London: Thomas Nelson & Sons Ltd.

Buchan, M. (1977), 'The Social Organisation of Fisher-Girls', Conference Paper, Aberdeen.

Buchan, N. and P. Hall (eds) (1973), *The Scottish Folksinger,* Glasgow: Collins.

Buchan, P. (1992), *Collected Poems and Short Stories,* Edinburgh: Gordon Wright.

Buckle, H. (1970), *On Scotland and the Scotch Intellect,* Chicago: University of Chicago Press.

Butchart, L. (1968), 'Montrose: an Industrial History', Unpublished MA Thesis in Geography for the University of St Andrews.

Butcher, D. (1987), *Following the Fishing,* Newton Abbot: Tops'l Books.

Button, J. (ed.) (1978), *The Shetland Way of Oil,* Sandwick, Shetland: Thuleprint.

Byron, R. (1975), 'Economic Functions of Kinship Values in Family Businesses: Fishing Crews in North Atlantic Communities', *Sociology and Social Research,* 60: 147–60.

—— (1986), *Sea Change: a Shetland Society, 1970–1979,* St. John's Newfoundland: Institute of Social and Economic Research.

—— (1994), 'The Maritime Household in Northern Europe', *Comparative Study of Society and History,* 271–92.

—— and Chalmers, D. (199), 'The Fisherwomen of Fife: History, Identity and Social change', in *Ethnologia Europaea* 23: 2.

Cage, R. (1981), *The Scottish Poor Law, 1745–1845*, Edinburgh: Scottish Academic Press.

Calder, A. (1994), *Revolving Culture: Notes from the Scottish Republic,* London: Tauris.

Callander, R. (1998), *How Scotland is Owned*, Edinburgh: Canongate

Cannizzo, J. (curator) (1999), *O Caledonia! Sir Walter Scott and the Creation of Scotland*. Exhibit at the Scottish National Portrait Gallery, Edinburgh.

Cargill, G. (1976), *Blockade '75*, Glasgow: Molendinar.

Carrier, J. and Carrier, A. (1987), 'Brigadoon, or; Musical Comedy and the Persistence of Tradition in Melanesian Ethnography', in *Oceania,* 57: 271–93.

Carrier, J. (1992), 'Occidentalism: The World Turned Upside Down', *American Ethnologist,* 19: 195–212.

—— (ed.) (1995) *Occidentalism: Images of the West,* Oxford: Clarendon Press.

Carson, R. (1962), *Silent Spring*, Boston: Houghton Mifflin.

Carter, I. (1974), 'The Highlands of Scotland as an Underdeveloped Region', in E. de Kadt and G. Williams (eds), *Sociology and Development*, London: Tavistock.

—— (1979), *Farm Life in Northeast Scotland 1840–1914.* Edinburgh: John Donald.

—— (1981), The Changing Image of the Scottish Peasantry, 1745–1980, in R. Samuels (ed.), *People's History and Socialist Theory*, London: Routledge & Kegan Paul.

Carwardine, R. (1979), *Transatlantic Revivalism*, Westport CT.

Chantraine, P. (1993), *The Last Cod Fish: Life and Death of the Newfoundland Way of Life,* Montreal: Robert Davies.

Chapman, M. (1978), *The Gaelic Vision in Scottish Culture*, London: Croom Helm

—— (1992), *The Celts,* New York: St Martin's.

Chitnis, A. (1976), *The Scottish Enlightenment*, London: Croom Helm.

Christensen, J. (1977), 'Motor Power and Women Power: Technological and Economic Change Among Fanti Fishermen in Ghana', in M.E. Smith (ed.), *Those Who Live from the Sea: A Study in Maritime Anthropology*, St Paul: West.

Clark, D. (1982), *Between Pulpit and Pew: Folk Religion in a North Yorkshire Fishing Village*, Cambridge: Cambridge University Press.

Clark, M. (1988), 'Managing Uncertainty: Family, Religion and Collective Action among Fishermen's Wives in Gloucester, Massachusetts', pp. 261–78 in Nadel-Klein and Davis (eds), *To Work and To Weep*, St John's, Newfoundland: ISER.

Clifford, J. (1986), 'Partial Truths', in J. Clifford and G. Marcus (eds), *Writing Culture: the Poetics and Politics of Ethnography*, Berkeley: University of California Press.

Cohen, A. (1982), *Belonging: Identity and Social Organisation in British Rural Cultures*, Manchester: Manchester University Press.

—— (1985), *The Symbolic Construction of Community*, London: Tavistock.

—— (1987), *Whalsay: Symbol, Segment and Boundary in a Shetland Island Community*, Manchester: Manchester University Press.

—— (1990), 'The British Anthropological Tradition, Otherness and Rural Studies' pp. 203–24 in P. Lowe and M. Bodiguel (eds), *Rural Studies in Britain and France*, London: Belhaven Press.

—— (1996), 'Personal Nationalism: a Scottish View of some Rites, Rights and Wrongs', *American Ethnologist* 23(4): 1–14.

—— (1999), 'Being Scottish? On the Problem of the Objective Correlative', in Bort, E. and Keat, R., (eds), *The Boundaries of Understanding: Essays in Honour of Malcolm Anderson*, Edinburgh: International Social Sciences Institute, University of Edinburgh.

Cole, J. (1977), 'Anthropology Comes Part-Way Home: Community Studies in Europe', in *Annual Review of Anthropology* 6: 349–78.

Cole, S. (1991), *Women of the Praia*, Princeton: Princeton University Press.

Colls, R. (1977), *The Collier's Rant: Song and Culture in the Industrial Village*, London: Croom Helm.

Connerton, P. (1989), *How Societies Remember*, Cambridge: Cambridge University Press.

Cook, J. (1984), *Close to the Earth: Living Social History of the British Isles*, London: Routledge & Kegan Paul.

Cooper, D. (1992), *The Road to Mingulay*, London: Warner Books.

Cooper, H. (1986), *Winslow Homer Watercolors*, Washington: National Gallery of Art.

Cooper, S. (1986), *The Dark is Rising*, Collier Books.

Cordell, J. (1989) (ed.), *A Sea of Small Boats,* Cambridge MA: Cultural Survival.

Coull, J. (1969), 'Fisheries in the North-East of Scotland Before 1800', *Scottish Studies*, 13: 17–31.

—— (1971), *Crofter Fishermen in Norway and Scotland*, O'Dell Memorial Monograph No. 2. Aberdeen: University of Aberdeen.

—— (1972), *The Fisheries of Europe: an Economic Geography,* London: G. Bell & Sons.

—— (ed.) (1983), *The Personal and Family Story of Gilbert Buchan in the History of the Herring Industry*, Buckland Occasional Papers: No. 1.

—— (1986), 'The Scottish Herring Fishery 1800–1914: Development and Intensification of a Pattern of Resource Use', *Scottish Geographical Magazine* 4–17.

—— (1989), 'The Fisherfolk and Fisher Settlements of the Grampian Region', in J.S. Smith and D. Stevenson (eds), *Fermfolk and Fisherfolk*, Aberdeen: Aberdeen University Press.

—— (1992), 'The Development of the Fishery Districts of Scotland', *Northern Scotland* 12: 117–32.

—— (1996), *The Sea Fisheries of Scotland: A Historical Geography*, Edinburgh.

Craig, C. (1996), *Out of History*, Edinburgh: Polygon.

Currie, S. (1996), *The Glace Bay Miners' Museum,* Wreck Cove, Cape Breton Island: Breton Books.

Czerkawska, L. (1975), *The Fisher-Folk of Carrick: a History of the Fishing Industry in South Ayrshire*, Glasgow: Molendinar.

Daiches, D. (1975), *Was*, Glasgow: Richard Drew Publishing.

Danforth, L. (1989), *Fire Walking and Religious Healing*, Princeton: Princeton University Press.

Davies, M. (1982) 'Corsets and Conception: Fashion and Demographic Trends in the Nineteenth Century', *Comparative Studies in Society and History* 24(4): 611–41.

Davis, D. (1983), *Blood and Nerves*, St. John's, Newfoundland: Insitute for Social and Economic Research.

—— (1988), '"Shore Skippers" and "Grass Widows" Active and Passive Women's Roles in a Newfoundland Fishery', in Nadel-Klein, J. and Davis, D., *To Work and To Weep: Women in Fishing Economies*, St John's, Newfoundland: ISER.

Davis, D. and Nadel-Klein, J. 'Terra Cognita? A Review of the Literature', in Nadel-Klein, J. and Davis, D., *To Work and to Weep: Women in Fishing Economies*, St John's, Newfoundland: ISER.

Dennis, N., Henriques, F. and Slaughter, C. (1969), *Coal is Our Life: An Analysis of a Yorkshire Mining Community,* London: Tavistock.

Devine, T. (1984), 'Women Workers, 1850–1914', in T. Devine (ed.), *Farm Servants and Labour in Lowland Scotland 1770–1914,* Edinburgh: John Donald.

Dodgshon, R. (1980), 'Medieval Settlement and Colonisation', in M.Parry and T. Slater (eds), *The Making of the Scottish Countryside*, London: Croom Helm.

Donaldson, G. (1972), *Scotland: Church and Nation Through Sixteen Centuries*, New York: Harper & Row.

Dorian, N. (1981), *Language Death: the Life Cycle of a Scottish Gaelic Dialect*, Philadelphia: University of Pennsylvania Press.

Dorst, J. (1987), *The Written Suburb: An American Site. An Ethnographic Dilemma*, Philadelphia: University of Pennsylvania Press.

Douglas, A. (1857), *History of the Village of Ferryden*, Montrose.

Douglass, D. and Krieger, J. (1983), *A Miner's Life*, London: Routledge & Kegan Paul.

Dugmore, R. (1972), *Puttenham under the Hog's Back*, London: Philliback.

Duncan, D. (n.d.), *The Montrose Lifeboat*, Montrose.

Durie, A. and Ingram, J. (1994), *George Washington Wilson in St. Andrews and Fife*, Aberdeen: Aberdeen University Library Publishing.

Edwards, D.H. (1971), *Among the Fisherfolk of Usan and Ferryden*, Brechin: Brechin Advertiser.

Elliott, C. (1978), Sailing *Fishermen in Old Photographs*, Reading: Tops'l Books.

—— (1979), *Steam Fishermen in Old Photographs*, Reading: Tops'l Books.

Ennew, J. (1980), *The Western Isles*, Cambridge: Cambridge University Press.

Eyre-Todd, G. (1947), *Scotland, Picturesque and Traditional*, Stirling: Eneas Mackay.

Fife 93 (1993) *A Free Guide*, Glenrothes: Glenrothes Tourist Information Centre.

Finlay, I. (1998), 'Hesiod: an Epigram on the Common Fisheries Policy', in Finlay, A. (ed.), *Green Waters: An Anthology of Boats and Voyages*, Edinburgh: Polygon, p. 33.

Fitchen, J. (1991), *Endangered Spaces, Enduring Places: Change, Identity, and Survival in Rural America*, Boulder: Westview.

Flinn, M. (ed.) (1977), *Scottish Population History: from the Seventeenth Century to the 1930s*, Cambridge: Cambridge University Press.

Forsythe, D. (1974), *Escape to Fulfilment: Urban-Rural Migration and the Future of a Small Island Community*, unpublished Ph.D. thesis. Cornell University.

—— (1980), 'Urban Incomers and Rural Change: the impact of Migrants from the City on Life in an Orkney Community', *Sociologica Ruralis*, xx: 4.

Frank, A.G. (1969), *Capitalism and Underdevelopment in Latin America*, Harmondsworth: Penguin.

Frankenberg, R. (1957), *Village on the Border*, London: Cohen & West.

Frankenberg, R. (1966) 'British Community Studies: Problems of Synthesis', in M. Banton (ed.), *The Social Anthropology of Complex Societies*, London: Tavistock.

—— (1969), *Communities in Britain: Social Life in Town and Country*, Harmondsworth: Penguin.

Fraser, D. (1971), *The Smugglers*, Montrose: Standard Press.

—— (1974), *East Coast Oil Town*, Montrose: Standard Press.

Fraser, D. (1983), *The Christian Watt Papers*, Edinburgh: Paul Harris.

Fried, M. (1975), *The Notion of Tribe*, Menlo Park: Cummings.

Friedman, J. (1997), 'Simplifying Complexity: Assimilating the Global in a Small Paradise', in Olwig, K. and Hastrup, K. (eds), *Siting Culture: The Shifting Anthropological Object,* London and New York: Routledge.

Frykman, J. (1987), 'Clean and Proper', in J. Frykman and O. Lofgren, *Culture Builders,* New Brunswick: Rutgers University Press.

Gable, E. and Handler, R. (1996), 'After Authenticity at an American Heritage Site', in *American Anthropologist* 98(3): 569–78.

Gaffin, D. (1996), *In Place: Spatial and Social Order in a Faeroe Islands Community,* Prospect Heights: Waveland Press.

Garner, A. (1960), *The Weirdstone of Brisingamen*, London: Collins.

Garry, F. (1988), 'To Suffie, The Last of the Buchan Fishwives', in A. Lawrie, H. Matthews and D. Ritchie (eds), *A Glimmer of Cold Brine: A Scottish Sea Anthology*, Aberdeen: Aberdeen University Press.

Gathercole, P. (1991), 'The Fetishism of Artefacts', in S. Pearce (ed.), *Museum Studies in Material Culture,* Washington DC: Leicester University Press and Smithsonian Institution Press.

Geertz, C. (1983), *Local Knowledge: Further Essays in Interpretive Anthropology*, New York: Basic Books.

Gewertz, D. and Errington, F. (1999), *Emerging Class in Papua New Guinea: the Telling of Difference,* Cambridge: Cambridge University Press.

Gibbon, L. G. (1971), *Sunset Song*, London: Longman.

Gibson, W.M (1994), *Fishing in Old East Lothian: Cockenzie, Port Seton, Fisherrow and Prestonpans,* East Lothian District Library.

Gilchrist, J. (1999), 'A Wordy Cause', in *The Scotsman*, 22 May: 13.

Gill, A. (1993), *Superstitions: Folk Magic in Hull's Fishing Community*, Beverley, North Humberside: Hutton.

Gmelch, G. (1977), *The Irish Tinkers*, Menlo Park CA: Cummings.

Goddard, V., Llobera, J and Shore, C. (eds), 1994, *The Anthropology of Europe: Identities and Boundaries in Conflict*, Oxford: Berg.

Goffman, E. (1963). *Stigma*, Englewood Cliffs: Prentice Hall.

Gold, J. and Gold, M. (1995), *Imagining Scotland: Tradition, Represent-ation and Promotion in Scotish Tourism since 1750,* Aldershot: Scolar Press.

Gomme, G. (1890), *The Village Community: with Special Reference to the Origin and Form of its Survivals in Britain*, New York: Scribner & Welford.

Gordon, E. (1990), 'Women's Spheres', in W.H. Fraser and R.J. Morris (eds), *People and Society in Scotland vol. II, 1830–1914,* Edinburgh: John Donald.

Gordon, E. and Breitenbach, E. (eds), 1990, *The World is Ill Divided: Women's Work in Scotland in the Nineteenth and Early Twentieth Centuries*, Edinburgh: Edinburgh University Press.

Gould, S.J. (1996), *The Mismeasure of Man*, New York: W.W. Norton.

Gourlay, G. (1879) *Fisher Life; or, the Memorials of Cellardyke and the Fife Coast*, Cupar.

Grant, I.F.(1961), *Highland Folk Ways*, London: Routledge & Kegan Paul.

Gray, M. (1967), 'Organisation and Growth in the East-Coast Herring Fishing 1800–1885', in P. Payne (ed.), *Studies in Scottish Business History,* New York: A.M.Kelley.

—— (1978), *The Fishing Industries of Scotland, 1790–1914,* Oxford: Oxford University Press.

—— ( n.d.), 'Foreword', in J. Waterman, *Aberdeen and the Fishing Industry in the Eighteen Seventies*, Aberdeen: Centre for Scottish Studies.

—— (1984), 'Farm Workers in North-East Scotland', in Devine, T. (ed.), *Farm Servants and Labour in Lowland Scotland, 1770–1914*, Edin-burgh: John Donald, pp. 10–28.

—— (1993), 'The Fishing Industry from 1800', in G. Jackson and S. Lythe (eds), *The Port of Montrose: a History of its Harbour, Trade and Shipping*, Tayport: Hutton Press.

Green. F. (1936), 'Rural and Coastal Settlement in the Moray Firth Lowlands', in *Scottish Geographical Magazine*, March: 97–118.

Greenlaw, L. (1999), *The Hungry Ocean,* New York: Hyperion.

Greenwood, D. (1989), 'Culture by the Pound: an Anthropological Persp-ective on Tourism as Cultural Commoditization', in V. Smith (ed.), *Hosts and Guests: the Anthropology of Tourism,* Philadelphia: Uni-versity of Pennsylvania Press.

Grimes, Marsha (1989), *The Old Silent*, New York: Onyx.

—— (1993), *The Horse You Came In On*, New York: Onyx.

Gunn, N. (1941), *The Silver Darlings*, London: Faber & Faber.

Gupta, A. and Ferguson, J. (1997), 'Discipline and Practice: "The Field" as Site, Method and Location in Anthropology', in A. Gupta and J. Ferguson (eds), *Anthropological Locations: Boundaries and Grounds of a Field Science,* Berkeley: University of California Press.

Habermas, J. (1973), *Legitimation Crisis,* Boston: Beacon Press.

Handler, R. (1985) , On Having a Culture: Nationalism and the Preservation of Quebec's Patrimoine', in G. Stocking (ed.), *Objects and Others: Essays on Museums and Material Culture*, Madison: University of Wisconsin Press.

—— (1988), *Nationalism and the Politics of Culture in Quebec*, Madison: University of Wisconsin Press.

Hardin, G. (1968), 'The Tragedy of the Commons', in *Science* 162: 1243–48

Hardy, F. (1990), *Scotland in Film,* Edinburgh: Edinburgh University Press.

Harrison, I. (1992), *En Kin Ee Mine Es?* Buckie: Moray District Council.

Harvie, C. (1977), *Scotland and Nationalism*, London: Allen & Unwin.

—— (1992), *Cultural Weapons: Scotland and Survival in a New Europe,* Edinburgh: Polygon.

Hay, E. and Walker, B. (1985), *Focus on Fishing: Arbroath and Gourdon*, Dundee: Abertay Historical Society Publication number 23.

Hechter, M. (1975), *Internal Colonialism*, London: Routledge & Kegan Paul.

Henderson, I. (1990), *Discovering Angus and the Mearns*, Edinburgh: John Donald.

Hendry, J. (1992), 'Snug in the Asylum of Taciturnity: Women's History in Scotland' , in I. Donnachie and C. Whatley (eds), *The Manufacture of Scottish History*, Edinburgh: Polygon.

Herzfeld, M. (1987), *Anthropology Through the Looking Glass: Critical Ethnography in the Margins of Europe*, Cambridge: Cambridge University Press.

—— (1991), *A Place in History*, Princeton: Princeton University Press.

Hewison, R. (1987), *The Heritage Industry: Britain in a Climate of Decline,* London: Methuen.

Hobsbawm, E and Ranger, T. (eds) (1983), *The Invention of Tradition*, Cambridge: Cambridge University Press.

Holy, L. and Stuchlik, M. (1981), 'The Structure of Folk Models', in L. Holy and M. Stuchlik (eds), *The Structure of Folk Models*, London: Academic Press.

Hooper-Greenhill, E. (1991), *Museum and Gallery Education*, Leicester: Leicester University Press.

——— (1992), *Museums and the Shaping of Knowledge*, London: Routledge.

House, J. (ed.) (1986), *Fish Vs. Oil: Resources and Rural Development in North Atlantic Societies*, Social and Economic Papers No. 16, St. Johns, Newfoundland: Institute for Social and Economic Research.

Houston, J.M. (1948) 'Village Planning in Scotland, 1745–1845', in *Advancement of Science* V: 129–33.

Houston, R. (1989), 'Women in the Economy and Society of Scotland, 1500–1800', in R. Houston and I. Whyte (eds), *Scottish Society 1500–1800*, Cambridge: Cambridge University Press.

Hoyau, P. (1988), 'Heritage and "the conserver society": the French case', in Lumley, R. (ed.), *The Museum Time-Machine*, London: Routledge, pp. 27–35.

Huby, G. (1992), 'Trapped in the Present: the Past, Present and Future of a Group of Old People in East London', in S. Wallman (ed.), *Contemporary Futures: Perspectives from Social Anthropology*, London: Routledge.

Hume, J. and J. Storer (1997), *Industry and Transport in Scottish Museums*, Edinburgh: The Stationery Office.

Hunt, D. (1976), 'The Sociology of Development: its Relevance to Aberdeen' in the *Scottish Journal of Sociology* 1(2): 135–54.

Hunter, James (1976), *The Making of the Crofting Community*, Edinburgh: John Donald.

Hutcheson, G. (1988), *Days of Yore or Buckie and District in the Past*, Buckie: Provost Publications.

Huth, A. (1998), *Wives of the Fishermen*, New York: St Martin's Press.

Jackson, B. (1968), *Working Class Community*, New York: Praeger.

James, S. (1999), *The Atlantic Celts: Ancient People or Modern Invention*, Madison: University of Wisconsin Press.

Jedrej, C. and Nuttall, M. (1996), *White Settlers: The Impact of Rural Repopulation in Scotland*, Luxembourg: Harwood.

Junger, P. (1997), *The Perfect Storm*, New York: Harper/Collins.

Kalland, A. (1995), *Fishing Villages in Tokugawa Japan*, Richmond, Surrey: Curzon.

Kapferer, B. (1990), 'From the Periphery to the Centre: Ethnography and the Critique of Ethnography in Sri Lanka', in Fardon, R. (ed.), *Localizing Strategies: Regional Traditions of Ethnographic Writing*, Edinburgh: Scottish Academic Press.

Karakasidou, Anastasia, 1997. *Fields of Wheat, Hills of Blood*, Chicago: University of Chicago.

Kay, B. (1993), *Scots: The Mither Tongue*, Ayrshire: Alloway.

Kearns, G. and Philo, C. (eds) (1993), *Selling Places: The City as Cultural Capital, Past and Present*, Oxford: Pergamon.

Kellas, J. (1968), *Modern Scotland: the Nation Since 1870*, New York: Praeger.

Kellas, J. and Fotheringham, P. (n.d.), 'The Political Behaviour of the Working Class', in A. MacLaren (ed.), *Social Class in Scotland, Past and Present*, Edinburgh: John Donald.

King, M. ( n.d.), *An Auchmithie Album,* Forfar: Angus District Council Libraries and Museums Service.

—— (1992–93), 'A Partnership of Equals: Women in Scottish East Coast Fishing Communities' *Journal of Ethnological Studies* 31: 2–35.

Kirschenblatt-Gimblett, B. (1998), *Destination Culture: Tourism, Museums and Heritage,* Berkeley: University of California Press.

Knipe, E. (1984), *Gamrie: an Exploration in Cultural Ecology*, Lanham: University Press of America.

Knox, W. (1990), 'The Political and Workplace Culture of the Scottish Working Class, 1832–1914', in W. Hamish Fraser and R.J. Morris (eds), *People and Society in Scotland Volume II, 1830–1914*, Edinburgh: John Donald.

Kuklick, H. (1993), *The Savage Within: The Social History of British Anthropology, 1885–1945*, Cambridge: Cambridge University Press.

Kunstler, J. (1993), *The Geography of Nowhere: the Rise and Decline of America's Man-Made Landscape*, New York: Simon & Schuster.

Lantenari, V. (1963), *The Religions of the Oppressed*, New York.

Laslett, P. (1984), *The World We Have Lost: Further Explored*, New York: Charles Scribner's Sons.

Lawrie, A., Matthews, H., and Ritchie, D. (eds) (1988), *Glimmer of Cold Brine: a Scottish Sea Anthology*, Aberdeen: Aberdeen University Press.

Lebow, N. (1976), *White Britain Black Ireland: The Influence of Stereotypes on Colonial Policy,* Philadelphia: Institute for the Study of Human Issues.

Lenman, B. (1981), *From Esk to Tweed: Harbours, Ships and Men of the East Coast of Scotland*, Glasgow: Blackie.

—— (1977), *An Economic History of Modern Scotland*, Hamden, Connecticut: Archon Books.

Levi. L. (1883), *The Economic Condition of Fishermen*, London: William Clowes & Sons.

Linares, O. (1985), 'Cash Crops and Gender Constructs: the Jola of Senegal', in *Ethnology* 24(2): 83–94.

Lindsay, M. (1980), *Lowland Scottish Villages*, London: Robert Hale.

Littlejohn, J. (1963), *Westrigg: the Sociology of a Cheviot Parish,* London: Routledge & Kegan Paul.

Livingstone (1996), *Scottish Customs*, New York: Barnes & Noble Books.

Lockhart, D. (1982), Patterns of Migration and Movement of Labour to the Planned Villages of North East Scotland in *Scottish Geographical Magazine*, April: 35–47.

Lockhart, W. (1997), *The Scots and Their Fish*, Edinburgh: Birlinn.

Lofgren, O. (1972), 'Resource Management and Family Firms: Swedish West Coast Fishermen', in R. Andersen and C. Wadel (eds), *North Atlantic Fishermen: Anthropological Essays on Modern Fishing*, Toronto: Memorial University of Newfoundland

—— (1987), 'The Nature Lovers' in J. Frykman and O. Lofgren, *Culture Builders*, New Brunswick: Rutgers University Press.

Lohr, S. (1989), 'Guarding Britain's Treasures' in *Historic Preservation*, November/December: 42–9.

Low, J. (1943), *Industry in Montrose,* Brechin: Pitnolen.

Lowenthal, D. (1985), *The Past is a Foreign Country*, Cambridge: Cambridge University Press.

—— (1992), 'The Death of the Future', in S. Wallman, (ed.), *Contemporary Futures: Perspectives from Social Anthropology*, London: Routledge.

—— (1994), 'Identity, Heritage, and History', in J. Gillis (ed.), *Commemorations: the Politics of National Identity,* Princeton: Princeton University Press.

—— (1998), *The Heritage Crusade and the Spoils of History*, Cambridge: Cambridge University Press.

Lummis. T. (1977), 'The Occupational Community of East Anglian Fishermen: an Historical Dimension Through Oral Evidence', *British Journal of Sociology* XXXVIII(1): 51–74.

—— (1985), *Occupation and Society: The East Anglian Fishermen 1880–1914*, Cambridge: Cambridge University Press.

Lutz, C and Collins, N. (1993), *Reading National Geographic*, Chicago: University of Chicago Press.

Lynch, M. (1992), *Scotland, a New History*, London: Pimlico.

Lythe, S. (1993), 'Early Modern Trade, c. 1550–1707' in G. Jackson and S. Lythe (eds), *The Port of Montrose: a History of its Harbour, Trade and Shipping*, Tayport: Hutton Press.

MacCannell, D. (1989), *The Tourist: A New Theory of the Leisure Class*, New York: Schocken.

McCay, B. (1989), 'Sea Tenure and the Culture of the Commoners', in J. Cordell (ed.) *A Sea of Small Boats*, Cambridge, MA: Cultural Survival, Inc.

Macdonald, S. (1987), *Social and Linguistic Identity in the Scottish Gaidhealtachd,* Unpublished D. Phil. Thesis, Oxford University.

—— (ed.) (1993), *Inside European Identities: Ethnography in Western Europe*, Oxford: Berg.

—— (1997a), *Reimagining Culture: Histories, Identities and the Gaelic Renaissance,* Oxford: Berg.

—— (1997b), 'A People's Story: Heritage , Identity and Authenticity', in C. Rojek and J. Urry (eds), *Touring Cultures: Transformation of Travel and Theory,* London: Routledge.

Mackay, G. (1986), 'The Conflicts Between the Oil and Fishing Industries in the North Sea', in J. House (ed.), *Fish Vs. Oil: Resources and Rural Development in North Atlantic Societies,* Social and Economic Papers No. 16, St. John's, Newfoundland: Institute for Social and Economic Research, Memorial University of Newfoundland.

MacLaren, A. (ed.) (1976), *Social Class in Scotland, Past and Present,* Edinburgh: John Donald.

Malinowski, B. (1948), *Magic, Science and Religion and other Essays,* Boston: Beacon.

Martin, A. (1995), *Fishing and Whaling,* Edinburgh: National Museums of Scotland.

Martin, P. (1991), *What to See in St Monans: a Guided Walk,* Cupar, Fife.

Mather J. (1969), 'Aspects of the Linguistic Geography of Scotland III: Fishing Communities of the East Coast (Part 1)', in *Scottish Studies,* 13: 1–16.

Matless, D. (1994), 'Doing the English Village, 1945–91: An Essay in Imaginative Geography', in P. Cloke, M. Doel, D. Matless, M. Phillips and N. Thrifts (eds), *Writing the Rural: Five Cultural Geographies,* London: Paul Chapman.

McArthur, C. (1998), 'Scotland and the "Braveheart" Effect', in *Journal for the Study of British Cultures* 5 (1): 27–30.

McBeth (1998), 'Dewar Calms Fears of Lairds', http://w.w.w.scotsman.com/news/ne15eigg981014.1.html

McBryde, I. (ed.) (1985), *Who Owns the Past?* Melbourne: Oxford University Press.

McCarthy, J. (1998), *An Inhabited Solitude: Scotland, Land and People,* Edinburgh: Luath Press.

McCay, B. (1989), 'Sea Tenure and the Culture of the Commoners', in J. Cordell (ed.), *A Sea of Small Boats,* Cambridge, MA: Cultural Survival.

McCrone, D. (1992), *Understanding Scotland: The Sociology of a State-less Nation,* London: Routledge

—— (1996), 'We're A' Jock Tamson's Bairns: Social Class in Twentieth-Century Scotland', in Devine and Finlay (eds), *Scotland in the Twentieth Century,* Edinburgh: Edinburgh University Press.

McCrone, D., Morris, A. and Kiely, R. (1995), *Scotland – the Brand: The Making of Scottish Heritage,* Edinburgh: Edinburgh University Press.

McCrone, D. Stewart, R., Kiely, R. and Bechhofer, F. (1998) 'Who are we? Problematising National Identity' in *The Sociological Review*: 629–52.

McEwen, J. (1981), *Who Owns Scotland*, Edinburgh: EUSPB.

McGoodwin, J. (1990). *Crisis in the World's Fisheries: People, Problems and Policies*, Stanford: Stanford University Press.

McGrath, J. (1974), *The Cheviot, The Stag, and the Black, Black Oil*, Kyleakin: West Highland Publishing Company.

McIlvanney, W. (1985), *The Big Man*, London: Sceptre.

McIvor, A. (1992), 'Women and Work in Twentieth Century Scotland', in A. Dickson and J. Treble (eds), *People and Society in Scotland Volume III, 1914–1990*, Edinburgh: John Donald.

McKinney, R. (1999), *Old Tunes for New Times: Contemporary Scottish Nationalism and the Folk Music Revival*, unpublished Ph.D. thesis, Department of Social Anthropology, University of Edinburgh.

McLennan, J. ([1865] 1970), *Primitive Marriage*, P. Riviere, (ed.), Chicago.

McMillan, R. (n.d.), *Broughty Ferry in the Days of Sail*, Dundee.

Mead, M. (1980), 'On the Viability of Villages', in P. Reining and B. Lenkerd (eds), *Village Viability in Contemporary Society*, Boulder: American Association for the Advancement of Science.

Mellor, A. (1991), 'Enterprise and Heritage in the Dock' in Corner, J. and Harvey, S. (eds), *Enterprise and Heritage: Crosscurrents of National culture*, London: Routledge.

Mencher, J. (1982), 'Muddy Feet, Dirty Hands: Rice Production and Female Agricultural Labour', *Economic and Political Weekly* 17: 52.

Miely, D. (1984), *Scottish Entrepreneurs Across Three Generations: the Fishing Town of Pittenweem*, unpublished Ph.D. dissertation in anthropology for Rutgers University. Ann Arbor: University Microfilms.

Miles, R. (1993), 'The Articulation of Racism and Nationalism: Reflections on European History' in Wrench, J. and Solomos, J. (eds), *Racism and Migration in Western Europe*, Oxford: Berg.

Miller, J. (1999), *Salt in the Blood: Scotland's Fishing Communities Past and Present,* Edinburgh: Canongate.

Miller, D., (1995), 'Introduction: Anthropology, Modernity and Consumption', in *Worlds Apart: Modernity Through the Prism of the Local*, London: Routledge.

Miller, D. (ed.) (1995), *Worlds Apart: Modernity Through the Prism of the Local*. London: Routledge

Millman, R. (1975), *The Making of the Scottish Landscape,* London: Batsford.

Mitchell, H. (1896), *A Brief Memorial of Ferryden Free Church*, Montrose.

Mitchell, W. (1860), *A Memoir of William Guthrie*, Montrose.

Mitchison, R. (1978), *Life in Scotland*, London: Batsford.

—— 'The Making of the Old Scottish Poor Law', *Past and Present*, 6: 58–93.

Moerman, D. (1984), 'Common Property and the Common Good: Ecological Factors among Peasant and Tribal Fishermen', in Gunda, *The Fishing Culture of the World,* Budapest: Academiai Klado.

Moore, R. (1982), *The Social Impact of Oil: the Case of Peterhead*, London: Routledge & Kegan Paul.

Morgan, L. H. (1877), *Ancient Society*, New York.

Morton, H.V. (1933), *In Scotland Again,* London: Methuen.

Muir, E. (1935), *Scottish Journey,* Edinburgh: Mainstream.

Mullen, P. (1978), *I Heard the Old Fisherman Say*, Austin: University of Texas Press.

Murphy, R. and Murphy, Y. (1974), *Women of the Forest,* New York: Columbia University Press.

Murray, M. (1986), *The Skipper's Notebook,* Anstruther: Scottish Fisheries Museum.

Myerhoff, B. (1978), *Number Our Days*. London: Simon & Schuster.

Nadel, J. (1983), 'Houston's Little Sisters: A Cross-Cultural Perspective on Offshore Oil', in *Human Organization* 42(2): 167–72.

—— (1984), 'Stigma and Separation: Pariah Status and Community Persistence in a Scottish Fishing Village', *Ethnology* XXIII(2): 101–15.

—— (1986), 'Burning with the Fire of God', *Ethnology* XXV (1): 49–60.

Nadel-Klein, J., 'A Fisher Laddie Needs a Fisher Lassie: Endogamy and Work in a Scottish Fishing Village', in Nadel-Klein, J. and Davis, D. *To Work and to Weep: Women in Fishing Economies*, St John's, Newfoundland: ISER.

—— (1991a), 'Reweaving the Fringe: localism, Tradition and Representation in British Ethnography', *American Ethnologist* 18(3): 500–15.

—— (1991b), 'Picturing Aborigines: A Review Essay on *After Two Hundred Years: Photographic Essays on Aboriginal and Islander Australia Today*', *Cultural Anthropology* 414–23.

—— (1995), 'Occidentalism as a Cottage Industry: Representing the Autochthonous 'Other ' in British and Irish Rural Studies', in J. Carrier, (ed.), *Occidentalism: Images of the West*, Oxford: Clarendon Press.

—— (1997), 'Crossing a Representational Divide: From West to East in Scottish Ethnography', in James, A., Hockey, J. and Dawson, A. (eds), *After Writing Culture*, London: Routledge.

—— (2000), 'Granny Baited the Lines: Perpetual Crisis and the Changing Role of Women in Scottish Fishing Communities' in *Women's Studies International Forum* 23(3): 363–72.

Nadel-Klein, J. and Davis, D.L. (eds) (1988), *To Work and To Weep: Women in Fishing Economies*, St John's, Newfoundland: ISER.

Nader, L. (1972), 'Up the anthropologist – perspectives gained from studying up' in D. Hymes (ed.), *Reinventing Anthropology*, New York: Pantheon.

Nairn, T. (1977), *The Break-Up of Britain*, London: NLB.

—— (1997), *Faces of Nationalism*, London: Verso.

Nemec, T. (1972) 'I Fish with my Brother: The Structure and Behaviour of Agnatic-Based Fishing Crews in a Newfoundland Irish Outport', in R. Andersen and C. Wadel (eds), *North Atlantic Fishermen*, Toronto: Memorial University of Newfoundland.

Neville, G.K. (1979) 'Community Form and Ceremonial Life in Three Regions of Scotland', *American Ethnologist* 6 (1): 93–109.

*New Statistical Account of the Parish of Craig 1835.*

Newby, H. (1987), *Country Life: A Social History of Rural England*, Totowa, New Jersey: Barnes & Noble.

Norbeck, E (1967), *Takashima. A Japanese Fishing Community*, Salt Lake City: University of Utah Press.

O'Hanlon, M. (1993) *Paradise: Portraying the New Guinea Highlands*, London: British Museum Press.

Okely, J. (1983), *The Traveller-Gypsies,* Cambridge: Cambridge University Press.

O'Shea, P. (1985), *The Hound of the Morrigan*, Oxford: Oxford University Press.

Paine, R. (1963), in F. Barth, *Entrepreneurship in Northern Norway*, Oslo: Scandinavian University Books.

Palsson, G. (1995) *The Textual Life of Savants,* Chur, Switzerland: Harwood.

Pardo, M. (1956) *Curtain of Mist*, New York: Funk & Wagnalls.

Parman, S. (1972), *Sociocultural Change in a Scottish Township*, unpublished Ph.D. thesis, Rice University, Austin, Texas.

—— (1990), *Scottish Crofters,* Fort Worth: Holt, Rinehart & Winston.

Parry, M.L. and Slater, T.R. (eds) (1980), *The Making of the Scottish Countryside*, London: Croom Helm.

Paterson, N. (1950), *Behold Thy Daughter*, London: Hodder & Stoughton.

Pedregal M. (1996), 'Tourism and Self-Consciousness in a South Spanish Coastal Community' in J. Boissevain (ed.), *Coping with Tourists*, Providence: Bergahn.

Phillipson, N. and Mitchison, R. (eds) (1970), *Scotland in the Age of Improvement*, Edinburgh: Edinburgh University Press.

Porter, M. (1985), 'Marginal Regions: Marginal Women? Sexual Divisions on the Periphery'. Paper presented to International Seminar on Marginal Regions, Galway.

Postel-Coster, E. and J. Heijmarin (1973), *Fishing Communities on the Scottish East Coast*, Leiden: Institut voor Culturele Antropologie en Sociologie der neit-Westerse Volken, Rijksuniversiteit.

Pratt, M. (1986), 'Fieldwork in Common Places' in J. Clifford and G. Marcus (eds), *Writing Culture: the Poetics and Politics of Ethnography*, Berkeley: University of California Press.

Prebble, J. (1963), *The Highland Clearances*, Harmondsworth: Penguin.

Price, R. and Price, S. (1995) 'Executing Culture: Musee, Museo, Museum', *American Anthropologist* 97(1): 97–109.

Puijk, R. (1996) 'Dealing with Fish and Tourists: a Case Study from Northern Norway', in J. Boissevain (ed.), *Coping With Tourists: European Reactions to Mass Tourism*, Providence: Bergahn.

Rapport, N. (1993), *Diverse World Views in an English Village,* Edinburgh: Edinburgh University Press.

Ray, C. (2001), *Highland Heritage: Scottish Americans in the American South*. Chapel Hill: University of North Carolina Press.

Reade, C. (1855), Christie Johnstone, Boston: Tickner and Fields.

Redfield, R. (1955), *The Little Community*, Chicago: University of Chicago Press.

Renwanz, M. (1981), *From Crofters to Shetlanders: the Social History of a Shetland Island Community's Self-image, 1872–1978*, upublished Ph.D. thesis, Stanford University.

Rich, G. (1998), in Finlay, A. (ed.), *Green Waters: an Anthology of Boats and Voyages*, Edinburgh: Polygon.

Robben, A. (1989), *Sons of the Sea Goddess: Economic Practice and Discursive Conflict in Brazil*, New York: Columbia University Press.

Rodman, M. (1992), 'Empowering Place: Multilocality and Multivocality', *American Anthropologist* 94: 640–56.

Rodgers, S. (1993), 'Women's Space in a Men's House: the British House of Commons', in S. Ardener, *Women and Space,* Oxford: Berg.

Rojek, C. (1997), 'Indexing, Dragging and Social Construction' in C. Rojek and J. Urry (eds), *Touring Cultures: Transformations of Travel and Theory,* London: Routledge.

Rojek, Chris and Urry, J. (eds) (1997), *Touring Cultures: Transformations of Travel and Theory*, London: Routledge.

Rosaldo, R. (1993), *Culture and Truth: The Remaking of Social Analysis*, Boston: Beacon Press.

Rosie, G. (1992), 'Museumry and the Heritage Industry', in I. Donnachie and C. Whatley (eds), *The Manufacture of Scottish History,* Edinburgh: Polygon.

Ross, J. (1999), 'Residents Win Fight for Knoydart', *The Scotsman,* 3 March: p. 7.

Rubenstein, L, (2001), *A Season in Dornoch: Golf and Life in the Scottish Highlands,* New York: Simon & Schuster.

Ruffins, F. (1992), 'Mythos, Memory and History' in Karp et al (eds), *Museums and Communities,* Washington: Smithsonian.

Russell, M. (1998), *In Waiting: Travels in the Shadow of Edwin Muir,* Glasgow: Neil Wilson.

Sahlins, M. (1976), *Culture and Practical Reason,* Chicago: University of Chicago Press.

Said, E. (1978), *Orientalism,* New York: Vintage Books.

Schneider, D. (1968), *American Kinship,* Englewood Cliffs NJ: Prentice-Hall.

Scott, J. (1985), *Weapons of the Weak,* New Haven: Yale University Press.

Scott, W. (1907 [1816]), *The Antiquary,* London: J.M. Dent & Sons.

Scott-Moncrieff, G. (1949), *The Lowlands of Scotland,* London: Batsford.

Scottish Tourist Board (1998) 'Tourism in Scotland 1997', Edinburgh: Scottish Tourist Board.

Sher, R. (1993) 'An "Agreeable and Instructive Society": Benjamin Franklin and Scotland', in John Dwyer and Richard Sher (eds), *Sociability and Society in Eighteenth Century Scotland,* Edinburgh: The Mercat Press.

Short, B. (1997), *Land and Society in Edwardian Britain,* Cambridge: Cambridge University Press.

Shostak, M. (1983) *Nisa: The Life and Words of a !Kung Woman,* New York: Random House.

Sider, G. (1988), *Culture and Class in Anthropology and History: a Newfoundland Illustration,* Cambridge: Cambridge University Press.

Simpson, A. and Stevenson, S. (1981), 'Historic Pittenweem: the Archaeological Implications of Development', *Scottish Burgh Survey,* Department of Archaeology, University of Glasgow.

Sinclair, J. (1791–9), Statistical Account of Scotland, London.

Slaven, A. (1994), 'The Origins and Economic and Social Roles of Scottish Business Leaders, 1860–1960', in T. Devine (ed.), *Scottish Elites,* Edinburgh: John Donald.

Smith, J.S. and Stevenson, D. (eds) (1989), *Fermfolk and Fisherfolk,* Aberdeen: Aberdeen University Press.

Smith, M.E. (ed.) (1977), *Those Who Live From the Sea,* St Paul: West.

Smith, P. J. 'Edinburgh: Catching up with a City in Transition', in *The New York Times Magazine* Pt. 2: September 26.

Smith P. (1985), *The Lammas Drave and the Winter Herrin': a History of the Herring Fishing from East Fife*, Edinburgh: John Donald.

Smith, R. (1991), *One Foot in the Sea*, Edinburgh: John Donald.

Smith, V. (ed.) (1989), *Hosts and Guests: the Anthropology of Tourism*, Philadelphia: University of Pennsylvania Press.

Smout, T.C. (1969), *A History of the Scottish People 1560–1830*, London: Fontana/Collins.

—— (1970), 'The Landowner and the Planned Village in Scotland, 1730–1830', in Phillipson, N. and Mitchison, N. (eds), *Scotland in the Age of Improvement*, Edinburgh: University of Edinburgh Press.

—— (1986), *A Century of the Scottish People 1830–1950*, New Haven: Yale University Press.

Smout, T.C. and Wood, S. (1991), *Scottish Voices 1745–1960,* London: Fontana.

Solomos, J. (1993), *Race and Racism in Britain*, New York: St Martin's.

Stevenson, S. (1991), *Hill and Adamson's The Fishermen and Women of the Firth of Forth*, Edinburgh: Scottish National Portrait Gallery.

Stewart, W. (n.d.), *A Fishing History of Lossiemouth*. Lossiemouth.

Stocking, G. Jr. (1987), *Victorian Anthropology*, New York: The Free Press.

—— (1992), *The Ethnographer's Magic and Other Essays in the History of Anthropology*, Madison: University of Wisconsin Press.

Strathern, M. (1981), *Kinship at the Core: an Anthropology of Elmdon, a Village in North-west Essex, in the 1960s*, Cambridge: Cambridge University Press.

Summers (1995), *Fishing off the Knuckle: the Fishing Villages of Buchan*, Aberdeen.

Sutherland, I. (n.d.), *From Herring to Seine Net Fishing on the East Coast of Scotland*, Wick: Camps Bookshop.

Sutherland, G. (1998), letter to the editor, *Fishing Monthly* 35: 18.

Sutherland, G. (ed.) (1994), *'A Stranger on the Bars': The Memoirs of Christian Watt Marshall of Broadsea*, Banff: Banff and Buchan District Council Department of Leisure and Recreation.

Taylor, J. (1994), *A Dream of England: Landscape, Photography and the Tourist's Imagination*, Manchester: Manchester University Press.

Taylor, J. (n.d.), *From Whinnyfold to Whitehills: Fishing The North East*, Gartocharn: Northern Books.

—— (n.d.), *Fishing the North East: a Guide to the People, the Places and their Craft*, Gartocharn: Northern Books from Famedram.

Taylor, J. and Taylor, L. (n.d.), *Fraserburgh Means Fish*, Turriff: Banff and Buchan Enterprise Trust.

Teal, J. and Teal, M. (1969), *Life and Death of a Salt Marsh*, Boston: Atlantic Monthly Press.

Telford, S. (1998), *'In a World A Wir Ane'*: *a Shetland Herring Girl's Story*, Lerwick: The Shetland Times.

Theroux, P. (1983), *Kingdom By the Sea*, New York: Washington Square Press.

Thompson, E. P. (1968), *The Making of the English Working Class*, Harmondsworth: Penguin.

Thompson, P., Wailey, T., and Lummis, T. (1983), *Living the Fishing*, London: Routledge & Kegan Paul.

Thomson, D. (1988), 'The Herring Girls', in A. Lawrie, H. Matthews and D. Ritchie (eds), *Glimmer of Cold Brine: A Scottish Sea Anthology*, Aberdeen: Aberdeen University Press.

Tilly, C. (1994), 'Political Memories in Space and Time' in J. Boyarin (ed.), *Remapping Memory* Minneapolis: University of Minnesota Press.

Tonnies, F. (1955 [1987]), Community and Society, Gemeinschaft und Gesellschaft. Translated and edited by C. Loomis, East Lansing: State University Press.

Trevor-Roper, H. (1983), 'The Invention of Tradition: the Highland Tradition of Scotland', in Hobsbawm, E. and Ranger, T. (eds), *The Invention of Tradition*, Cambridge: Cambridge University Press.

Tylor, E.B. (1899), 'On a Method of Investigating the Development of Institutions, Applied to Laws of Marriage and Descent', in *Journal of the Royal Anthropological Institute* 18: 245–69.

Urry, J. (1984), 'Englishmen, Celts and Iberians: The Ethnographic Survey of the United Kingdom, 1892–1899', in G. Stocking, (ed.), *Functionalism Historicized: Essays on British Social Anthropology*, Madison: University of Wisconsin Press.

—— (1990), *The Tourist Gaze*, London: SAGE Publications.

—— (1995), *Consuming Places*, London: Routledge.

Wallerstein, I. (1974), *The Modern World-System*, New York: Academic Press.

—— (1980), *The Modern World-System II*, New York: Academic Press.

Walsh (1992), *The Representation of the Past: Museums and Heritage in the Post-modern World*, London: Routledge.

Ward, B. (1955) 'A Hong Kong Fishing Village' in *Journal of Oriental Studies* 1: 195–214.

Warner, W. (1983), *Distant Water: the Fate of the North Atlantic Fisherman*, Harmondsworth: Penguin.

Watson, W. (1964) 'Social Mobility and Social Class in Industrial Communities' in M. Gluckman (ed.), *Closed Systems and Open Minds: the Limits of Naivety in Social Anthropology*, Chicago: Aldine.

Watson, Harry D. (1992), '"Poetry Peter" Smith: The Fisherman-Poet of Cellardyke'

Webster, B. (1975) *Scotland from the Eleventh Century to 1603*, Ithaca: Cornell University Press.

Weld, C. (1991 [1860]) *Two Months in the Highlands,* cited in C.Smout and S. Wood (eds), *Scottish Voices 1745–1960*, London: Fontana/Collins.

Welsh, I. (1993), *Trainspotting,* New York: W.W. Norton.

West, B. (1988), 'The Making of the English working past: a critical view of the Ironbridge Gorge Museum', in R. Lumley (ed.), *The Museum Time Machine,* London: Routledge.

Whatley, C. (1988), 'The Experience of Work' in T. Devine and R. Mitchison (eds), *People and Society in Scotland, 1760–1830,* Edinburgh: John Donald.

Whitehead, A. (1976), 'Sexual Antagonism in Herefordshire', in D.L. Barker and S. Allen (eds), *Dependence and Exploitation in Work and Marriage*, London: Longman.

Whyte, C. (1995), 'Fishy Masculinities', in C. Whyte (ed.), *Gendering the Nation*, Edinburgh: Edinburgh University Press.

Wightman, A. (1997), *Who Owns Scotland*, Edinburgh: Canongate

Wilk, R. (1995), 'Learning to be Local in Belize: global systems of common difference', in D. Miller (ed.), *Worlds Apart: Modernity Through the Prism of the Local*, London: Routledge.

Williams, R. (1973), *The Country and the City*, New York: Oxford University Press.

—— (1976), *Kewords*, London: Fontana.

Wilson, W. (1980), *Ebb Tide,* Berwick-upon-Tweed.

Withers, C. (1992), 'The Historical Creation of the Scottish Highlands', in Donnachie, I. and Whatley, C. (eds), *The Manufacture of Scottish History*, Edinburgh: Polygon.

Withrington, D. 'Schooling, Literacy and Society', in T. Devine and R. Mitchison (eds), *People and Society in Scotland Vol. I, 1760–1830,* Edinburgh: John Donald

Wolf, E. (1966), *Peasants*, Englewood Cliffs, N.J.: Prentice-Hall.

—— (1982), *Europe and the People Without History*, Berkeley: University of California Press.

Wood, E. (1998), *Notes From the North,* Edinburgh: Luath Press.

Wood, L. (1998), *The Berwickshire Coast,* Ochiltree, Ayrshire: Stenlake.

Wood, R. and Deppen, M. (1994), 'Cultural Tourism: Ethnic Options and Constructed Otherness', paper presented at the International Socio-logical Association meetings, Bielefeld, Germany.

Wright, P. (1985), *On Living in an Old Country,* London: Verso.

# Index

# Index

# Index